THE NEW DEAL
COLLECTIVE
BARGAINING POLICY

A Da Capo Press Reprint Series

FRANKLIN D. ROOSEVELT
AND THE ERA OF THE NEW DEAL

GENERAL EDITOR: FRANK FREIDEL

Harvard University

THE NEW DEAL COLLECTIVE BARGAINING POLICY

By

IRVING BERNSTEIN

DA CAPO PRESS • NEW YORK • 1975

Library of Congress Cataloging in Publication Data

Bernstein, Irving, 1916-
    The New Deal collective bargaining policy.

    (Franklin D. Roosevelt and the era of the New Deal)
    Original t.p., at head of title: Institute of
Industrial Relations, University of California.
    Reprint of the ed. published by University of Cali-
fornia Press, Berkeley.
    "National labor relations act": p.
    Bibliography: p.
    Includes index.
    1. Collective bargaining — United States — History.
2. Labor policy — United States — History. I. California. University. Institute of Industrial Relations.
II. United States. Laws, statutes, etc. National
labor relations act. 1975. III. Title. IV. Series.
[HD8072.B374   1975]   331.89'0973   75-8997
ISBN 0-306-70703-9

This Da Capo Press edition of *The New Deal Collective Bargaining Policy*
is an unabridged republication of the first edition published in Berkeley and
Los Angeles in 1950. It is reprinted with the permission of University of
California Press and reproduced from a copy in the collections of The New
York State Library.

Published by Da Capo Press, Inc.
A Subsidiary of Plenum Publishing Corporation
227 West 17th Street, New York, N.Y. 10011

THE NEW DEAL
COLLECTIVE BARGAINING POLICY

INSTITUTE OF INDUSTRIAL RELATIONS
UNIVERSITY OF CALIFORNIA

THE NEW DEAL
COLLECTIVE
BARGAINING POLICY

By

IRVING BERNSTEIN

UNIVERSITY OF CALIFORNIA PRESS

BERKELEY AND LOS ANGELES

1950

UNIVERSITY OF CALIFORNIA PRESS

BERKELEY AND LOS ANGELES

CALIFORNIA

◇

CAMBRIDGE UNIVERSITY PRESS

LONDON, ENGLAND

PRINTED IN THE UNITED STATES OF AMERICA
BY THE UNIVERSITY OF CALIFORNIA PRESS

TO THE MEMORY OF

MY PARENTS

FOREWORD

THE Institute of Industrial Relations, Southern Division, offers this monograph as part of a growing research program in labor-management relations. Other studies in article, pamphlet, and monograph form have been published or are under way.

Collective bargaining now plays a significant role in the economic life of the nation, commanding the increasing attention of the public and scholars alike. The bargaining process itself is the product of several forces, of which the affirmative intervention of the federal government has not been the least important. *The New Deal Collective Bargaining Policy* recounts the development of this intervention in its formative period. It should serve as an historical introduction for those interested in legislative policy concerned with collective bargaining.

The views expressed in this study are the author's. The Institute seeks to promote independent scholarly research in industrial relations and neither approves nor disapproves of the conclusions reached in publications such as this one.

EDGAR L. WARREN, *Director*
Southern Division
Los Angeles, California

PREFACE

THE EMERGENCE of a national collective bargaining policy in the early years of the New Deal facilitated the large-scale organization of labor in the United States and was therefore a development charged with significance for our society. Although unionism might have become an important force in any event, federal intervention hastened the process. The statutes considered together constitute a wedge in the penetration of government into economic life, recognizing that the right of workers to associate and bargain collectively is clothed with a public interest. These laws—the New Deal collective bargaining policy—embrace two lines of development, one beginning with Sec. 7(a) of the National Industrial Recovery Act and leading to the Wagner Act, the other commencing with the Railway Labor Act of 1926 and culminating in the 1934 amendments to that statute. Although it incorporated related principles, Title III of the Guffey Bituminous Coal Conservation Act of 1935 is not considered since the Supreme Court declared it unconstitutional at the outset.[1]

The New Deal marked a basic change in governmental policy toward economic affairs. Theretofore government, with notable exceptions, left primary responsibility for decision-making to individuals—private citizens and corporations. The Great Depression, however, led to a shift in emphasis from an individual to a collective responsibility, applied alike to business, to agriculture, and to labor. The National Industrial Recovery Act reversed an historic antitrust policy to permit businessmen collectively to fix prices, determine rates of output, and make other decisions jointly. The Agricultural Adjustment Act developed a related policy for farmers. The Wagner Act and the Railway Labor Act expressed a similar philosophy, collective over individual bargaining, in the area of labor-management relations. This study traces the emergence of this new concept of the role of government.

It is cause for wonder that the labor statutes were enacted when they are viewed against the determination of the opposition, the division within the Administration, and the mixed feelings of union leadership. The monograph therefore seeks to explain this departure in public policy in light of the times: the condition of the union movement, the crystallization of fundamental ideas, and the nature of the "first" New Deal. Rather than take the measure of the statutes as isolated experiences in law or public administration, I have endeavored to place them in their historical context, to reveal their collective role as a response to

---

[1] *Carter v. Carter Coal Co.* (1936), 298 U.S. 278.

contemporary conditions. Consequently their administration is developed only where necessary to illuminate the broad formulation of policy.

The emphasis, therefore, is historical rather than current and deals with the years 1933–1935. It is important to bear in mind that the locus of concern was different then from now. At that time the absorbing issue was the elementary right of workers to organize into unions for the purpose of collective bargaining. Hence the New Deal statutes were directed to this question. Mainly because the legislation was successful—we now have large and powerful unions and collective bargaining is widespread—the locus has shifted. Recent discussion and legislation have been primarily concerned with new issues, for example, restricting strikes that affect the public welfare and regulating union excesses. These problems, however, were not of major significance in the period that this monograph examines.

In the body of the study I have sought to recount this development of public policy without consciously intruding my own views. Conclusions are reserved for the final chapter. Since they are drawn, the reader should be apprised of the frame of reference within which they rest.

I am persuaded that collective bargaining can be a constructive institution in a democratic society. This, at bottom, is because I feel it politically, economically, and socially desirable for all major interest groups to be organized in approximate equality in order to prevent any one from gaining dominance.[2] *The Federalist* (No. 51) put it this way: "It is of great importance in a republic, not only to guard the society against the oppression of its rulers; but to guard one part of the society against the injustice of the other part. Different interests necessarily exist in different classes of citizens." Although such differences do exist between workers and employers, I do not subscribe to the view that class conflict is inevitable and irremediable. In fact, I am convinced that the bargaining mechanism is an alternative—perhaps the only one—to such conflict.

With respect to the economic effects of collective bargaining, I am more impressed with the division among theorists than with their separate conclusions. These views range the spectrum from an extreme holding that collective wage determination produces high levels of output and employment to another arguing that bargaining misallocates resources with undesirable effects upon the volume of employment and production. The least that can be said in favor of bargaining is that theory is far from crystallized and that there certainly is no compelling evidence that it is damaging to the economy in the long term. My inclination, however, is to go a good deal further. Some collective wage decisions, quite obviously, have more desirable economic effects than others.

[2] For a different view, cf. Henry C. Simons, *Economic Policy for a Free Society* (Chicago: 1948).

In any case, I would regard the theoretical consideration as subsidiary to the balance of power concept stated above.

At the institutional level it is generally agreed that bargaining can produce desirable results: shorter hours, the orderly disposition of individual grievances, improved productive efficiency, stability of employment and wage income within the firm and the industry, removal of intraplant and intraindustry wage inequities, a channel of communication between management and workers, the removal of industrial hazards, and others. Collective bargaining, of course, does not inevitably produce these results, but it does provide the mechanism by which they may be approached.

History is usually written either so soon after the event that significant materials are kept under cover and issues are beclouded with controversy or so long afterward that the objectivity gained is at the price of valuable sources. This study has had the advantage of striking a balance. Enough time has elapsed to permit passions to cool; important collections of unpublished documents have been opened; and many participants in the events retain vivid recollections.

Senator Wagner's assistants during these years, Judge Simon H. Rifkind, Leon H. Keyserling, and Philip Levy, provided much information through discussion, while the last two opened documents of inestimable value. Judge Charles E. Wyzanski, Jr., and Boris Shishkin gave generously of their time and materials. Donald R. Richberg, Dr. Meyer Jacobstein, Lloyd K. Garrison, Judge Jerome N. Frank, and Dr. W. Jett Lauck illuminated many dark corners. Others too numerous to mention supplied information through correspondence. The librarians and archivists of the Labor Department, National Archives, Library of Congress, Brookings Institution, Interstate Commerce Commission, Federal Reserve Board, Department of Interior, Harvard University, and the University of California were most helpful. Dr. Fred W. Shipman, Director of the Franklin D. Roosevelt Library, placed his facilities at my disposal.

The manuscript has benefited immeasurably from the critical reading and helpful suggestions of the following: Professor Arthur M. Schlesinger of Harvard; the staff of the Institute of Industrial Relations at both Los Angeles and Berkeley and particularly Dr. Frank C. Pierson, Michael I. Komaroff, and Benjamin Aaron; Professor Malcolm M. Davisson of the University of California, Berkeley; Professor John T. Dunlop of Harvard; and a reading committee of the Institute consisting of Dean Neil H. Jacoby, Professor Brainerd Dyer, and Dean D. E. McHenry of the University of California, Los Angeles. Mrs. Anne P. Cook prepared the index. I herewith express my gratitude to each of them. Responsibility for errors and the viewpoint, of course, remain my own.

IRVING BERNSTEIN

CONTENTS

I. THE CONDITION OF THE UNION MOVEMENT

IN A FEW YEARS following the first inauguration of Franklin D. Roosevelt public policy with respect to collective bargaining crystallized. The right of employees to organize and bargain collectively through representatives of their own choosing was underwritten by the federal government in Section 7(a) of the National Industrial Recovery Act, in Public Resolution No. 44, in the 1934 amendments to the Railway Labor Act, in the Guffey Act, and in the Wagner Act. From this legislative foundation union membership advanced from less than three million in 1933 to almost fifteen million in 1946.[1]

In retrospect these statutes appear as a natural product of the early New Deal. At the time, however, their enactment appeared far from inevitable. As an observer on the scene wrote, "We who believed in the [Wagner] Act were dizzy with watching a 200-to-1 shot come up from the outside."[2] It is necessary, therefore, to examine with care the historical antecedents. The purpose of this chapter is to analyze the position of trade unions in the United States in the period immediately preceding the New Deal. The following chapter seeks to trace the historical emergence of the concepts that were to take shape in the New Deal statutes.

The trade union movement at the advent of the New Deal was weak and ineffective as a consequence of secular tendencies which set in after World War I and as a result of the Great Depression. An amateur analyst graphically noted that "the American Federation of Labor, and the Railway Union, constitute but a volstead per-centage of the employee [sic] of these United States."[3] In diagnosing the Federation in 1932, Louis Adamic found it beset with a host of ailments and his prognosis was not more cheerful:

> The body is undoubtedly a sick body. It is ineffectual—flabby, afflicted with the dull pains of moral and physical decline. The big industrialists and conservative politicians are no longer worried by it. Indeed, the intelligent ones see in it the best obstacle— temporary at least—to the emergence of a militant and formidable labor movement. . . . The ten year decline of the whole organization, I think, has already gone too far to be rejuvenated by anybody.[4]

[1] Leo Wolman, *Ebb and Flow in Trade Unionism* (New York: 1936), p. 34; Bureau of Labor Statistics, Bull. No. 909, *Extent of Collective Bargaining and Union Recognition* (1946), p. 1.

[2] Malcolm Ross, *Death of a Yale Man* (New York: 1939), p. 170. Cf. also Twentieth Century Fund, *Labor and the Government* (New York: 1935), p. 63.

[3] William Cattingham to Perkins, July 4, 1933, National Archives, Labor Department, 167/2283.

[4] Louis Adamic, "The Collapse of Organized Labor," *Harper's Monthly Magazine*, CLXIV (1932), 167, 171. For similar contemporary analyses, cf. Louis Stanley, "The

Union membership declined from 5,047,800 in 1920 to 2,973,000 in 1933, a loss of 2,074,800 members—1,605,200 in the years 1920–1929 and 469,600 during the depression. By 1933 membership retrogressed to the level of 1917 and, if the growth of the labor force is considered, fell to that of 1910.[5] Most severe losses were suffered in the early twenties due mainly to unemployment accompanying the postwar depression. Decline later in the decade stemmed principally from the retreat of the Mine Workers, bitter struggle between right and left within the Ladies Garment Workers, and shrinkage in the number employed in manufacturing, particularly skilled workers.[6] The defection of less than half a million in the depression years is surprisingly small in view of the volume of unemployment. "That the loss was not larger can be explained only by the fact that so much had already been surrendered since 1920." By 1930 only 10.2 per cent of nonagricultural workers were organized as contrasted with 19.4 a decade earlier.[7]

Unions, in addition, covered only fragments of the working population primarily in the traditional crafts with only a few penetrations of basic industries such as coal, construction, and railroads. In manufacturing and the mechanical industries extensive inroads had been made into printing, clothing, and shoe manufacturing. There was, however, little membership in the majority of the industries in this category, for example, steel, automobiles, electrical equipment, rubber, oil, and cement. Among clerical employees only postal and railroad groups were organized. Unionization of professional workers was confined to small units of actors, draftsmen, and teachers as well as the powerful musicians. In domestic and personal service only barbers and hotel and restaurant employees revealed significant organization.[8]

The union movement demonstrated little interest or effectiveness in organizing the unorganized. Fainthearted attempts were made to unionize the automobile industry and the South, while steel remained inviolate after the defeat of the 1919 strike. By 1930 the AFL even ceased to form international unions out of federal locals in the same industry. The aggressive morale needed for organization was absent, nor were funds available to contest the large corporations. Many labor leaders

Collapse of the A. F. of L.," *The Nation,* CXXXI (1930), 367, and Lyle W. Cooper, "The American Labor Movement in Prosperity and Depression," *American Economic Review,* XXII (1932), 641.

[5] Wolman, *op. cit.,* pp. 16, 33–34.

[6] Sumner H. Slichter, "The Current Labor Policies of American Industries," *Quarterly Journal of Economics,* XLIII (1929), 427.

[7] Wolman, *op. cit.,* pp. 40–41, 112–19.

[8] *Ibid.,* pp. 118–21.

were more concerned with maintaining a hold on existing crafts and spent their energies on jurisdictional disputes.[9]

Contemporary observers generally agreed that the quality of union leadership deteriorated. A letter, cited as typical of several written by frank AFL spokesmen, described the leaders as "about played out and . . . mostly labor politicians, anyhow." It went on to characterize office-holders as derelict in their obligations to the membership, while organizers "are either burned out or never had that passion for the movement which is necessary to stir and inspire others." Of the top echelon of the Federation it was said ". . . the high officials seem unable to formulate policies to meet the great problems of today. They are merely carrying over the minds of earlier years." Without direction from above, city central bodies and state federations were "lifeless."[10] Symptomatically, in Middletown a promising young leader gave up the union movement and became a minor functionary in the dominant political machine.[11] Adamic concluded that the Federation's Executive Council and the leaders of state federations and international unions "have exhibited intellectual, intestinal, and moral inadequacy, if not total bankruptcy, as leaders of labor and social-minded men."[12]

In collective bargaining the limited measuring rods of real wages, hours, and strikes indicate that on balance members of labor organizations gained little more than unaffiliated employees.[13] The figures compiled by Professor Paul H. Douglas reveal that real hourly earnings of employees in selected union manufacturing industries and those of employees in predominantly unorganized manufacturing industries rose the same amount, 32 per cent, between 1914 and 1926. Organized employees in the building trades and coal did moderately better than the

---

[9] Lewis L. Lorwin, *The American Federation of Labor, History, Policies, and Prospects* (Washington: 1933), pp. 279–80; H. M. Douty, "The Trend of Industrial Disputes, 1922–1930," *Journal of the American Statistical Association,* XXVII (1932), 171–72; Adamic, *op. cit.,* p. 171; Stanley, *op. cit.,* pp. 367–68.

[10] Adamic, *op. cit.,* p. 168.

[11] Robert S. and Helen Merrell Lynd, *Middletown, a Study in Contemporary American Culture* (New York: 1929), p. 80.

[12] Adamic, *op. cit.,* p. 172. Similar views were expressed by Stanley, *op. cit.,* p. 368; Twentieth Century Fund, *op. cit.,* pp. 7–8. Weak leadership was given as a principal reason for the failure to organize steel. Carroll R. Daugherty, Melvin G. deChazeau, and Samuel S. Stratton, *The Economics of the Iron and Steel Industry* (New York: 1937), II, 937, 945.

[13] This analysis assumes that unions can raise the real wages of their members as compared with unorganized workers. The assumption is by no means universally accepted. Recent investigations, however, tend to substantiate this view both with regard to comparisons between organized and unorganized industries and between union and nonunion jobs within the same industry. Cf. Arthur M. Ross, *Trade Union Wage Policy* (Berkeley, Calif.: 1948) chap. vi, and Joseph Shister, *Economics of the Labor Market* (Philadelphia: 1949), p. 186, n.

manufacturing employees. In full-time real weekly earnings, however, the unionized manufacturing workers gained 25 per cent between 1914 and 1926 as compared with an increase of only 18 per cent for unorganized manufacturing employees. The affiliated building tradesmen, coal miners, and railroad workers advanced 31, 30, and 21 per cent respectively.[14]

With regard to hours of work, on the other hand, unorganized employees achieved greater advances than union workers. Hours in Douglas's nonunion manufacturing group declined from an average of 56.6 per week in 1918 to 52.2 in 1926, or 4.4 hours. In the union manufacturing industries weekly hours decreased from 47.2 to 45.9, or only 1.3 hours. The former was an 8.4 per cent drop as compared with 2.8 per cent for the latter. If the unorganized manufacturing industries are compared with the building trades and coal, the advantage is even more impressive. Hours in construction declined less than 1 per cent between 1918 and 1926, while coal miners worked virtually the same hours at both ends of the period.[15]

The period 1921–1932 proved to be remarkably quiescent in use of the strike weapon. To the extent that strike activity measures an affirmative bargaining policy the disuse into which the strike fell may be regarded as a sign of waning union vitality. The table (p. 5) shows the drop in the national strike-load during the 1920's and the depression as contrasted with 1910 and 1920.[16]

The weakness of the AFL permitted the creation of a left-wing dual-union movement. In the 1920's the Communist line called for "boring from within" existing organizations. In 1929 this policy was reversed with the formation of the Trade Union Unity League. It urged "the organization of new and revolutionary industrial unions in industries

---

[14] *Real Wages in the United States, 1890–1926* (Cambridge, Mass.: 1930), pp. 98, 104, 135, 164, 120, 127, 137, 162, 168. These data have been subjected to methodological criticism primarily on the grounds of comparing percentage increases. A contrast of absolute changes leads to the opposite conclusion: between 1890 and 1926 average hourly earnings in the unionized group rose 68 cents, while those of the nonunion category increased only 34 cents. Cf. Ross, *op. cit.*, pp. 128–32.

[15] Douglas, *op. cit.*, pp. 112–17, 136, 163. These conclusions must be qualified to the extent that the unorganized were in this period catching up with gains made earlier by unions. The industries primarily responsible for bringing the nonunion category down, men's clothing and steel, were affected by trade unionism; the activities of the Amalgamated Clothing Workers and the steel strike of 1919 had the result of reducing hours.

[16] John I. Griffin, *Strikes, a Study in Quantitative Economics* (New York: 1939), pp. 38–39, 43–44. Douty has made this point even more effectively by establishing a relationship between the volume of strikes and the number of industrial workers, thereby correcting for the growth of the labor force. The disputes index number of 100 in 1916–1921 fell to 34 in 1922–1925 and to 18 in 1926–1930. Douty, *op. cit.*, p. 170.

wheie there are no unions and in industries where the existing unions are corrupt and impotent."[17] A number of industrial organizations were formed, including the National Miners Union, the National Textile Workers, the Needle Trades Workers International Union, the Marine Workers Industrial Union, the Auto Workers Union, and the Steel and Metal Workers Industrial Union. TUUL sought to organize the unskilled and semiskilled in the mass production industries. Most success was attained, however, in unionized industries, such as coal, clothing, and textiles. By 1934 the TUUL reached a peak membership of 125,000.[18]

Year	Strikes	Workers involved
1910	3,334	824,000
1920	3,411	1,463,000
1925	1,301	428,000
1926	1,035	330,000
1927	707	330,000
1928	604	314,000
1929	921	289,000
1930	637	183,000
1931	810	342,000
1932	841	324,000

The causes of the decline of the union movement after 1920 derived from the psychological and sociological motivations of workers, the play of economic forces, the structural weaknesses of the AFL, and the antiunion policies of employers which were protected by the law. "The average working stiff is too indifferent and sour, or selfish . . . ," a union leader wrote.[19] Postwar prosperity with its rising standard of living and materialism nurtured individualistic rather than concerted tendencies among workers. Even those who remained members were apathetic. In Middletown, for example, the Molders found it necessary to impose fines on absentees in order to get the membership together. Prosperous workers identified themselves socially with the middle class, engaging in emulative spending and sending their children to college. They came to believe that they were "getting ahead" and that there was a place for them or their progeny in an expanding future. "The desire for steady employment and higher earnings became more dominant in the minds of the workers than the feeling for industrial freedom and independ-

[17] *Handbook of American Trade-Unions,* Bureau of Labor Statistics, Bull. No. 618, p. 14.
[18] *Ibid.,* pp. 13–16; Lorwin, *op. cit.,* p. 269.
[19] Adamic, *op. cit.,* p. 168.

ence."[20] New devices, the automobile, the radio, and the movies, absorbed their time and scattered their interests with a consequent sapping of the vitality of unionism. One organizer declared that "the Ford car has done a lot of harm to the unions."[21] Since unions contributed little to their improved status, workers saw no point in joining.

Economic forces contributed to the same result. In 1926 the wage earner in manufacturing purchased thirty per cent more with his average annual earnings than he bought in 1914. Two-thirds of this increase in real wages was effected after the Armistice, largely in 1922 and 1923.[22] It stemmed principally from a sharp rise in productivity in a period—after 1922—of relative price stability. This accelerated application of new invention incidentally diluted the skills or made technologically unemployed those most likely to organize. That great boon to unionization, a rise in the cost of living, did not put in an appearance.[23]

A feature of the era was the trustification and concentration of American industry. The structure and policies of the AFL were geared to small-scale operations and were most effective in industries characterized by diversity of control, such as construction, printing, and soft coal. They were hardly able to cope with the aggregations of capital which had taken form by 1929 and the unions, in effect, drifted into an eddy outside the main stream of American economic life.

"The huge corporation . . . has come to dominate most major industries if not all industry in the United States."[24] By 1930 almost 200 nonbanking corporations had assets of over $100 million and fifteen exceeded one billion. The combined assets of the 200 largest were nearly half the corporate wealth of the country and totaled $81 billion. In 1929 they received 43.2 per cent of the net income of nonbanking corporations. The rate of concentration among the largest was half again that of smaller corporations. With concentration appeared a tendency for ownership and control to be divorced, the latter being exercised by a few with interlocking relationships among them. Berle and Means concluded: "The rise of the modern corporation has brought a concentration of economic power which can compete on equal terms with the modern state. . . ."[25]

[20] Lorwin, *op. cit.*, p. 239; Lynds, *op. cit.*, pp. 78, 80; Douty, *op. cit.*, pp. 171–172; Cooper, *op. cit.*, p. 643.

[21] Lynds, *op. cit.*, pp. 80, 254.

[22] Douglas, *op. cit.*, p. 244.

[23] *Ibid.*, p. 590; Douty, *loc. cit.*; Wolman, *op. cit.*, pp. 36–37; Cooper, *op. cit.*, p. 684.

[24] A. A. Berle, Jr., and Gardiner C. Means, *The Modern Corporation and Private Property* (New York: 1932), p. 44.

[25] *Ibid.*, p. 357. For the extent of concentration by industry, cf. Harry W. Laidler, *Concentration of Control in American Industry* (New York: 1931), pp. 435 ff.

A common aspect of these combinations was the virtual absence of unionism among their employees. The very fact of size created an imbalance of bargaining power with the individual employee, permitting the corporation to fix the terms of the employment contract unilaterally. It could resist organization by transferring production from one plant to another and by putting pressure upon smaller concerns within its orbit of supply or distribution. The merger process for the employer reduced competition from low-wage firms.[26] These enterprises had an almost unanimous opposition to unionism. As a result, organization was virtually nonexistent in industries where combination was marked: steel, automobiles, aluminum, rubber, electrical equipment, telephones, glass, tobacco, and baking.[27]

The prosperity of the 1920's was uneven and in both its unfavorable and favorable aspects militated against unionism. Unemployment in no year of the decade fell below 1,500,000.[28] The worker had to calculate before striking that there would be someone to take his job. Business expanded largely outside the organized industries, for example, in automobiles, chemicals, public utilities, distribution, and the services. On the other hand, several unionized industries were depressed, such as coal, clothing, and textiles (in New England). Furthermore, there was a fugitive movement in textiles and coal to the nonunion South and of clothing to unorganized communities.[29]

The craft structure of most AFL unions had evolved in small-scale enterprises in the nineteenth century and was poorly adapted to an age of mass production. Mechanization diluted or obliterated crafts and lowered the ratio of skilled to semiskilled and unskilled workers. The craftsman became a rarity and even then his trade often failed to fit the unions' jurisdictional framework.[30] The Federation failed to conform structurally to the new era in large part because of the character of its leadership. Those in power feared the loosing of forces beyond their control.[31]

The direct antiunion practices of employers protected by law perhaps constituted the most formidable road block to organization, a conclusion supported by the fact that millions of workers joined unions after these policies were made illegal by the New Deal. It was not true, however,

---

[26] Myron W. Watkins, "Trustification and Economic Theory," *American Economic Review*, XXI, supp. (1931), pp. 59–61.

[27] *Ibid.*, p. 61; Laidler, *op. cit.*, p. 457.

[28] Meredith B. Givens, cited in John R. Commons and associates, *History of Labour in the United States* (New York: 1935), III, 141–42.

[29] Wolman, *op. cit.*, pp. 35–38.

[30] *Ibid.*, pp. 36–38; Cooper, *op. cit.*, pp. 649–50; Daugherty *et al.*, *op. cit.*, p. 195.

[31] Adamic, *op. cit.*, pp. 168–71.

as sometimes charged, that the law was tilted in favor of employers. Labor relations law, statutory and, to a lesser extent, decisional, was characterized by a spirit of toleration. In theory there was essential equality. Workers might lawfully organize and bargain collectively, while employers with equal legality might frustrate freedom of association and refuse to bargain. In the realities of the market place this hypothetical balance gave the employer the advantage.[32] As Leiserson has noted:

> The law recognized the equal freedom of the employers to destroy labor organizations and to deny the right of employees to join trade unions. An employer could coerce or threaten his employees to keep them from organizing. He could discharge them if they joined a union, and he could refuse to hire anyone who was a member. He could decline to deal with any union of his employees or to recognize the organization or any of its officers or agents as representatives of the employees. He was free to organize a company union of his own and force his employees to join it. It was not illegal for him to employ detectives to spy on his employees in order to find out whether they talked unionism among themselves, and he could send his spies into the labor organization to become members and officers so that they might be in a better position to report union activities to him and recommend effective disciplinary action designed to stop such activities. Under such circumstances, to speak of labor's right to organize was clearly a misuse of terms. All that the employees had was a right to try to organize if they could get away with it; and whether they could or not depended on the relative economic strength of the employers' and employees' organizations.[33]

In a yellow-dog contract the worker agreed as a condition of employment not to join a union or attempt to organize his fellow-employees. It became prominent in the New England textile industry in the 1870's and after World War I was generally used in the coal, hosiery, street railway, and shoe industries. Although 16 states outlawed yellow-dogs the statutes were evaded and were finally declared unconstitutional.[34] The Hitchman case legalized injunctions restraining union organizational activities on the ground of inducing breach of (yellow-dog) contract.[35] In West Virginia the Mine Workers were virtually barred from the state by an injunction obtained by 316 coal companies enforcing their contracts.[36]

---

[32] Edwin E. Witte, *The Government in Labor Disputes* (New York: 1932), pp. 230–31; Calvert Magruder, "A Half Century of Legal Influence upon the Development of Collective Bargaining," *Harvard Law Review*, L (1937), 1078.

[33] William M. Leiserson, *Right and Wrong in Labor Relations* (Berkeley, Calif.: 1938), pp. 24–27.

[34] *Coppage v. Kansas* (1915), 236 U.S. 1.

[35] *Hitchman Coal & Coke Co. v. Mitchell* (1917), 245 U.S. 229.

[36] *United Mine Workers v. Red Jacket Consolidated Coal & Coke Co.* (1927), 18 Fed. (2d) 839, cert. den., 275 U.S. 536. Cf. Joel I. Seidman, "The Yellow-Dog Contract," *Quarterly Journal of Economics*, XLVI (1932), 349; "Employer Interference with Lawful Union Activity," *Columbia Law Review*, XXXVII (1937), 820–21.

The labor injunction first appeared in the 1880's and became common after 1900. The usual variety was the temporary restraining order, often granted *ex parte* without notice or hearing. Typically the employer filed a complaint that a strike, actual or prospective, was an unlawful interference with the conduct of his business. If in the court's judgment the danger of injury was imminent, it issued an order prohibiting the union from striking. Witnesses were seldom called and there was no trial by jury, while the court's action was reviewable only on restricted grounds. During the period of strike suspension the employer was free to undermine the union. Resentment arose from the expansion of a simple judicial device "to an enveloping code of prohibited conduct, absorbing *en masse*, executive and police functions and affecting the livelihood, and even lives, of multitudes."[37]

The Norris-LaGuardia Act of 1932 made the yellow-dog contract unenforceable in the federal courts and established safeguards for the issuance of injunctions in labor cases. Similar legislation was enacted in many of the states.[38]

The simplest and probably commonest devices of the employer to destroy a union were discrimination against and discharge of members. In more highly developed form a group of firms maintained a blacklist of workers whom they would fire or refuse to hire. The effectiveness of these practices "in hindering successful organization is hardly open to dispute."[39] They were condemned in the 1902 and 1915 reports of the industrial commissions which recommended remedial legislation.[40] The courts, however, upheld the employer's right to refuse to hire and to discharge at will on the grounds that it was repugnant to compel him to enter an unwilling personal relationship. As a result legislation protecting the employee against discrimination based on membership was held invalid.[41]

Industrial espionage, developed after the Civil War, was another anti-union employer practice. One union leader testified, ". . . there is no gathering of union members large enough to be called a meeting that

[37] Felix Frankfurter and Nathan Greene, *The Labor Injunction* (New York: 1930), p. 200.

[38] *U. S. Stat. at Large*, XLVII, 70; Osmond K. Fraenkel, "Recent Statutes Affecting Labor Injunctions and Yellow-Dog Contracts," *Illinois Law Review*, XXX (1936), 854.

[39] *Columbia Law Review*, XXXVII (1937), 817; "Violations of Free Speech and Rights of Labor," *Sen. Rep.*, 75th Cong., 1st sess., no. 46, pt. 3 (Dec. 21, 1937), p. 8, hereafter cited as *La Follette Comm. Rep.*; National Labor Relations Board, *Governmental Protection of Labor's Right to Organize* (Washington: 1936), pp. 15–16.

[40] *Report of the Industrial Commission, 1902*, pp. 890–93; *Report of the Commission on Industrial Relations*, p. 90.

[41] *Adair v. United States* (1908), 208 U.S. 161; Magruder, *op. cit.*, pp. 1082–84; *Columbia Law Review*, XXXVII (1937), 817–20.

is small enough to exclude a spy."[42] The La Follette Committee uncovered a list of corporations using espionage that "reads like a blue book of American industry," while the NLRB estimated the number of spies in 1936 as 40 to 50 thousand. The Pinkerton agency alone, one of some 200, employed over 1,200 spies and operated in 93 unions in about one-third of which agents held office. The annual income of three agencies during the 1920's was about $65 million.[43] Espionage was supplied by detective agencies, employers' associations, and corporations themselves. The La Follette Committee concluded that it was the most efficient system to prevent unions from forming, to weaken them once they gained a foothold, and to wreck them when they tried to test their strength.[44]

This technique called for placing spies and *agents provocateurs* in the plant and the union. Key objectives were: to secure the names of members and advance strike plans, to precipitate calling of a strike, and to discredit leadership with the membership. Spy reports were useful throughout the campaign against the union: in forming the blacklist, in discrimination and discharge, in breaking strikes, in initiating the company union, and in supplying affidavits for an injunction.[45] There were no effective legal safeguards. Federal legislation did not exist, while state statutes were unenforceable. "For all practical purposes espionage remains unchecked despite legislation."[46]

Strikebreaking and espionage were linked policies. "Spies precede strikes; strikeguards and strikebreakers accompany them. The connection between the two forms of service is convenient for the employer who wishes to destroy a union, and therefore lucrative for the agency that supplies them."[47] Private armies to suppress unions existed only in the United States, growing out of a history of employer antipathy to collective bargaining and of turbulence in industrial relations. Prior to 1900, corporations recruited strikebreakers themselves, but thereafter detective agencies and employer associations professionalized the service. By 1910 distinct occupational types developed, at first, immigrants enlisted for their gullibility, but later, "strikebreakers by calling," primarily the socially maladjusted and criminals. The lowest echelon consisted of strikebreakers, "finks," who replaced strikers. Above them were strikeguards, "nobles," who carried arms and "protected" loyal workers and property, often deputized as police officers. Another type was the propagandist, or "missionary," who posed as a neutral and spread de-

[42] *La Follette Comm. Rep.*, pt. 3, p. 8.
[43] *Ibid.*, pp. 22, 26–28; NLRB, *op. cit.*, p. 15; *Columbia Law Review*, XXXVII (1937), 839.
[44] *La Follette Comm. Rep.*, pt. 3, pp. 9, 17.
[45] *Ibid.*, pt. 3, pp. 45–69; *Columbia Law Review*, XXXVII (1937), 838.
[46] *Columbia Law Review*, XXXVII (1937), 840.
[47] *La Follette Comm. Rep.*, "Strikebreaking Services" (Jan. 26, 1939), p. 35.

fcatism. At the top were the strike lieutenants, who organized and executed the operation. All looked with contempt upon "scabs," those who permanently replaced strikers. The strikebreaker was unqualified by character or training to labor, his function being to shock the morale of the strikers and intimidate them into returning to work. Violence was a consequence of strikebreaking since workers detested the intruders and any encounter was apt to be a spark which set off the charged atmosphere.[48]

There were no effective statutory restrictions upon strikebreaking. There was no federal legislation, while the courts upheld the strikebreaker's "right to work." State "Pinkerton" laws prohibiting importation of armed guards from other states were evaded by shipping guards and arms separately or by recruiting within the state. The La Follette Committee reported, ". . . the detective agencies engaged in furnishing strikeguards today ignore these statutes."[49]

Very large employers, particularly in steel, and those with operations in isolated communities, as in coal and metal mining, developed the private police system. These police were originated in pioneering days by the railroads to protect property because public forces were inadequate. Even at the start, however, they defended the employer's interests with no final accountability to the public. Like espionage and strikebreaking this system was marked by "a long and bloodstained history." There were no legal safeguards and, in fact, Pennsylvania, Maryland, and South Carolina statutes specifically legalized company police.[50]

When private police operated within a company town the result was virtual peonage. U. S. Steel, for example, in the communities it dominated sealed its workers against outside influences. They lived in company houses, received utilities from the Corporation, and were subject to surveillance in their social activities. Housing, electricity, and water became instruments of labor policy. A union organizer entering such a town was soon spotted. The operation of these towns was not only legal but law officers were often controlled by the companies.[51]

The fact that some of these practices ultimately involved force led to industrial munitioning. It began prior to 1890 and thereafter became a large business. Sales correlated with antiunion employer policies and organizational strikes; steel, for example, provided the largest market. The weapons, tear and sickening gas, shells and guns to discharge them, and machine guns, were usually purchased in anticipation of a strike.

---

[48] *Ibid., passim;* "Strikebreaking," *Fortune,* XI (Jan., 1935), 58–60, 89.

[49] *La Follette Comm. Rep.,* pp. 14–17; *Columbia Law Review,* XXXVII (1937), 833–34.

[50] *La Follette Comm. Rep.,* pt. 2, "Private Police Systems," pp. 1–4, 6, 11.

[51] *Ibid.,* p. 4; "U. S. Steel III: Labor," *Fortune,* III (1936), 136, 138, 142.

The munitions companies followed labor difficulties in their sales campaigns, while the detective agencies often acted as commission agents. Frequently private purchasers supplied public officers with weapons prior to a dispute. There was no federal regulatory legislation. Several states required licenses for gas or machine guns but they were easy to obtain because the laws set no standards for issuance.[52]

Company unions were sometimes established to resist unionism, usually during an organizational drive or strike or after breaking a strike. Employers had the added purpose of improving personnel relations through machinery to air employee grievances. Finally, after World War I, company unionism became the fashion and some firms introduced it on that note.[53] Though introduced at the turn of the century few plans existed prior to 1915. Their number increased during and after World War I when employers were concerned with the development of unionism. In the late twenties and during the depression they declined as the independent organizations weakened.[54]

Of company unions the Bureau of Labor Statistics found that,

> The great majority ... were set up entirely by management. Management conceived the idea, developed the plan, and initiated the organization. ... The existence of a company union was almost never the result of a choice by the employees in a secret election in which both a trade union and a company union appeared on the ballot.[55]

Even in cases where employees took the initiative, it was impossible "to conceive of the establishment or the continued existence of a company union in the face of opposition from management."[56] The employer's technique of introduction varied from a statement of approval to firing those who joined a trade union or refused to join the company union.[57]

Company unions were limited to the employees of a single employer in both membership and representation. Some required and others permitted membership and the employer supplied financial support. Representatives were elected by the employees and time spent by them was paid for by the employer. Representatives were neither aware of nor had control over conditions in the industry as a whole. They met at stated intervals with management usually to discuss individual grievances. Occasionally, arbitration was permitted if they failed to agree. Management, however, reserved the right to hire and fire, strikes were

[52] *La Follette Comm. Rep.*, pt. 3, "Industrial Munitions," *passim*.

[53] Bureau of Labor Statistics, Bull. No. 634, *Characteristics of Company Unions, 1935*, pp. 80–81; National Industrial Conference Board, *Collective Bargaining through Employee Representation*, pp. 12–13.

[54] National Industrial Conference Board, *op. cit.*, pp. 6–10, 16.

[55] Bureau of Labor Statistics, *op. cit.*, p. 199.

[56] Twentieth Century Fund, *op. cit.*, p. 67.

[57] Bureau of Labor Statistics, *op. cit.*, pp. 86–89.

prohibited, and representatives were allowed no voice in the basic determination of wages and hours. Company unionism therefore was the
denial of collective bargaining.[58]

It was more common among large than among small employers. A
survey in 1933 found company unions in seventy per cent of plants with
over 10,000 workers and in only fourteen per cent of those with fewer
than fifty.[59] Large corporations found the company union useful in opposing trade unionism and in bridging the gulf to employees.

The legality of company unions was protected except on the railroads.
The affirmation of freedom of association in the Railway Labor Act of
1926 was interpreted by the Supreme Court to make a company union
unlawful.[60] As will be pointed out, this decision was honored more in
the breach than in the observance.

Opposition to unionism was the main purpose of some employer associations. They organized by industry (the National Metal Trades Association), by area (the Associated Industries of Cleveland), to contest a
particular strike (so-called "citizens' committees"), and as federations
(the National Association of Manufacturers). They began to develop on
a broad scale at the turn of the century. The Industrial Relations Commission in 1915, remarking on this growth, pointed out that, "the prime
function of the hostile associations is to aid their members in opposing
the introduction of collective bargaining."[61]

The NMTA, organized in 1899, represented hundreds of employers
in metal fabricating industries. The declaration of principles affirmed:
management's sole right to conduct a business, to refuse to deal with
strikers, to discharge with absolute freedom; and unilateral determination of wages and apprenticeship rules by the employer. To effectuate
these policies NMTA engaged in espionage, strikebreaking, and blacklisting. Its spy net was in operation by 1906 and three years later it had
a blacklist of over 200,000 names. Certificates of merit were awarded
employees who continued to work during a strike. NMTA rules required
that members obtain its approval of agreements with their employees
and prohibited resignation during a stoppage with penalties for violations. If a member faced a strike, NMTA experts assumed complete
control over the strikebreaking operation.[62]

---

[58] *Ibid.*, pp. 60–72, 99–100, 108–11, 200–03; Twentieth Century Fund, *op. cit.*, pp. 66
ff., 96 ff.

[59] National Industrial Conference Board, *Individual and Collective Bargaining under
the N.I.R.A.*, p. 18.

[60] *Texas & New Orleans R. R. Co. v. Brotherhood of Railway & Steamship Clerks*
(1930), 281 U.S. 548.

[61] *Report of the Commission on Industrial Relations*, p. 188.

[62] *La Follette Comm. Rep.*, pt. 4, "Labor Policies of Employers Associations. National
Metal Trades Association."

The NAM operated at the legislative and opinion-forming levels. In 1937 it represented, through allied groups, over 30,000 manufacturers with nearly 5,000,000 employees. Formed during the depression of 1893, it did not primarily concern itself with labor policy until the AFL drive of 1897–1903. NAM's declaration of labor principles, adopted in 1903, closely resembled that of the NMTA. It opposed legislation in conflict with the declaration and for many years was the leading spokesman for industry on labor questions. The NAM was thoroughly reorganized in 1932 and 1933; large employers took a more active role in its direction.[63]

In personnel policy the 1920's proved to be a decade of paternalism for many corporations. This policy, "welfare capitalism," may be regarded as the indirect practices of employers to check unionism. Employees received a financial stake in business through stock ownership, profit-sharing, and bonuses. Some were protected against the hazards of life by old-age pensions, accident and life insurance, and medical and nursing care. Many firms provided housing or its financing. Personnel management burgeoned, while new plants provided better and safer working conditions, as well as cafeterias, social halls, and athletic fields. In a few cases vacations were introduced and relief was provided during unemployment. The social functions of the union, in other words, were assumed by the factory.[64]

Employers had several motives for this paternalism, perhaps most important being the desire to prevent labor trouble by removing its causes. In addition, they perceived a relationship between the worker's morale and his productive efficiency. Finally, some felt a social responsibility for their employees since bargaining hardly existed. Welfare capitalism retarded unionism in the areas it failed to penetrate, but had little effect upon the decline in membership or the shrinkage in the number of strikes. Its efficacy in winning the loyalty of workers depended basically upon how well capitalism worked. In the sunny year of 1929, Professor Sumner H. Slichter wrote, "Modern personnel methods are one of the most ambitious social experiments of the age, because they aim, among other things, to counteract the effect of modern technique upon the mind of the worker, to prevent him from becoming class conscious and from organizing trade unions."[65]

The dikes of paternalism against the spread of unionism were swept away in the flood of the Great Depression. National income plummeted 40 per cent, from $81 billion in 1929 to $49 billion in 1932. Wages sustained the heaviest losses, 60 per cent, as compared with 57 for divi-

---

[63] *Ibid.*, pt. 6, "Labor Policies of Employers Associations. The National Association of Manufacturers."

[64] Lynds, *op. cit.*, p. 78; Slichter, *op. cit.*, p. 397; Lorwin, *op. cit.*, pp. 236–39; Twentieth Century Fund, *op. cit.*, p. 59.

[65] *Op. cit.*, p. 432.

dends, 55 for rents and royalties, 41 for salaries, and 3 for interest. In these years wage payments dropped from $17 billion to under $7 billion. The industrial groups hit hardest were those into which unionism had made inroads—construction, 72 per cent; mining, 61; manufacturing, 54; and transportation, 40.[66]

Shrinkage in income accompanied a precipitous decline in employment. It was estimated that there were over 15,000,000 unemployed in early 1933.[67] Between 1929 and 1933 employment contracted 77 per cent in construction, 69 in metalliferous mining, 64 in bituminous coal, 46 in anthracite, and 43 in manufacturing and on the railroads. Encouraged by "share-the-work" programs, short days, short weeks, and other varieties of irregularity and dilution were introduced. A study of representative firms in 25 industries revealed that hours worked per week declined from 48.4 in 1929 to 34.9 in 1932, or 28 per cent.[68]

While those employed suffered a reduction in wages, real wages did not decline to the same extent due to the lowered cost of living.[69] The depression, however, created distortions within the wage structure, disparities growing up between competing plants. Wage cuts varied widely and concerns that cut deepest gained competitively in the shrinking market. Substandard rates, not revealed in the averages, became common, for example, 10 cents per hour. Industrial homework spread and women and children replaced adult males. In the face of such conditions, it was almost impossible for unions to maintain scales.[70]

The depression accentuated the secular tendencies to decline already manifest in the union movement. The total loss of close to half a million members came entirely from the groups strongest in 1929, the building trades and transportation and communication.[71] Unemployment among members was very severe, rising within the AFL from 8.2 per cent in 1929 to 25.3 in 1933. In addition, between 1931 and 1933 the proportion of AFL members working part time ranged from 19 to 21 per cent.[72] The major effort of the Federation to resist wage reductions collapsed by the spring of 1930.[73]

[66] Simon Kuznets, *National Income, 1929–32,* National Bureau of Economic Research, Bull. No. 49 (June 7, 1934), pp. 3, 5, 9.

[67] The AFL estimated 15,635,000, the National Industrial Conference Board 15,439,000. Cited in Royal E. Montgomery, "Labor," *American Journal of Sociology,* XLVII (1942), 932.

[68] Meredith B. Givens, *Employment during the Depression,* National Bureau of Economic Research, Bull. No. 47 (June 30, 1933), pp. 2, 4.

[69] Leo Wolman, *Wages during the Depression,* National Bureau of Economic Research, Bull. No. 46 (May 1, 1933), pp. 2–3.

[70] Twentieth Century Fund, *op. cit.,* p. 4.

[71] Wolman, *Ebb and Flow,* p. 41.

[72] *53rd Convention American Federation of Labor, 1933,* p. 87.

[73] Lorwin, *op. cit.,* pp. 289–90.

The impact of depression on the union movement can best be seen in the histories of individual unions, the United Mine Workers, International Ladies Garment Workers, and International Typographical Union being illustrative. Decline in coal began in the mid-twenties and by 1932 the bituminous area was "a badly frightened country. . . . Its livelihood was gone."[74] In West Virginia miners worked only two to four days a week with net earnings from 80 cents to $1.00 a day, while coal sold at 75 cents to $1.25 a ton, often below the cost of production. John L. Lewis wrote to President Hoover, "The fare of the workers and their dependents is actually below domestic animal standards."[75]

The effect was that the "union was nigh unto death, except in the fields west of Indiana, and in the Pennsylvania anthracite region."[76] Membership in the UMW dropped precipitously; District 5 in western Pennsylvania, for example, had only 293 dues-paying members out of 45,000 coal diggers in 1930. The union's financial position was critical and most of the district organizations went under. The UMW, in addition, was racked with factionalism and dual-unionism. A bitter battle raged between Lewis and Farrington over control of District 12 in Illinois, fought with fists, injunctions, and rival conventions, with Lewis emerging the victor. An insurgent group called out 30,000 anthracite miners in 1931 and was put down only after denunciation by the international and a costly struggle. The Communist National Miners Union raided several locals and kept the fields in turmoil with strikes.[77] The executive officers informed the 1932 convention, "Never in the history of organized labor . . . has the task of preserving the economic standards and social welfare of its membership been so difficult as is the case today."[78]

The Ladies Garment Workers sank to the lowest point reached since emerging as a nationwide organization in 1910. Membership dropped to 40,000; the ILG was heavily in debt; and in many trades there was no more than a skeleton organization.[79]

In Chicago, for example, the cloak and suit and raincoat organizations disintegrated as the result of bankruptcies and the exodus of shops to nonunion towns. In dresses, wages were cut and hours increased so that by 1930 only a fraction of the firms had contracts. The cloak indus-

---

[74] Ross, *op. cit.*, p. 91.

[75] *United Mine Workers Journal* (Jan. 1, Feb. 1, 1932).

[76] David J. McDonald and Edward A. Lynch, *Coal and Unionism, a History of the American Coal Miners' Union* (Silver Spring, Md.: 1939), p. 182.

[77] *Ibid.*, pp. 183–85, 190, 192; McAlister Coleman, *Men and Coal* (New York: 1943), pp. 138–41.

[78] *United Mine Workers Journal* (Feb. 1, 1932).

[79] Joel Seidman, *The Needle Trades* (New York: 1942), p. 188.

try, the core of ILG strength, insisted on a return to piecework to save the market. After the largest firm locked its employees out and announced its removal to Gary the union agreed not only to give up week work but also accepted a ten per cent wage cut. Drastic salary cuts for officers in 1932 proved inadequate. Manufacturers violated contracts and imposed further wage reductions in early 1933. In the face of internal despondency and growing factionalism it seemed that the union would disappear.[80]

The Typographical Union weathered the depression with a minimum of distress, facing no dual-unionism and little loss of membership. Unemployment, however, was very severe and earnings of members declined from $180 million in 1929 to $123 million in 1933. For the first three years of the depression the ITU succeeded in holding the wage line but in 1933, 760 locals accepted decreases while only 78 maintained the same rates. Share-the-work devices were used and employed members were taxed to support those without jobs. The pension system was strained as older men, who had continued work after becoming eligible, applied for benefits. In 1933, $650,000 was expended in excess of income and the balance was soon to be exhausted.[81]

New Deal intervention to protect the right of wage earners to bargain collectively was grounded on the assumption that they were unable adequately to organize themselves. The weakness of the union movement, the product of secular decline combined with depression, was clear in 1933. At this time, however, the organizations began to shape policies based upon officially established principles that were to lead to the revitalization of the movement.

---

[80] Wilfred Carsel, *A History of the Chicago Ladies Garment Workers Union* (Chicago: 1940), pp. 197–206.

[81] *76th Session International Typographical Union* (1931), pp. 2–5, 35; *77th Session International Typographical Union* (1932), pp. 1, 24; *International Typographical Journal*, LXXXIII, supp., Aug., 1933, pp. 1–5, 30, 35, 66, 108; Bureau of Labor Statistics, Bull. No. 675, *Union Wages, Hours and Working Conditions in the Printing Trades, June 1, 1939*, p. 7.

II. SOURCES OF IDEAS

THE FUNDAMENTAL PRINCIPLES embodied in the New Deal collective bargaining legislation may be summarized as follows:

1) Employees shall have the right to self-organization and may designate representatives of their own choosing for the purpose of collective bargaining.

2) Conversely, employers shall not interfere with, restrain, or coerce employees in organizing or selecting representatives.

3) Representatives for collective bargaining may be determined by an election conducted by secret ballot; those elected by the majority shall represent all the employees.

4) The employer shall recognize and deal with the representatives designated by his employees.

These ideas had been officially expressed on repeated occasions prior to March 4, 1933—in reports of industrial commissions, court decisions, rulings of administrative bodies, and legislation. The New Deal, in effect, gathered up the historical threads and wove them into law.

This line of policy began with the landmark decision of the Supreme Judicial Court of Massachusetts in 1842 in *Commonwealth v. Hunt* in which the right of workers to associate was established. The Boston Journeymen Bootmakers' Society was charged with being an unlawful conspiracy since it practiced the closed shop. The court ruled that combination in itself was not conspiracy and that the tests of legality were the purposes and the means employed. The maintenance of labor conditions through the closed shop met these standards.[1]

After the Pullman Strike in 1894, President Cleveland appointed a commission to inquire into its causes. It found that the company did not recognize the right of its employees to combine and that wages and working conditions were fixed unilaterally. Hence the commission urged employers to accept unions, also recommending that the yellow-dog contract be made illegal.[2]

In 1898 Congress attempted to eliminate discrimination, particularly antiunion contracts, on the railroads. Sec. 10 of the Erdman Act provided that

Any employer subject to the Act, ... who shall require an employee, or any person seeking employment as a condition of such employment to enter into an agreement ..., not to become or remain a member of any labor ... organization; or shall threaten any employee with loss of employment, or shall unjustly discriminate against any employee because of his membership in such a labor ... organization, ... is hereby declared to be guilty of a misdemeanor. ...[3]

---

[1] *Commonwealth v. Hunt* (1842), 4 Metcalf, 111.

[2] *Report on the Chicago Strike of June–July 1894,* United States Strike Commission (Washington: 1894), xxvi, xlvii, liv.

[3] *U. S. Stat. at Large,* XXX, 424. This provision was declared unconstitutional in *Adair v. United States* (1908), 208 U.S. 161.

Labor difficulties at the turn of the century led to an exhaustive study and report by the Industrial Commission in 1902. It concluded that collective bargaining was beneficial to workers, employers, and the public and could not exist in the absence of strong labor organizations. The commission therefore proposed legislation to restrict the injunction and to prohibit employment of strikeguards and the blacklist.[4]

In 1914 in the Clayton Act, Congress declared that labor organizations as such were not to be considered illegal combinations in restraint of trade under the antitrust laws. The courts were limited in their authority to issue injunctions in labor disputes unless necessary to prevent irreparable injury and there was no proper remedy at law.[5]

The Commission on Industrial Relations in 1915 urged the right of workers to organize and condemned interferences by employers, arguing that antiunion policies constituted a major cause of unrest. A constitutional amendment was recommended to guarantee freedom of association to be followed by legislation to prohibit unfair labor practices.[6]

The principles proposed by management and labor during World War I, imposing equal rights and obligations on both, served as the policy base for the first National War Labor Board. They agreed that:

1) The right of workers to organize in trade-unions and to bargain collectively, through chosen representatives, is recognized and affirmed. This right shall not be denied, abridged, or interfered with by the employers in any manner whatsoever.

2) The right of employers to organize in associations or groups and to bargain collectively, through chosen representatives, is recognized and affirmed. This right shall not be denied, abridged, or interfered with by the workers in any manner whatsoever.

3) Employers shall not discharge workers for membership in trade-unions, nor for legitimate trade-union activities.

4) The workers, in the exercise of their right to organize, shall not use coercive measures of any kind to induce persons to join their organizations, nor to induce employers to bargain or deal therewith.[7]

The NWLB in several hundred cases not only asserted the right of association and disallowed restraining practices, but also evolved the election to determine representatives and flirted with requiring the employer to bargain. Despite its equalizing authority, the board's awards were concerned exclusively with employer unfair practices, reflecting the nature of the market. Employers were forbidden to discriminate against workers for union membership or activity; employees discrim-

---

[4] *Final Report of the Industrial Commission* (Washington: 1902), XIX, 844, 890–93.

[5] *U. S. Stat. at Large*, XXXVIII, 735. The injunction exemption was nullified in *Duplex Printing Press v. Deering* (1926), 254 U.S. 443.

[6] *Final Report of the Commission on Industrial Relations* (Washington: 1915), *passim.* The report was signed by four of the nine members of the commission.

[7] *National War Labor Board*, Bureau of Labor Statistics, Bull. No. 287, p. 32.

inatorily discharged were reinstated with compensation for time lost; blacklists and yellow-dog contracts were forbidden; peaceful striking was held no bar to reëmployment; and employees could not be required to join company unions. Where no union existed the board determined representatives by a secret ballot election, usually directing the workers to elect a fixed number from each department who in turn selected a plant committee. Where the board itself conducted the election it stipulated that management deal with the representatives, all of whom were employees.[8]

In 1921 Chief Justice Taft, formerly co-chairman of NWLB, declared that labor unions

were organized out of the necessities of the situation. A single employee was helpless in dealing with an employer. . . . Union was essential to give laborers an opportunity to deal on equality with their employer. They united to exert influence upon him and to leave him in a body in order by this inconvenience to induce him to make better terms with them. . . . The right to combine for such a purpose has in many years not been denied by any court.[9]

Since the Transportation Act of 1920 did not deal adequately with collective bargaining, the Railroad Labor Board the following year found it necessary to erect the entire structure of principles.

The right of railway employees to organize for lawful objects shall not be denied, interfered with, or obstructed. The right of such lawful organization to act toward lawful objects through representatives of its own choice, whether employees of a particular carrier or otherwise, shall be agreed to by management. No discrimination shall be practiced by management as between members and non-members of organizations or as between members of different organizations, nor shall members of organizations discriminate against non-members or use other methods than lawful persuasion to secure their membership. Espionage by carriers on the legitimate activities of labor organizations or by labor organizations on the legitimate activities of carriers should not be practiced. The right of employees to be consulted prior to a decision of management adversely affecting their wages or working conditions shall be agreed to by management. This right of participation shall be deemed adequately complied with if and when the representatives of a majority of the employees of each of the several classes directly affected shall have conferred with the management. . . . The majority of any craft or class of employees shall have the right to determine what organization shall represent members of such craft or class. Such organization shall have the right to make an agreement which shall apply to all employees in such craft or class.[10]

The Railway Labor Act of 1926 codified these decisional precepts except for the election and majority rule. Section 2 read as follows:

[8] *Ibid.*, pp. 52–67.

[9] *American Steel Foundries v. Tri-City Central Trades Council* (1921), 257 U.S. 184. The Chief Justice's remarks here were *obiter dictum*. The decision actually sustained an injunction restraining unlawful picketing on the grounds of intimidation.

[10] H. D. Wolf, *The Railroad Labor Board* (Chicago: 1927), pp. 184–86.

First, It shall be the duty of all carriers, their officers, agents, and employees to exert every reasonable effort to make and maintain agreements concerning rates of pay, rules, and working conditions, and to settle all disputes, whether arising out of the application of such agreements or otherwise, in order to avoid any interruption to commerce or to the operation of any carrier growing out of any dispute between the carrier and the employees thereof.

Second, All disputes between a carrier and its employees shall be considered, and, if possible, decided, with all expedition, in conference between representatives designated and authorized so to confer, respectively, by the carriers and by the employees thereof interested in the dispute.

Third, Representatives, for the purposes of this Act, shall be designated by the respective parties in such manner as may be provided in their corporate organization or unincorporated association, or by other means of collective action, without interference, influence, or coercion exercised by either party over the self-organization, or designation of representatives, by the other.[11]

The Supreme Court, in upholding the disestablishment of a company union in the railway clerks case in 1930, unanimously sustained the validity of the statute. Chief Justice Hughes declared,

Freedom of choice in the selection of representatives on each side of the dispute is the essential foundation of the statutory scheme. . . . The entire policy of the act must depend for success on the uncoerced action of each party through its own representatives to the end that agreements satisfactory to both may be reached and the peace essential to the uninterrupted service of the instrumentalities of interstate commerce may be maintained. There is no impairment of the voluntary character of arrangements for the adjustment of disputes in the imposition of a legal obligation not to interfere with a free choice of those who are to make such adjustments. On the contrary, it is of the essence of a voluntary scheme, if it is to accomplish its purpose, that this liberty should be safeguarded.

The legality of collective action on the part of employees in order to safeguard their proper interests is not to be disputed. It has long been recognized. . . . Congress was not required to ignore this right of the employees but could safeguard it and seek to make their appropriate collective action an instrument of peace rather than of strife. Such collective action would be a mockery if representation were made futile by interferences with freedom of choice. Thus the prohibition by Congress of interference with the selection of representatives for the purpose of negotiation and conference between employers and employees, instead of being an invasion of the constitutional right of either, was based on the recognition of the rights of both.[12]

The policy declaration of the Norris-LaGuardia Act of 1932, based upon the Tri-City case, the Railway Labor Act, and the decision sustaining it,[13] reads as follows:

Whereas under prevailing economic conditions developed with the aid of governmental authority for owners of property to organize in the corporate and other forms

---

[11] *U. S. Stat. at Large*, XLIV, 577.

[12] *Texas & New Orleans R. R. Co. v. Brotherhood of Railway and Steamship Clerks* (1930), 281 U.S. 548.

[13] 72d Cong., 1st sess., H.R., Hearings before Comm. on Jud. on H.R. 5315, *Defining and Limiting the Jurisdiction of Courts Sitting in Equity* (Feb. 25, 1932), p. 11.

of ownership association, the individual unorganized worker is commonly helpless to exercise actual liberty of contract and to protect his freedom of labor, and thereby to obtain acceptable terms and conditions of employment, wherefore, though he should be free to decline to associate with his fellows, it is necessary that he have full freedom of association, self-organization, and designation of representatives of his own choosing, to negotiate the terms and contracts of his employment, and that he shall be free from the interference, restraint, or coercion of employers of labor, or their agents, in the designation of such representatives or in self-organization or in other concerted activities for the purpose of collective bargaining or other mutual aid or protection.[14]

The labor provisions of the Bankruptcy Act of March 3, 1933, the terminal point in the pre-New Deal line of policy, were suggested by the railway unions and sponsored by Senator George W. Norris. Sec. 77(p) and (q) provided that no one receiving bankrupt railroad property might

deny or in any way question the right of employees . . . to join the labor organization of their choice . . . [or] interfere in any way with the organizations of employees, or . . . use the funds of the railroad . . . in maintaining so-called company unions, or . . . influence or coerce employees in an effort to induce them to join or remain members of such company unions. [Or],

. . . require any person seeking employment . . . to sign any contract or agreement promising to join or to refuse to join a labor organization, and if such contract has been enforced . . . then the said judge . . . shall notify the employees . . . that said contract has been discarded and is no longer binding on them in any way.[15]

Before President Roosevelt took office the right of employees to associate and designate representatives had thus been asserted in *Commonwealth v. Hunt,* the 1894 report of the Strike Commission, the Clayton Act, the report of the Commission on Industrial Relations, the decisions of the NWLB, the American Steel Foundries case, the rulings of the Railroad Labor Board, the Railway Labor Act, the railway clerks case, and the Norris-LaGuardia Act. Similarly, the principle that employers shall not interfere with these rights was affirmed by the Strike Commission, the Erdman Act, the 1902 Industrial Commission, the Commission on Industrial Relations, the rulings of NWLB and the Railroad Board, the Railway Labor Act, the railway clerks case, the Norris-LaGuardia Act, and the Bankruptcy Act. NWLB and the Railroad Labor Board employed the secret ballot election and majority rule. The responsibility of the employer to deal with the representatives of his employees was declared by the Strike Commission, the Industrial Commission, the War Labor Board, the Railroad Board, and the Railway Labor Act.

The motive power in converting these principles into legislation came from the union movement and political leaders sympathetic with its

---

[14] *U. S. Stat. at Large,* XLVII, 70.
[15] *Ibid.,* XLVII, 1467.

aims. The right to organize and bargain was, in fact, the presumption of existence and unions had always struggled to assert them in dealings with employers.[16]

The next step, insistence that the *government* enforce these policies, required that the AFL rid itself at least in part of the philosophy of voluntarism. Gompers embedded in labor thinking the concept of self-help. "So long as we have held fast to voluntary principles," he declared, in what was in effect his last will and testament, " . . . we have made our labor movement something to be respected and accorded a place in the councils of our Republic."[17] Voluntarism was grounded on a deep suspicion of government for, as Gompers declared,

The mass of the workers are convinced that laws necessary for their protection against the most grievous wrongs cannot be passed except after long and exhausting struggles; that such beneficent measures as become laws are largely nullified by the unwarranted decisions of the courts; that the laws which stand upon the statute books are not equally enforced; and that the whole machinery of government has frequently been placed at the disposal of the employers for the oppression of the workers.[18]

The breakdown of voluntarism was a function of adversity, the unions coming to the government for assistance when hard times set in. The process began with those traditional pacemakers, the railway organizations and the miners, and finally encompassed the AFL itself. With the first this took shape in the Railway Labor Act, whose principal draftsman was Donald R. Richberg, counsel of the Railway Labor Executives Association. Disastrous defeat in the shop crafts strike of 1922 taught the unions to rely on legislation rather than strikes, resulting in the 1926 statute. The Act imposed the duty on both sides to exert every reasonable effort to reach agreement; each was given the right to organize and select representatives without interference; and a procedure was devised for handling disputes. "The keystone of this 'peace arch' lay in the provision guaranteeing freedom of association and the right of collective bargaining."[19]

The Mine Workers turned to the government as a result of the sickness of the coal industry in the late 1920's, having exhibited a fleeting interest as early as 1919. In 1928 the union instigated a congressional investigation of conditions in the fields and drafted the Watson-Rathbone bill. It proposed stabilization by producers' selling pools outside the

[16] Cf. Samuel Gompers, "The President's Industrial Conference," *American Federationist*, XXVI (1919), 1041–44.

[17] *44th Convention American Federation of Labor, 1924*, p. 5.

[18] Quoted by G. G. Higgins, *Voluntarism in Organized Labor in the United States, 1930–1940* (Washington: 1944), p. 31.

[19] Donald R. Richberg, *The Rainbow* (Garden City, N.Y.: 1936), p. 51; Wolf, *op. cit., passim.*

antitrust laws with labor gaining an equalizing freedom to organize. It would be the obligation of operators and employees to bargain collectively; workers might select representatives without interference; the yellow-dog contract would be illegal; and the closed shop would be safeguarded. The bill, however, got nowhere.[20]

As the depression racked the industry the union had essentially the same measure reintroduced in 1932, as the Davis-Kelly coal stabilization bill. Sec. 5 carried over the labor provisions with these additions: the right of assembly to discuss organized labor and collective bargaining; employees would not be required to purchase from company stores and would be free to select their own checkweighmen; and weights and scales would be open to public inspection. It would be inequitable, the UMW argued, for miners to work under individual and yellow-dog contracts while operators collectively fixed the price of coal. Further, since labor constituted a major cost factor, it was necessary to establish wage uniformity through collective bargaining to stabilize the industry.[21]

The seriousness with which the miners advocated governmental intervention is evident in Lewis' testimony:

> The coal industry needs the helping hand of the Federal Government. I say that reluctantly. I am one who for long years in the councils of the miners and operators of this country opposed any form of Government regulation. . . . I have reluctantly come to the conclusion that the industry itself is so impotent that it cannot and will not work out its own salvation. . . . The industry is beggared. Its people are in misery, and it petitions Congress for help.[22]

The Mine Workers in 1932–1933 took every occasion to press for federal assistance. Delegations headed by Vice-President Philip Murray called upon candidate Roosevelt repeatedly during the 1932 campaign to obtain a commitment to support collective bargaining in coal.[23] In hearings in January, 1933, on the Thirty-Hour bill the UMW proposed amendments outlawing the yellow-dog contract and guaranteeing the right of workers to select their own representatives.[24] The following month Lewis urged action to foster collective bargaining as a means of combating Communism and of preserving free institutions.[25]

[20] *United Mine Workers Journal* (Dec. 1, 1931).

[21] *Ibid.* (Feb. 1, 1932); *To Create a Bituminous Coal Commission,* 72d Cong., 1st sess., Sen., Hearings before Subcomm. on Mines on S. 2935 (Mar. 14–Apr. 22, 1932), pp. 1–3, 61.

[22] *To Create a Coal Commission,* Sen. Hearings, pp. 1346–47.

[23] David J. McDonald and Edward A. Lynch, *Coal and Unionism, a History of the American Coal Miners' Union* (Silver Spring, Md.: 1939), pp. 193–94. McDonald to the writer, Nov. 24, 1947.

[24] *Thirty-Hour Work Week,* 72d Cong., 2d sess., Sen., Hearings before Subcomm. on Jud. on S. 5267 (Jan. 5–19, 1933), pp. 288–89.

[25] *Investigation of Economic Problems,* 72d Cong., 2d sess., Sen., Hearings before Comm. on Finance pursuant to S. Res. 315 (Feb. 13–28, 1933), p. 300.

The AFL moved at a slower pace and did not discard voluntarism in overt policy until the spring of 1933. The drift appeared in August 1931, however, when the Executive Council called for anti-injunction legislation representing the ideas of such staid leaders as Matthew Woll, John P. Frey, and Victor A. Olander.[26] When the Norris-LaGuardia Act became law, moreover, the council hailed the declaration of policy as "a most distinct step forward in the government attitude toward organizations of labor and collective bargaining."[27] Perhaps most dramatic was the reversal on unemployment insurance at the 1932 convention where the Executive Council, in defiance of the Gompers tradition of voluntary assistance, called for federal intervention in this field.[28]

At the same time, the AFL asked the government to expand its activity in the collective bargaining area. Green gave the labor provisions of the Davis-Kelly bill the Federation's blessing. In April 1933 the AFL proposed an amendment to the Thirty-Hour bill to guarantee to workers the right to belong to unions and to bargain through freely chosen representatives.[29] At this time, however, the AFL's prime interest was unemployment, since the right to join a union did little good if the worker was on the streets. Moreover, the protagonists of voluntarism, though now a minority, were not to be ignored.[30]

Between Governor Roosevelt's nomination for the presidency in the summer of 1932 and his inauguration the following March the union movement did not seek a commitment on collective bargaining from him except in the limited area of coal. Although he and his advisers considered an extraordinary variety of legislative proposals, they gave little thought to encouraging unionism and collective bargaining.[31] Roosevelt's campaign, in fact, left the public largely unaware of the policies he would represent.[32] As Frances Perkins has noted,

The New Deal was not a plan with form and content. It was a happy phrase he [Roosevelt] had coined during the campaign. . . . The notion that the New Deal had a preconceived theoretical position is ridiculous. The pattern it was to assume was not clear or specific in Roosevelt's mind, in the mind of the Democratic party, or in the

[26] *New York Times*, Aug. 15, 1931; AFL, *Weekly News Service*, Aug. 22, 1931.

[27] *52d Convention American Federation of Labor, 1932*, p. 66.

[28] Higgins, *op. cit.*, pp. 59–72.

[29] *To Create a Coal Commission*, Sen. Hearings, pp. 76–78; *Thirty-Hour Bill*, 73d Cong., 1st sess., H.R., Hearings before Comm. on Labor on S. 158 and H.R. 4557 (Apr. 25–May 5, 1933), pp. 66, 69.

[30] Shishkin interview; Slichter, *op. cit.*, p. 272.

[31] Frank interview.

[32] Walter Millis, "Presidential Candidates," *The Yale Review*, XXI (1932), 13–15; Oswald Garrison Villard, "The Democratic Trough at Chicago," *The Nation*, CXXXV (1932), 27.

mind of anyone else taking part in the 1932 campaign. There were no preliminary conferences of party leaders to work out details and arrive at agreements.[33]

The New Deal was made possible by Roosevelt's awareness of social evils, receptiveness to ideas, and willingness to employ the power of government in economic life. If this "constituted a national program, then a man's intention to build a house constitutes the work of the architect, of the contractor, and of the carpenters."[34]

Raymond Moley has shrewdly characterized Roosevelt as a "patron" of labor. He had a profound concern for the hardships imposed upon workers by depression, perceiving them as people in trouble rather than as tables of statistics. As governor of New York he had sponsored a program of social welfare, with AFL support, including ceilings on hours and minimum wages for women and children, workmen's compensation, factory inspection, relief and public works, and a study of unemployment insurance and old-age pensions.[35] These measures reveal a faith in direct legislation to assist the needy rather than a desire to nurture unionism as an instrument to raise their standards. There were, in addition, blank spots in the fields of his interest. He showed little concern with collective bargaining as contrasted with foreign affairs, finance, and military and naval policy. The details bored him and he relied, therefore, on the advice of his experts.[36]

For his own education and to prepare material for campaign addresses, the Governor established the "brain trust" under Moley. Specialists recruited largely from Columbia University formulated policies for agriculture, the tariff, finance, international debts, power, relief, the railroads, governmental economy, and presidential power. No expert in the labor relations field was called in except Donald Richberg, who worked exclusively on the railways. The brain trusters themselves, with the exception of Rexford G. Tugwell, exhibited little concern with trade unions.[37] Tugwell was disturbed by their submissiveness, by their acquiescence in rule by business, and he criticized the AFL's craft structure, the backwardness of its leadership, and its failure to employ the services of experts.[38]

[33] Frances Perkins, *The Roosevelt I Knew* (New York: 1946), pp. 166–67.

[34] Raymond Moley, *After Seven Years* (New York: 1939), pp. 13–14; Ernest K. Lindley, *The Roosevelt Revolution, First Phase* (New York: 1933), p. 11.

[35] Moley, *op. cit.,* p. 13; Perkins, *op. cit.,* chaps. vii and viii; *The Public Papers and Addresses of Franklin D. Roosevelt,* ed. by Samuel I. Rosenman (New York: 1938), I, 83–84, 90–91, 104–05, 123.

[36] Richberg, Keyserling, Wyzanski interviews.

[37] Moley, *op. cit.,* pp. 15 ff. Cf. also, A. A. Berle, Jr., and Gardiner C. Means, *The Modern Corporation and Private Property* (New York: 1932); Hugh S. Johnson, *The Blue Eagle from Egg to Earth* (New York: 1935); Unofficial Observer, *The New Dealers* (New York: 1934); Lindley, *loc. cit.;* Rexford G. Tugwell, *The Industrial Discipline and the Governmental Arts* (New York: 1933).

[38] Tugwell, *op. cit.,* pp. 5–6, 133, 157.

The 1932 campaign evoked little discussion of unionism. The spirit of the Democratic platform was supplied by the elder statesmen of the Wilson era and emphasized a balanced budget, sound currency, encouragement of competition and small business, less intervention by the federal government, and the repeal of prohibition, but did contain a plank, at AFL insistence, favoring shorter hours.[39] Except for the Boston address of October 31st, none of Roosevelt's major speeches dealt primarily with the problems of workers. Its preparation involved the only important rift within the brain trust. Berle and Tugwell urged a direct attack upon business abuses and a broad affirmative program, while Moley, General Johnson, Senator Key Pittman, and Senator James F. Byrnes cautioned moderation. Roosevelt sided with conservative counsel and indulged largely in generalities. On the positive side, however, he pledged direct relief and public works for the destitute, supported the Wagner employment service bill, and reasserted the platform statement on hours. No mention was made of collective bargaining[40] but in minor speeches at Indianapolis and Terre Haute he promised to call a conference of miners and operators and, if they were unable to agree on a stabilization program, to recommend legislation.[41]

Although not a member of the brain trust, Frances Perkins was one of Roosevelt's closest advisers on labor matters, particularly where they impinged upon social welfare. She had worked on factory safety, women in industry, workmen's compensation, and related problems for over twenty years and was his industrial commissioner in the State Department of Labor. Roosevelt's regard for her is revealed in the fact that he named her Secretary of Labor in the face of vigorous AFL opposition. When offered the post, she outlined a broad prospective program which received his approval. It covered unemployment relief, public works, minimum wages and maximum hours, unemployment and old-age insurance, abolition of child labor, and an employment service. Again, a collective bargaining policy was notably absent for Miss Perkins had little confidence in the union movement as an instrument of social advancement.[42]

The man who was to provide the principal link between the unions and the New Deal was Senator Robert F. Wagner of New York, who had the former's complete confidence. Wagner had been an outstanding

---

[39] Walter Lippmann, *Interpretations, 1931–1932*, ed. by Allan Nevins (New York: 1932), pp. 308–10; Irving Bernstein, "Labor and the Recovery Program, 1933," *Quarterly Journal of Economics*, LX (1946), 272.

[40] Moley, *op. cit.*, pp. 62–63; *Roosevelt Public Papers*, I, 842–55.

[41] Lawrence Dwyer to Roosevelt, Mar. 9, 1933, Berle to Marvin McIntyre, Apr. 10, 1933, White House, O.F. 175, Coal; McDonald to the writer, Nov. 24, 1947.

[42] Perkins, *op. cit.*, pp. 150–52; Frances Perkins, "Eight Years as Madame Secretary," *Fortune*, XXIV (1941), 77; Wyzanski interview.

progressive in the New York Assembly and Senate (1905–1918) and sponsored the resolution, following the Triangle shirtwaist fire, that created the Factory Investigation Commission. The commission under his chairmanship laid the basis for a notable factory code and workmen's compensation law. As a judge he is credited with granting the first injunction to a union restraining an employer from interfering with lawful activities.[43] With his law partner and later legislative secretary, Simon H. Rifkind, he was instrumental in preparing a key case assaulting the Hitchman doctrine, the New York Court of Appeals holding a yellow-dog contract unenforceable and no basis for an injunction.[44] This in turn led him to prevail upon Senator Norris, chairman of the Judiciary Committee, to seek expert assistance in formulating the anti-injunction bill. By 1933, in fact, Wagner was recognized as the member of Congress most active in the labor field, having sponsored measures dealing with unemployment compensation, public works and relief, employment exchanges, and a census of those out of work.[45]

In Wagner's view there was an essential relationship between collective bargaining and democracy. He observed that,

The development of a partnership between industry and labor in the solution of national problems is the indispensable complement to political democracy. And that leads us to this all-important truth: there can no more be democratic self-government in industry without workers participating therein, than there could be democratic government in politics without workers having the right to vote.... That is why the right to bargain collectively is at the bottom of social justice for the worker, as well as the sensible conduct of business affairs. The denial or observance of this right means the difference between despotism and democracy.[46]

[43] Oswald Garrison Villard, "Pillars of Government, Robert F. Wagner," *Forum & Century*, XCVI (1936), 124–25; I. F. Stone, "Robert F. Wagner," *The Nation*, CLIX (Oct. 28, 1944), 507; Owen P. White, "When the Public Needs a Friend," *Collier's*, XCIII (June 2, 1934), 18, 60; Perkins, *The Roosevelt I Knew*, pp. 17, 22.

[44] *Interborough Rapid Transit Co. v. Green* (N. Y., 1928), 131 Misc. 682. For its significance, cf. Felix Frankfurter and Nathan Greene, *The Labor Injunction* (New York: 1930), pp. 40–42, 270–72, and Homer F. Carey and Herman Oliphant, "The Present Status of the Hitchman Case," *Columbia Law Review*, XXIX (1929).

[45] Rifkind interview; Keyserling to the writer, June 11, 1948.

[46] Quoted by Leon H. Keyserling, "Why the Wagner Act?" *The Wagner Act: After Ten Years*, ed. by Louis G. Silverberg (Washington: 1945), pp. 12–13.

III. FIRST STEP: SECTION 7(a)

THE PRIME PROBLEM facing the new administration on March 4, 1933, was the stimulation of business with a consequent reduction in the number of the unemployed. Among the hundreds of proposals advanced to achieve these purposes four received the support of important interest groups and leaders and were incorporated in varying degrees in the New Deal's basic revival measure, the National Industrial Recovery Act. The first called for the spread of available employment by compulsory shortening of hours, urged by the AFL and such public officials as Senator Hugo L. Black of Alabama and Governor John G. Winant of New Hampshire. The creation of jobs and mass purchasing power through public works was the second, proposed by the AFL, many economists, and Senators Wagner, Robert M. La Follette, Jr., of Wisconsin, and Edward P. Costigan of Colorado. The third would suspend the antitrust laws, permitting businessmen through trade associations to regulate prices, production, and labor standards. It was pressed by the Chamber of Commerce, the NAM, independent business leaders like Bernard M. Baruch, General Johnson, Gerard Swope, and Dr. Meyer Jacobstein, and was conditionally acceptable to organized labor. The final proposal, backed by unions, particularly the Mine Workers, urged a guarantee of the right of workers to organize and bargain collectively.[1]

The shorter hours group seized the initiative on December 21, 1932, when Black introduced the Thirty-Hour bill. It would have barred interstate commerce to articles produced in establishments "in which any person was employed or permitted to work more than five days in any week or more than six hours in any day."[2] In hearings before a Senate subcommittee in January, 1933, AFL President William Green described the measure as a fundamental attack upon the depression by spreading work and reducing technological unemployment. Though doubtful as to its constitutionality, he warned that the Federation might call general strikes to obtain passage.[3] Philip Murray for the miners, however, pointed out that employers would lower wages if hours were reduced. Since the bill faced the formidable constitutional hurdle of the child labor case,[4] he proposed that labor protect its wages by collective bargaining, suggesting an amendment to prohibit shipment in commerce of articles in whose manufacture "it is made a condition of employment

---

[1] Irving Bernstein, "Labor and the Recovery Program, 1933," *Quarterly Journal of Economics,* LX (1946), 270–71; *Staff Studies,* National Archives, NRA, pp. 113–18.

[2] *Cong. Record,* LXXVII, pt. vi, 5901.

[3] *Thirty-Hour Work Week,* 72d Cong., 2d sess., Sen., Hearings before Subcomm. on Jud. on S. 5267, pt. i (Jan. 5–19, 1933), pp. 2–22.

[4] *Hammer v. Dagenhart* (1918), 247 U.S. 251.

that the workers engaged in such manufacture or production shall not belong to, remain, or become a member of a labor organization, or in which they shall be denied the right to collectively bargain for their wages through chosen representatives of their own."[5] Industry except for a few hosiery employers denounced the Black bill as unconstitutional and bad economics.[6]

On March 30th, after Roosevelt had summoned Congress into special session, the Judiciary Committee reported the bill favorably with a reservation on constitutionality.[7] When Senate debate began on April 3, it became evident that the measure would be passed. The Administration would then be presented with a recovery program without having taken a hand in its formulation. After a hurried White House conference, Senate majority leader Joseph T. Robinson on April 5th therefore introduced an amendment to raise maximum hours to 36 per week and 8 per day. The Administration amendment was defeated 48 to 41, however, and the following day the Senate adopted the bill, 53 to 30.[8]

The President was exercised since he regarded it as unconstitutional and so rigid as to be economically unworkable. Wagner felt it inadequate for recovery, while Raymond Moley and General Johnson, regarding the bill as "utterly impractical," recommended that it be killed. Roosevelt decided, nevertheless, to support the Secretary of Labor's efforts to gain flexibility in amendments addressed on April 25th to the House Labor Committee.[9] These changes, approved by several cabinet members but not submitted to the AFL, called for a sliding scale of hours, from thirty to forty weekly with a maximum of eight daily, as well as minimum wages. In both cases tripartite boards with union representation where possible would make determinations.[10]

Green then told the committee that the AFL would accept the amendment on hours, but only because it represented an Administration policy. Minimum wages, however, were rejected except for women and children since the AFL felt that minima tended to become maxima and thereby reduced skilled rates. Inasmuch as tripartite boards could not possibly represent workers in the absence of unions, he proposed

[5] *Thirty-Hour Work Week,* Sen. Hearings, pp. 288–97.

[6] *Ibid.,* pp. 190 ff., 272–73.

[7] Sen. Rep. No. 114, 73d Cong., 1st sess. (Mar. 30, 1933).

[8] *Cong. Record,* CXXVII, pt. ii, 1178–99, 1244–1350; Raymond Moley, *After Seven Years* (New York: 1939), p. 186.

[9] Frances Perkins, *The Roosevelt I Knew* (New York: 1946), pp. 192–96; Moley, *op. cit.,* p. 186; Rifkind interview.

[10] C. F. Roos, *NRA Economic Planning* (Bloomington, Ill.: 1937), p. 40; AFL, *Weekly News Service,* Mar. 4, 1933; *Thirty-Hour Bill,* 73d Cong., 1st sess., H.R., Hearings before Comm. on Labor on S. 158, H.R. 4557 (Apr. 25–May 5, 1933), pp. 2–18, 26.

an amendment: "Workers . . . shall not be denied by their employer the free exercise of the right to belong to a *bona fide* labor organization and to collectively bargain for their wages through their own chosen representatives."[11] Industry vigorously opposed the Secretary's amendments.[12]

On May 10th the committee issued a unanimous report, conceding fully to organized labor with respect to collective bargaining. A tripartite Trade Regulation Board, chaired by the Secretary of Labor, would license firms to engage in commerce which were affiliated with trade associations that made agreements with unions, or unaffiliated but in compliance with such contracts, or willing to accept board regulations regarding wages, conditions, and limitations on production. Licensees would maintain the five-day week and six-hour day and pay wages sufficient for standards of decency. A license would be denied for articles in the production of which children or enforced labor were employed, nor would one be issued to a firm in which

any worker who was a signatory to any contract of employment prohibiting such worker from joining a labor union or employees' organization, was employed, or any goods, articles, or commodities [were] produced by any person whose employees were denied the right to organization and representation in collective bargaining by individuals of their own choosing.[13]

The Black bill was doomed even before the committee reported since Roosevelt had thrown his full weight behind an Administration substitute. Despite a direct appeal by the AFL Executive Council, he withdrew support on May 1, burying the report in the Rules Committee. The President had concluded that the endorsement of industry, denied to the Black bill, was vital. Hence activity on the Administration bill proceeded under forced draft.[14]

The President, in fact, in March, 1933, had asked Wagner, the Congressional focal point of recovery planning and a trusted adviser as well, to shape a legislative policy. During the previous fall Jacobstein had suggested the trade association idea to halt deflation and, to examine this plan, the Senator called together a representative group in April. Leading members, in addition to Wagner, Rifkind, and Jacobstein, were: Harold Moulton of the Brookings Institution; Virgil D. Jordan of the National Industrial Conference Board; M. C. Rorty, an industrial economist; Fred I. Kent of the Bankers Trust Company;

[11] House Hearings, *Thirty-Hour Bill,* p. 66.

[12] *Ibid.,* pp. 91–92, 199, 511, 707, 713.

[13] H.R. Rep. No. 124, 73d Cong., 1st sess. (May 10, 1933).

[14] *Staff Studies,* National Archives, NRA, p. 120; Moley, *op. cit.,* p. 187; *Cong. Record,* LXXVII, pt. vi, 5805; AFL, *Weekly News Service,* May 6, 1933.

James H. Rand, Jr., of Remington-Rand; the trade association attorney David L. Podell; W. Jett Lauck, economist of the Mine Workers; and Representative M. Clyde Kelly, cosponsor of the coal bill. Convinced after several sessions that the group was too large and represented irreconcilable elements, Wagner appointed a drafting committee consisting of Moulton, Jacobstein, Podell, and Lauck. Their measure provided for self-regulation of business through trade associations, a public works program, and a guarantee of the right to bargain collectively. Moulton, Jacobstein, and Podell emphasized the first; the Senator insisted upon the second; and Lauck, with Wagner's support, backed the miners' leading demand. This last they justified on the ground that businessmen would have unfettered control over wages and hours unless labor organized as a counterbalance. Jerome N. Frank, Counsel of the Agricultural Adjustment Administration, and John Dickinson, Assistant Secretary of Commerce, then joined the group, but only the former interested himself in the labor provision.[15]

On April 11th Roosevelt instructed Moley to work on a recovery measure without informing him of the activities already under way. Laden with other responsibilities, Moley on April 25th passed on the assignment to General Johnson, who cared only about a program of self-regulation for business. Although neither regarded labor policy as relevant to recovery, the AFL's political strength demonstrated in the Black bill compelled a concession. Hence they called on Donald R. Richberg, who drafted a collective bargaining statement based upon his experience with the Railway Labor Act and the Norris-LaGuardia Act, emphasizing freedom of association in the designation of bargaining representatives.[16]

Early in May the President summoned both groups to the White House where they agreed to include the trade association formula, a guarantee of collective bargaining, and public works. By this combination he hoped to win the support of business and labor, since he regarded the backing of both as necessary for the success of the program. A drafting committee, consisting of Budget Director Lewis W. Douglas, Wagner, Johnson, Richberg, Dickinson, Assistant Secretary of Agriculture Rexford G. Tugwell, and Secretary Perkins, started to work on a unified bill, but after several meetings the last three dropped out, leav-

---

[15] Jacobstein, Lauck, Rifkind, Frank interviews; Roos, *op. cit.*, pp. 38–39.

[16] Moley, *op. cit.*, pp. 187–88; Hugh S. Johnson, *The Blue Eagle from Egg to Earth* (Garden City, N.Y.: 1935), pp. 201–03; Donald R. Richberg, *The Rainbow* (New York: 1936), p. 106; John T. Flynn, "Whose Child Is the NRA?" *Harpers Magazine*, CLXIX (1934), 390–92; Lauck interview. Richberg insists that he had not seen the Wagner version prior to drawing his own. Richberg interview; Richberg to N. von Hoershelman, Sep. 26, 1933, National Archives, NRA, No. 3706.

ing the final drafting to Douglas, Wagner, Johnson, and Richberg. An NAM delegation appealed to Roosevelt to revise the labor section drastically. He referred them to the committee, which, under Wagner's influence, refused to make the changes.[17]

Sec. 7(a) of the National Industrial Recovery bill, submitted to Congress by the President on May 17, 1933, required that

> Every code of fair competition, agreement, and license approved, prescribed, or issued under this title shall contain the following conditions:
> 1) that employees shall have the right to organize and bargain collectively through representatives of their own choosing,
> 2) that no employee and no one seeking employment shall be required as a condition of employment to join any organization or to refrain from joining a labor organization of his own choosing, and
> 3) that employers shall comply with the maximum hours of labor, minimum rates of pay, and other working conditions approved or prescribed by the President.[18]

Since wages, hours, and working conditions were already determined by bargaining in some industries, 7(b) empowered employers and employees to reach agreements which, when approved by the President, would have the force of codes of fair competition. Where collective bargaining did not exist, Sec. 7(c) authorized the President to fix maximum hours, minimum rates, and other conditions which would then have the effect of codes.

Immediately preceding the hearings of the House Ways and Means Committee on May 18th, an emergency conference of the AFL in Washington voted to insist on changes in both clauses (1) and (2) of 7(a).[19] On May 19th Green proposed to the committee that the first, after guaranteeing to employees the right to organize, should continue, "and shall be free from the interference, restraint, or coercion of employers of labor or their agents, in the designation of such representatives or in self-organization or in other concerted activities for the purpose of collective bargaining or other mutual aid or protection."[20] This language, taken verbatim from the Anti-injunction Act, aimed to buttress these rights against employer restrictions. He also recommended that in the second clause "company union" be substituted for "organization," to read, "that no employee and no one seeking employment shall be required as a condition of employment to join a *company union,* or to

---

[17] Richberg, Frank, Jacobstein interviews; Roos, *op. cit.,* pp. 39–40; Richberg, *op. cit.,* pp. 107–09; *Violations of Free Speech and Rights of Labor,* 76th Cong., 1st sess., Sen., Hearings before Subcomm. on Edu. and Labor on S. Res. 266, pt. 17, 7414, hereafter cited as *La Follette Comm. Hearings.*

[18] 73d Cong., 1st sess., H.R. 5664 (May 17, 1933).

[19] *53d Convention American Federation of Labor, 1933,* p. 41.

[20] *National Industrial Recovery,* 73d Cong., 1st sess., H.R., Hearings on H.R. 5664 before Comm. on Ways and Means (May 18–20, 1933), p. 117.

refrain from joining a labor organization of his own choosing."[21] The intent was to safeguard the closed shop, which might be defined as "any organization," thereby outlawing agreements in which membership in a trade union was a condition of employment. He did not, however, suggest rewording the first clause for the same purpose. With these amendments the AFL offered to endorse the bill without qualification.[22]

Henry I. Harriman of the Chamber of Commerce did not discuss the labor provisions in his testimony. In fact, no representative of industry objected to Sec. 7(a) or the AFL's amendments. The Federation and the Chamber, indeed, had agreed privately that the former would accept the trade association features in return for the Chamber's pledge to accept the labor section, the NAM refusing to accede.[23] Senator Wagner, speaking for the Administration before the committee, supported the AFL proposals. On May 23d the Ways and Means Committee reported the bill out with Sec. 7(a) in the AFL form.[24]

The House adopted the recovery bill in only two days, debate being limited by the cloture rule and amendments restricted to those introduced by the committee. There was no discussion of the labor provisions or, with one minor exception, of the AFL amendments. The House on May 26th passed the bill with 7(a) in the committee's form by a vote of 325 to 76.[25]

The hearings of the Senate Finance Committee between May 22d and June 1st marked a sharp change in the attitude of employers, acquiescence giving way to disapproval as the initiative passed from the Chamber to the NAM. In a press statement NAM President Robert L. Lund denounced Sec. 7, declaring that employers would be required to deal with Communistic and racketeering organizations and that employee welfare plans might be destroyed.[26] He called an emergency meeting in Washington which on June 3d, despite Johnson's restraining efforts, proposed amendments "to make it clear that there is neither the intention nor the power to reorganize present mutually satisfactory employment relations, nor to establish any rule which will deny the right of employers and employees to bargain individually or collectively."[27]

James A. Emery, appearing for the NAM before the committee, charged that 7(a) would deprive Americans of their precious liberty

---

[21] *Ibid.*, p. 118. Italics mine.   [22] *Loc. cit.*

[23] Jacobstein, Shishkin interviews.

[24] *National Industrial Recovery*, House Hearings, pp. 122, 137; H.R. Rep. No. 159, 73d Cong., 1st sess. (May 23, 1933).

[25] *Cong. Record*, LXXVII, pt. iv, 4220–21; pt. v, 4373.

[26] *New York Times*, May 18, 1933.

[27] *Ibid.*, May 31, June 4, 1933; *La Follette Comm. Hearings*, pt. 17, 7561–63.

to associate or not associate by requiring that workmen join labor organizations. Employment relations would be molded into a single form, the trade union, despite the fact that three times as many workers were members of employee representation plans (company unions). Sec. 7(a) would disrupt existing satisfactory relationships and retard recovery. If, however, the committee believed that some statement was essential, Emery urged this substitute language:

> 1) that employers and employees shall have the right to organize and bargain collectively in any form mutually satisfactory to them through representatives of their own choosing,
> 2) that no employee and no one seeking employment shall be required as a condition of employment to join or refrain from joining any legitimate organization, nor shall any persons be precluded from bargaining individually or collectively.[28]

The stiffening of attitude appeared also in a letter from Harriman which, in contrast with his earlier silence, now recommended amendments to support the open shop.[29]

Spokesmen for the steel industry in particular opposed 7(a). Charles R. Hook of ARMCO warned that it endangered "the happy relationship which has existed between employer and employee in this country," and supported the NAM amendments to undermine the closed shop and protect the company union.[30] "The industry," Robert P. Lamont of the Iron and Steel Institute declared, "stands positively for the open shop." The steel companies, though prepared to deal with their own employees, refused to bargain with "outside organizations of labor or with individuals not its employees." Accordingly, the industry "most strongly objects" to 7(a) or even to language which "implies" that it might have to deal with unions. "If this position is not protected," he warned, "the industry is positive in the belief that the intent and purpose of the bill cannot be accomplished."[31]

John L. Lewis opposed the NAM amendments for both his union and the AFL. After assailing industry's reversal during the hearings, he charged that despite its protestations steel management practiced a "closed shop" by barring employment to union members. Although the bill virtually required employers to organize in trade associations they sought to deny their employees the less than equal right to associate in unions. Offering solace to industry, Lewis pointed out that 7(a) would

---

[28] *National Industrial Recovery,* 73d Cong., 1st sess., Sen., Hearings before Comm. on Fin. on S.1712 and H.R. 5755 (May 22– June 1, 1933), p. 288.
[29] *Ibid.,* p. 408.
[30] *Ibid.,* p. 389.
[31] *Ibid.,* pp. 394–95.

not destroy company unions if the employees wished to remain members, but only forbade an employer to require membership as a condition of employment.[32]

Senator David I. Walsh of Massachusetts then proposed an amendment to clause (2) of 7(a), supported by the AFL, so as to read [amendment italicized], "no employee and no one seeking employment shall be required as a condition of employment to join any company union or to refrain from joining, *organizing or assisting* a labor organization of his own choosing." He pointed out that yellow-dog contracts not only prohibited employees the right to join but also denied them the right to engage in these related activities. The committee accepted this language.[33]

The committee report of June 5th accepted industry's position with respect to "existing satisfactory relationships" in clause (1). A proviso proposed by Senator Champ Clark of Missouri won unanimous adoption and the endorsement of Richberg (who suggested "satisfactory") and Johnson. The amended clause read [changes italicized],

> That employees shall have the right to organize and bargain collectively through representatives of their own choosing, and shall be free from the interference, restraint or coercion of employers of labor, or their agents, in the designation of such representatives or in *self-organization* or in other concerted activities for the purpose of collective bargaining or other mutual aid or protection. *Provided, That nothing in this Title shall be construed to compel a change in existing satisfactory relationships between the employees and employers of any particular plant, firm, or corporation, except that the employees of any particular plant, firm, or corporation shall have the right to organize for the purpose of collective bargaining with their employer as to wages, hours of labor, and other conditions of employment.*[34]

This amendment not only sanctioned company unions but might have been construed to negate Sec. 7(a) entirely. The AFL denounced it at a later date, declaring itself opposed to the bill in that form.[35]

The Clark proviso, however, had been adopted on June 8th without debate when Senator Norris hastened into the chamber to insist upon reconsideration. After emphasizing its significance, he won the courtesy of full debate and a roll call. The proviso in his judgment legalized employer-dominated unions and nullified the preceding language. Employers might organize company unions, thereby creating "satisfactory" conditions, with the purpose of thwarting free association. Wagner voiced an additional fear lest it condone the yellow-dog contract. Clark,

---

[32] *Ibid.*, pp. 404–07.
[33] *Cong. Record*, LXXVII, pt. v, 4799.
[34] Sen. Rep. No. 114, 73d Cong., 1st sess. (June 5, 1933).
[35] AFL, *Weekly News Service*, June 10, 1933; *53d Convention American Federation of Labor, 1933*, p. 16.

decrying these views as exaggerations, emphasized that Richberg, a leading labor lawyer, had approved the proviso. Senator Burton K. Wheeler of Montana expressed incredulity, while La Follette pointed out that the attorney had acted in a private capacity rather than for the railway organizations. Norris's intervention bore fruit in the roll call; the proviso was defeated, 46 to 31.[36] The issue squarely tested the strength of those who supported the trade union as against those who preferred an equal status for it and the company union.

Wheeler then proposed a fourth clause to prohibit employers from transporting employees "from one State, county, city, or place to another for the purpose of taking the place of men out on strike," charging that strikebreaking was the chief cause of bloodshed in labor difficulties. The amendment, however, was rejected without a roll call.[37]

The conference committee of the House and Senate made no changes in 7(a) and the President signed the National Industrial Recovery Act on June 16, 1933.[38] The labor section read:

Every code of fair competition, agreement, and license approved, prescribed, or issued under this title shall contain the following conditions: (1) That employees shall have the right to organize and bargain collectively through representatives of their own choosing, and shall be free from the interference, restraint, or coercion of employers of labor, or their agents, in the designation of such representatives or in self-organization or in other concerted activities for the purpose of collective bargaining or other mutual aid or protection; (2) that no employee and no one seeking employment shall be required as a condition of employment to join any company union or to refrain from joining, organizing, or assisting a labor organization of his own choosing; and (3) that employers shall comply with the maximum hours of labor, minimum rates of pay, and other conditions of employment, approved or prescribed by the President.[39]

The impetus for including it in the Act came from the union movement, spearheaded by the Mine Workers. The principles of 7(a), in fact, closely resembled those in the Watson-Rathbone and Davis-Kelly coal bills.[40] The individuals most responsible for its inclusion and form were Lauck, Wagner, Rifkind, and Richberg. Secretary Perkins, though influential in shaping the wage and hour and public works features, took

---

[36] *Cong. Record,* LXXVII, pt. v, 5279–84.

[37] *Ibid.,* p. 5284.

[38] H.R. Rep. No. 243, 73d Cong., 1st sess. (June 10, 1933); S. Doc. No. 76, 73d Cong., 1st sess.; *New York Times,* June 17, 1933.

[39] *U. S. Stat. at Large,* XLVIII, 195.

[40] John L. Lewis, "Labor and the National Recovery Administration," *Annals of the American Academy of Political and Social Science,* CLXXII (1934), 58; David J. McDonald and Edward A. Lynch, *Coal and Unionism, a History of the American Coal Miners' Union* (Silver Spring, Md.: 1939), p. 194; McAlister Coleman, *Men and Coal* (New York: 1943), p. 148.

no hand in Sec. 7(a).[41] The amendments introduced in committee were the work of the American Federation of Labor.[42]

The press displayed singularly little interest in 7(a) during its legislative history. This was probably because the period was short—May 17th to June 16th; industry opposition did not crystallize until the Senate hearings; and the implications of the provision were not immediately apparent. Of fifteen newspapers eleven failed to comment.[43] The only approving paper was the Democratic *Cleveland Plain Dealer,* and it opposed the AFL amendments for fear they would outlaw the company union.[44] The *New York Herald Tribune, Chicago Tribune,* and *Los Angeles Times,* all Republican, were opposed.[45] Within the limited articulate area an embryonic line of opposition was discernible.

The AFL achieved in the Recovery Act, in one form or another, its leading legislative demands. In addition to 7(a), it won a public works program and the prospect of shorter hours through the codes and collective bargaining.[46] As Dan Tobin of the Teamsters later wrote, "I was in Washington in conference together with other Labor men during the discussion of this legislation . . . and the Bill went through about as good, and even better, than we expected it would go through the Senate."[47] The *New York Times* observed with amazement and concern that organized labor "has suddenly jumped into . . . sudden power."[48] Green described 7(a) as a "Magna Charta" for labor, while Lewis compared it with the Emancipation Proclamation.[49] Industry, though successful in obtaining exemption from the antitrust laws, grudgingly paid the price of the labor section. The NAM committed itself, however, to a program of firm opposition, promising to "fight energetically against any encroachments by Closed Shop labor unions."[50]

Sec. 7(a), a short and seemingly clear declaration of policy in a statute otherwise marked by complexity, lifted the lid of Pandora's box. The haste and inexperience from which it was derived were breeding grounds

---

[41] Frances Perkins, "Eight Years as Madame Secretary," *Fortune,* XXIV (September, 1941), 78–79; Frank interview.

[42] Shishkin interview.

[43] *Atlanta Constitution, Baltimore Sun, Boston Herald, Des Moines Register, New York Evening Journal, New York Post, New York Times, New York World-Telegram, Philadelphia Evening Bulletin, St. Louis Post-Dispatch,* and *Washington Post.* The *Baltimore Sun,* however, opposed NIRA as a whole, June 8, 1933, while the *New York World-Telegram* approved of the bill in its entirety, June 10, 1933.

[44] June 2, 1933.

[45] June 1, June 8, June 10, 1933.

[46] Bernstein, *op. cit.,* p. 288.

[47] Tobin to McIntyre, Dec. 11, 1933, White House, O.F. 142, AFL.

[48] May 7, 1933.

[49] William Green, "Labor's Opportunity and Responsibility," *American Federationist,* XL (1933), 693; Lewis, *op. cit.,* p. 58.

[50] *La Follette Comm. Hearings,* pt. 17, 7549, 7561.

of ambiguity; it raised more questions than it provided answers. Latent antagonism between unions and employers gained a point of focus and a furious battle was to rage for two years over its interpretation. The President, his advisers, and Congress, to win the support of both management and labor for the recovery program, had committed themselves, probably without realizing it, to a broad policy of intervention in collective bargaining that was to lead far beyond 7(a).

Of the four principles outlined in chapter ii, Sec. 7(a) affirmed only the first two, namely, the right of employees to organize and designate representatives and, conversely, the obligation of employers not to interfere with that right. The latter was made explicit in one respect with direct prohibition of the yellow-dog contract. The third and fourth, that is, the means of determining representatives and the duty of the employer to recognize and deal with them, did not appear. Nor did 7(a) establish a procedure for enforcement. In going only part way the statute left itself open to attack from all quarters. The Railway Labor Act, by contrast, was being shaped into an inclusive structure.

IV. BROADENING THE RAILWAY
LABOR ACT

WHILE THE NEW DEAL in Sec. 7(a) took a halting first step in the regulation of collective bargaining for industry at large, it at the same time placed the capstone on the statutory edifice for the railways. Government regulation in transportation, in fact, was firmly established long before 1933. Labor organization was extensive, particularly in train and engine service, by the opening of the present century. Railway labor has traditionally associated upon a craft basis, the five independent operating brotherhoods and the sixteen nonoperating unions affiliated with the AFL Railway Employees Department. The Railway Labor Executives Association composed of the union presidents has been the instrument of combined action in legislative matters. The organizations, unlike most American unions, have not sought the closed shop, the Trainmen alone deviating, and then sporadically, because of a jurisdictional dispute with the Switchmen.[1] Railway management has more willingly accepted collective bargaining than has industry as a whole, especially for the train and engine service crafts. Hence the main area of conflict has involved the nonoperating employees.

The carriers, their employees, and the public have long recognized that transportation is clothed with a public interest. Regulation began in the states with the Granger laws in the 1870's and reached the federal level in the Interstate Commerce Act of 1887. The public utility nature of the industry has circumscribed collective bargaining since general strikes have an immediate and disastrous effect. There have been only two national stoppages, 1922 and 1946, and in both cases the government stepped in to compel a resumption of operations. This weakness of economic power has led the organizations to insist upon government intervention, and they have, accordingly, developed political pressure with remarkable success. As a result the statutes have been pacemakers and railway labor relations have exhibited what Lloyd K. Garrison has called a "reign of law."[2]

The first federal legislation, enacted in 1888, provided for voluntary arbitration and alternatively for the appointment of investigating commissions by the President. The former was never invoked and the latter

---

[1] Cf. Jerome L. Toner, *The Closed Shop* (Washington: 1942), pp. 100–11. The Trainmen developed a variant of the closed shop, the "percentage contract," which required that a specified proportion of the employees join the union as a condition of employment. *Railroad Trainman*, LI (1934), 66.

[2] "The National Railroad Adjustment Board: a Unique Administrative Agency," *Yale Law Journal*, XLVI (1937), 569.

only during the Pullman strike. In 1898 Congress passed the Erdman Act to cover operating employees, adding mediation to voluntary arbitration and outlawing the yellow-dog contract. The parties after 1906 frequently employed the adjustment provisions. Failure in several important disputes, however, led to passage of the Newlands Act in 1913, which incorporated the provisions of the old law, adding to them a permanent Board of Mediation and Conciliation as well as arbitrators. The agency proved successful in a number of cases, but broke down in face of the 1916 controversy over the eight-hour day. It was settled only when Congress in effect constituted itself as an arbitration board and enacted the Adamson Law.[3]

World War I proved a seminal experience shaping collective bargaining and legislation on the railroads. Rising employment, a higher cost of living, and increased union effectiveness combined to produce a phenomenal growth in membership. Following federal seizure of the roads in 1917, the Railroad Administration fully accepted the right of employees to associate. Joint action by the unions won national agreements for the first time, while bipartisan national boards of adjustment created to hear grievances arising under these contracts achieved an impressive record of settlements. The carriers, however, determined to restore the old system at the first opportunity.[4]

The Transportation Act of 1920 returned the roads to private operation and created the tripartite Railroad Labor Board to hear and decide disputes but with no means of enforcement. The postwar depression curtailed employment and with the board's assistance lowered wages, with consequent reductions in union membership. Despite defensive strikes, the wartime system of national agreements and adjustment boards was demolished. In addition, the carriers launched a broad program of company unionism accompanied by yellow-dog contracts and discriminatory practices. Company unionism made great advances among shop and roundhouse employees, while clerks, maintenance of waymen, and telegraphers were affected on a few roads. The operating brotherhoods were hardly affected. The board, except for an extended academic controversy with the Pennsylvania, had neither heart nor authority to call a halt.[5]

The organizations, dissatisfied with both the Act and the board, prepared new legislation introduced as the Howell-Barkley bill in 1924.

[3] Harry D. Wolf, *The Railroad Labor Board* (Chicago: 1927), pp. 6–10; *First Annual Report of the National Mediation Board* (Washington: 1935), pp. 6–7.

[4] Garrison, *op. cit.*, p. 570; Wolf, *op. cit.*, chap. iii.

[5] Wolf, *op. cit.*, chaps. vi–xv; B. L. McKillips, "Company Unions on the Railroads," *Nation*, CXLII (1936), 48; Twentieth Century Fund, *Labor and the Government* (New York: 1935), pp. 86–87.

The measure, after being extensively revised by the carriers, received their endorsement and became the Railway Labor Act of 1926, establishing conditions for collective bargaining and laying down rules for its conduct.[6] Sec. 2 declared it the duty of carriers and their employees "to exert every reasonable effort to make and maintain agreements . . . and to settle all disputes . . . in order to avoid any interruption of commerce." Disagreements "shall be considered, and, if possible, decided . . . in conference between representatives designated and authorized so to confer, respectively, by the carriers and by the employees. . . . Representatives . . . shall be designated . . . without interference, influence, or coercion exercised by either party over the self-organization, or designation of representatives, by the other." In grievance cases the Act required both to confer provided that existing agreements were not violated, that is, protecting company union "contracts."

Sec. 3 created voluntary boards of adjustment to handle grievances. This provision was undermined by the condition that nothing shall "prohibit an individual carrier and its employees from agreeing upon . . . such machinery of contract and adjustment as they may mutually establish." Hence the roads might insist that boards be limited to one system or that there be no boards at all. To handle contract disputes Sec. 4 established an independent five member Board of Mediation, while the remainder of the Act set forth the duties of the parties and its procedures in these cases.

This statute, the most inclusive labor code of its time, met three of the four principles set forth in chapter ii. Employees won the right of self-organization and collective bargaining; employers could not lawfully interfere with their exercise; and the carriers must recognize and deal with employee representatives. The Act stated the first two comprehensively, the third in rudimentary form. The fourth, selecting representatives by elections, did not appear. In addition, the Act lacked enforcement machinery, imposing no effective penalties for noncompliance. As the chairman of the board put it, "the law was as full of holes as a . . . Swiss cheese."[7]

Although the Act proved successful in disposing of contract disputes, it failed to establish freedom of association where it did not exist and grievance machinery where carriers opposed its creation. The Mediation Board, described as "an asylum for needy politicians," even refrained

---

[6] *U. S. Stat. at Large*, XLIV, 577. The roads supported it out of expediency. As the price of endorsement they exacted important amendments eliminating national boards of adjustment, protecting company unions, and removing penalties. Wolf, *op. cit.*, pp. 417, 421–22, 426–29.

[7] *Railway Labor Act Amendments*, 73d Cong., 2d sess., H.R., Hearings before Comm. on Interstate Commerce on H.R. 7650 (May 22–25, 1934), p. 69, hereafter cited as House Hearings, *Railway Labor Act Amendments*.

from exercising available discretion in, for example, conducting elections.[8] In 1933, as a result, 147 of the 233 largest roads maintained company unions, virtually all established prior to the passage of the Act. The carriers dominated their formation, drafted constitutions, bylaws, and governing rules, intervened in nominations and elections, contributed financial support, participated in collecting dues, discriminated in favor of members, penalized nonmembers, maintained blacklists, and required employees to sign yellow-dog contracts.[9] Similarly, many roads refused to create adjustment boards, thousands of grievances thereby remained unsettled.[10] The impact of this decade upon the unions is revealed in the fact that only 38 per cent of the men were organized in 1930 as compared with over 53 per cent in 1920, despite a sharp drop in employment.[11]

These union difficulties were compounded by the Great Depression as the volume of traffic dropped precipitously after 1929. The government kept many roads afloat only by financial transfusions, while others went bankrupt. Employment sagged from 1,661,000 in 1929 to 1,041,000 in 1932, half the number of 1920, and was accompanied by demotions, furloughs, and part-time work. Annual earnings dropped from $1,543 to $1,275. As a result union membership declined by almost 300,000 from 1929 to 1933.[12]

The depression stimulated greater political participation by the organizations than they had engaged in since the Progressive campaign of 1924. Despite the fact that a Trainman, William N. Doak, was President Hoover's Secretary of Labor and some organizations were traditionally Republican, the leaders gave considerable support to Roosevelt in 1932. Donald Richberg, for example, organized the National Progressive Conference for this purpose.[13] After the election the labor executives met in Washington to draw up a legislative program emphasizing the need "to strengthen the right of self-organization and the power of collective bargaining as already provided in the Railway Labor Act."[14]

---

[8] McKillips, *op. cit.*, p. 50; Eastman to Roosevelt, June 28, 1934, FCT, National Archives, No. 026–408–2.

[9] Garrison, *op. cit.*, p. 571; *Regulation of Railroads*, 73d Cong., 2d sess., Sen. Doc. No. 119 (Jan. 22, 1934), p. 60.

[10] Wolf, *op. cit.*, p. 438; *Railway Clerk*, XXXII (1933), 49.

[11] Leo Wolman, *Ebb and Flow in Trade Unionism* (New York: 1936), 118.

[12] Social Science Research Council, J. Douglas Brown and associates, *Railway Labor Survey* (September, 1933), p. 120; Otto S. Beyer and Edwin M. Fitch, "Annual Earnings of Railroad Employees, 1924 to 1933," *Monthly Labor Review*, XLI (1935), 6–7, 11; Wolman, *op. cit.*, p. 41; Perkins to Roosevelt, Apr. 19, 1934, White House, O.F. No. 31, Railroads.

[13] Richberg interview.

[14] *Railway Clerk*, XXXII (1933), 47.

Opportunity struck for the unions even before the new administration took office. By early 1933 ten Class I railroads were in receivership and forty-five others were close behind, hoping for a more liberal Bankruptcy Act before taking the plunge. The unions feared that a new law might permit reorganizations to protect bondholders by squeezing out economies in wage cuts and canceled contracts.[15] With the prospect of key negotiations in the summer, therefore, they prevailed upon the House Judiciary Committee to insert an amendment declaring that "nothing in this Act shall be construed as amending or in any way altering the provisions of the Railway Labor Act."[16] When it reached the Senate they pressed for further changes to bolster the 1926 statute against company unions and yellow-dog contracts. Hence, Senator Norris inserted Sec. 77 (o), (p), (q) over the opposition of the carriers, and the Bankruptcy Act was signed by Hoover on March 3, 1933.[17]

These provisions forbade a receiver to "change the wages or working conditions of railroad employees except in the manner prescribed in the Railway Labor Act" or in the 1932 agreements between carriers and unions. They prohibited him to "deny or in any way question the right of employees . . . to join the labor organization of their choice, . . . to interfere in the organization of employees, or to use the funds of the railroad . . . in maintaining so-called 'company unions,' or to influence or coerce employees in an effort to induce them to join or remain members of such company unions." Finally, he might not require "any person seeking employment . . . to sign an agreement promising to join or refuse to join a labor organization," and such agreements in effect were illegal. This language outlawed both the yellow-dog contract and the closed shop.[18] For the organizations "the importance of these provisions in the new law cannot be overstated."[19]

The plight of the railroads in 1933 made federal intervention indispensable and one of Roosevelt's first acts was to appoint a committee to draft the necessary legislation. The members were: Secretary of Commerce Daniel C. Roper, chairman; Treasury Secretary William H. Woodin; Interstate Commerce Commissioner Joseph B. Eastman; Senator Clarence C. Dill and Representative Sam Rayburn, chairmen of the Senate and House Commerce Committees; and W. M. W. Splawn, counsel to the latter committee. This group soon agreed upon a program calling for an emergency transportation coördinator with power to compel the elimination of waste by promoting consolidation without

[15] *Ibid.*, pp. 76, 115.
[16] *Labor*, Feb. 7, 1933.
[17] *Cong. Record*, LXXVI, pt. v, 5118–22; *New York Times*, March 4, 1933.
[18] *U. S. Stat. at Large*, XLVII, 1467.
[19] *Railway Clerk*, XXXII (1933), 100.

regard to the antitrust laws, encouraging financial reorganization, and removing duplicating services. This "can be accomplished," Eastman wrote, "in very large part, by sacrifice of labor and decrease of employment."[20]

On April 3d, before the committee finished its work, A. F. Whitney, president of the Labor Executives Association, warned Roper that the plan would turn 50,000 to 350,000 men out and upset contracts, particularly seniority provisions. The government could justify such results only by guaranteeing absorptive employment, reducing capital obligations, protecting hard-hit communities and maintaining labor standards. Above all, there must be consultation with the organizations, which required

universal compliance with the Railway Labor Act.... Adequate and lawful employee representation cannot be provided unless the federal government, as a part of any legislation, is empowered to compel, and does compel, the carriers to comply with the law and to cease interferences with employee self-organization and designation of representatives of their own choosing.... Managements in general will only yield to federal compulsion.[21]

Many carriers and company unions were equally anxious to prevent federal underwriting of collective bargaining.[22]

The committee's report to the President on April 19th did not concede Whitney's demands. The bill merely empowered the coördinator to confer with the unions prior to issuing orders affecting employee interests and declared that exempting carriers from the antitrust laws did not relieve them of duties under the Railway Labor Act.[23] The President, submitting it to Congress on May 4th, declared vaguely that the coördinator might "render useful service in maintaining railroad employment at a fair wage."[24] The *Railway Clerk,* on the other hand, described it as "the worst bill that has been presented in the special session of congress," while the executives held an emergency meeting to prepare amendments.[25]

Richberg on May 10th voiced the labor executives' strenuous objection before the Senate Commerce Committee, proposing comprehensive changes. The unions should have a veto over orders affecting employees. The coördinator should prohibit company unions and yellow-dog contracts, enforce agreements and compliance with the Railway Labor Act,

[20] *Emergency Railroad Transportation Act, 1933,* FCT, National Archives, No. 026–17; *Cong. Record,* LXXVII, pt. v, 4853.
[21] Whitney to Roper, Apr. 3, 1933, FCT, National Archives, No. 026–17.
[22] L. M. Graham to Perkins, Apr. 6, 1933, *loc cit.*
[23] Roper to Roosevelt, Apr. 19, 1933, White House, O.F. No. 31-B, Railroads, FCT.
[24] *The Public Papers and Addresses of Franklin D. Roosevelt,* ed. by Samuel I. Rosenman (New York: 1938), II, 153.
[25] XXXII (1933), 154; *Labor,* May 9, 1933.

and establish regional boards of adjustment. Richberg would require the carriers to stabilize employment and provide old-age pensions and dismissal wages. Finally, the act should guarantee the right to strike. The roads, of course, strongly opposed these revisions.[26]

The committee determined, with the President's approval, to win labor support by accepting the essentials of the proposals in its report of May 22, 1933. The coördinator would consult with the standard organizations; there would be no reductions except as a result of death, retirement, or resignation and, in any case, they might not exceed five per cent of pay rolls; carriers would reimburse employees for losses incurred in transfers; the coördinator would create regional boards of adjustment; and the roads would comply with the labor provisions of the Bankruptcy Act.[27] Dill, presenting the report to the Senate on May 26th, emphasized that Roosevelt had accepted the labor amendments. That body then adopted the measure with the revisions proposed by the committee.[28]

The House Committee held hearings concurrently, during which suggested amendments and arguments followed the same pattern. The committee, in view of opposition to the labor revisions, withheld action until after Senate passage. On May 31st Roosevelt called Rayburn, Dill, Roper, Eastman, Splawn, W. J. Cummings (assistant to the Secretary of the Treasury), Whitney, George M. Harrison (president of the Railway Clerks), and Richberg to the White House. They agreed to press for the Senate bill except for a minor amendment to permit employees not union members to confer with the coördinator. On June 2d the committee reported it in this form and the House adopted it without a roll call the following day. The conference made no changes and Roosevelt signed the Emergency Railroad Transportation Act on June 16th, simultaneously with the Recovery Act.[29]

The union leaders felt that they achieved in the Act "one of the most impressive victories the railway labor organizations have ever won."[30] The labor features of the Bankruptcy Act were extended to the industry as a whole, while Eastman's appointment as Coördinator met with their

---

[26] *Emergency Railroad Transportation Act, 1933,*73d Cong., 1st sess., Sen., Hearings before Comm. on Interstate Commerce on S. 1580 (May 9–12, 1933), pp. 77, 85 ff., 152–53.

[27] *Emergency Railroad Transportation Act, 1933,* 73d Cong., 1st sess., Sen., Rep. No. 87, Comm. on Interstate Commerce (May 22, 1933), pp. 2, 5–6; *Cong. Record,* LXXVII, pt. v, pp. 4250–56; *New York Times,* May 18, 1933.

[28] *Cong. Record,* LXXVII, pt. v, pp. 4250–56, 4268–83.

[29] *Emergency Railroad Transportation Act, 1933,* 73d Cong., 1st sess., H.R., Hearings before Comm. on Interstate Commerce (May 8–22, 1933); House Rep. No. 193, June 2, 1933; House Rep. No. 213, June 9, 1933; *Cong. Record,* LXXVII, pt. v, pp. 4853, 4884, 4999; *Labor,* June 6, 13, 1933; *Railroad Telegrapher,* L (1933), 419.

[30] *Railway Clerk,* XXXII (1933), 154.

full approval. He revealed the significance of the amendments by declaring that they "converted my work very largely from action to research."[31]

The unions, fortified by the legislation, moved promptly to destroy company unionism by launching organizational drives unmatched since the war. Impressive results were quickly achieved, ending dominated organizations on such roads as the Rock Island, Union Pacific, Missouri-Pacific, Père Marquette, and Jersey Central. In October the executives announced that company unionism was "groggy."[32]

The Coördinator's enforcement program contributed to this end. His first step, an exhaustive study of company unionism and yellow-dog contracts, revealed the carriers illegally sponsoring both on a wide scale. In December he asked them voluntarily to cease interfering with self-organization, to post notices that employees were free to join or not to join labor organizations, to abrogate yellow-dog contracts, and to drop discriminatory practices. Many carriers complied, but some disregarded his warning to invoke the statute's severe penalties.[33] President W. W. Atterbury of the Pennsylvania, for example, informed him that the Act applied only to bankrupt roads, which his was not, and indicated readiness for a court test. Similarly, the carriers declined to establish adjustment boards and a growing number of grievances remained unsettled. Finally, the Illinois Central and Rock Island, according to union sources, unlawfully reduced wages.[34]

These violations and the one year duration of the Emergency Act convinced the organizations and the Coördinator that permanent legislation was necessary. The unions were anxious to capitalize on the favorable political climate to win a broad program from the congress opening in January, 1934. Hence the executives met in Washington to draw plans which Whitney addressed to Eastman on November 27th. He underlined the need for "unqualified acceptance throughout the industry of the requirements in letter and in spirit of the Railway Labor Act." Free representation could not exist "unless the federal government . . . is empowered to compel, and does compel, the carriers to comply with the law and to cease interferences with employee self-organization and designation of representatives of their own choosing."[35]

---

[31] *Railroad Telegrapher*, LI (1934), 430.

[32] *Labor*, Sept. 12, 26, Oct. 11, 24, 1933; *Railway Clerk*, XXXII (1933), 214, 232, 279; *Railroad Telegrapher*, L (1933), 420–21.

[33] Releases of the Federal Coördinator, Sept. 7, Dec. 8, 1933, Jan. 22, 1934; *Regulation of Railroads*, 73d Cong., 2d sess., Sen., Doc. No. 119 (Jan. 22, 1934), pp. 59–61.

[34] *Railway Age*, XCVI (1934), 666–67; *Railway Clerk*, XXXII (1933), 246; *Railroad Telegrapher*, LI (1934), 5; *Labor*, Jan. 2, 1934.

[35] Whitney to Eastman, Nov. 27, 1933, FCT, National Archives, No. 026–408–2; *Labor*, Oct. 24, Dec. 3, 1933.

On December 20th the organizations launched their program publicly in a large conference in Chicago. A virtually full-time legislative committee then descended upon Washington, consisting of Whitney, Harrison, B. M. Jewell, president of the AFL Railway Department, T. C. Cashen, president of the Switchmen, and C. M. Sheplar, Marine Engineers president, assisted by counsel and a research staff. On January 19th they called upon Roosevelt to ask support for bills dealing with pensions, the six-hour day, hours of service, the length of trains, full crews, workmen's compensation, regulation of motor carriers, and amendments to the Railway Labor Act.[36]

The revisions in the last aimed at the elimination of the company union and the yellow-dog contract and the creation of national grievance machinery, proposing no basic changes in the remainder of the Act. "Company union" was defined in Sec. 1 to lay the basis for legalizing the closed shop. Sec. 2, in language paralleling the Norris-LaGuardia Act, Sec. 7(a), and the contemporary Wagner bill, stated that there was an inequality of bargaining power between the employer and the worker. Though the latter should be free to decline to organize, "he should have the full freedom of association, self-organization, and designation of representatives of his own choosing, to negotiate the terms and conditions of his employment . . . free from the interference, influence, or coercion of his employer." Hence it would be unlawful for a carrier to change wages or conditions except in conformity with the Act; to deny workers the right to join a labor organization; to contribute funds to company unions; to induce employees to join or remain members of such organizations; or to impose yellow-dog contracts, while such agreements in effect would become void. By limiting several of these prohibitions to "company unions," the bill permitted carriers to negotiate closed shop agreements with standard organizations. Representatives for bargaining need not be employees of the carrier. In a dispute over representation the Mediation Board, upon the request of either party, would investigate and certify within thirty days the names of those designated by secret ballot vote or other proper means. Neither majority rule nor appropriate unit was mentioned. The Coördinator would enforce these provisions and violations of his orders were misdemeanors subject to heavy fine and/or imprisonment, each day of willful noncompliance constituting a separate offense.

Sec. 3 would create a bipartite National Board of Adjustment with forty-two members drawn equally from the carriers and the standard organizations. Sitting in Chicago, it would comprise four divisions,

---

[36] *Labor,* Dec. 26, 1933, Jan. 2, 9, 23, 30, 1934; *Railway Clerk,* XXXIII (1934), 3; Beyer to Eastman, Program Presented by Labor Executives to the President, n.d., FCT, National Archives, No. 026–408–2.

covering train and yard service; shopmen; station, maintenance of way, and miscellaneous; and maritime and longshore. The bill specifically named the twenty-one unions, giving them a favored position. The parties would bear the costs of their own members. Arbitrators would be selected if the boards were unable to agree.[37]

At the President's suggestion the labor leaders conferred with the Coördinator between January 24 and February 16, 1934, reaching agreement on fundamentals. FCT experience showed need for elimination of the company union and yellow-dog contract, while the continuous increase of grievances since 1926 and strike threats on several roads evidenced "an almost complete breakdown" of the voluntary adjustment system. Eastman balked at several details and suggested some features of his own. He, for example, rejected the definition of "company union." They agreed, however, upon "the complete divorcement of carrier management and employees in the matter of self-organization"; upon protecting the status of the outside organization; upon forbidding a road to interfere with employee association, use funds to maintain a labor organization (not a "company union"), collect dues, or impose yellow-dog contracts; upon the representation procedures; and, finally, upon heavy penalties for noncompliance. The Coördinator, however, would extend free association by outlawing the closed shop. He revised the adjustment boards provision by reducing membership to thirty-six and striking out the union names to permit others which might be formed in the future to gain representation. Eastman, concerned with the competence of the existing board in view of its added duties, proposed a new National Mediation Board of three. The number was reduced from five because the adjustment boards were expected to absorb grievance cases.[38]

When Eastman and the organizations reached tentative agreement they joined to urge the President's endorsement. The Coördinator emphasized that the unions were "more interested in this amendment than in any other plank in their platform," while they underlined that "it was imperative that we obtain the enactment of these amendments at this session of Congress."[39] Roosevelt, however, withheld his support and Eastman, accordingly, made no public report for a month, conferring meantime with the carriers, who were opposed, and with Board chairman Samuel E. Winslow, who was understandably unenthusiastic.

---

[37] *Railroad Trainman,* LI (1934), 71–75. This bill, introduced as H.R. 7650 and S. 2651, never reached the hearing stage.

[38] Beyer to Eastman, Program Presented by Labor Executives to the President, n.d., FCT, National Archives, No. 026–408–2.

[39] Eastman to Roosevelt, Feb. 6, 1934, White House, O.F. No. 31-B, Railroads, FCT; Whitney to Roosevelt, March 13, 1934, FCT, National Archives, No. 026–408–a.

A bombardment of letters and visits finally won the President's permission (but no endorsement) to send the report to the Hill on March 29th.[40]

On April 2d Dill introduced S. 3266, the Coördinator's bill, which differed markedly from the 1926 Act. The revised Sec. 1 defined "representative" to mean "any person or persons, labor union, organization, or corporation designated either by a carrier or group of carriers or by its or their employees, to act for it or them."

Sec. 2 declared that representatives "need not be persons in the employ of the carrier" and forbade influencing employees not to designate outside organizations. It guaranteed to employees the right to organize and bargain collectively through representatives of their own choosing. "The majority of any craft or class of employees shall have the right to determine who shall be the representative of the craft or class for the purposes of this Act." The draftsmen did not clarify whether they intended a "majority" of all employees or merely of those voting. It would be unlawful for a carrier to deny the right of employees to join, organize, or assist labor organizations, interfere with self-organization, contribute funds to or collect dues for a labor organization, or use influence or coercion to induce employees to join, not to join, to remain, or not to remain members. A proviso permitted individuals and local representatives to confer with management and carriers to furnish free transportation to employees while on the business of an employee association. No carrier "shall require any person seeking employment to sign any contract . . . promising to join or not to join a labor organization," and such agreements in effect were no longer binding. This explicitly outlawed both the yellow-dog contract and the closed shop.

Sec. 2 as well forbade carriers to change wages or conditions except in accordance with agreements or the Act. The railroads must notify employees that disputes would be handled under the statute, while the general rights of workers under it would be incorporated in all contracts. In case of dispute "among a carrier's employees" as to representation the board would investigate and certify within thirty days the names of those designated. This asserted the principle that representation was the exclusive concern of the employees. Upon certification the carrier "shall treat with the representative so certified as the representative of the craft or class of employees for the purposes of this Act." The board might take a secret ballot or utilize other appropriate means of deciding employee preferences. In conducting the election the "Board shall designate who may participate" and establish other rules, although no

[40] Whitney to Eastman, *op. cit.*, March 13, 1934; Eastman to McIntyre, Feb. 20, 1934, White House, O.F. No. 31, Railroads; Eastman to McIntyre, March 27, 1934, White House, O.F. No. 31-B, Railroads, FCT; Eastman to Early, March 31, 1934, FCT, National Archives, No. 026–408–2.

mention was made of appropriate unit. Failure of the carrier to comply with these duties was a misdemeanor subject to stiff fine and/or imprisonment, each day of noncompliance constituting a separate offense.

Sec. 3 would create a bipartite National Board of Adjustment of thirty-six members in four divisions in Chicago. Labor representatives would be named by organizations "national in scope, as have been or may be organized in accordance with the provisions of Section 2." The parties would assume the expenses of their members. In case they failed to reach a decision, a neutral referee would be selected, whose awards would be final and enforceable in the courts.

Sec. 4 would abolish the Board of Mediation and create a National Mediation Board of three appointed by the President and approved by the Senate for three-year terms. The remaining provisions of the 1926 statute carried over with minor revisions.[41]

In the hearings before the Senate Committee on April 10th Eastman observed, "The Railway Labor Act has brought about many good results, but experience has shown that it is in need of improvement." Hence the amendments sought "not to overturn but to perfect what has been done."[42] He urged that labor and management be wholly independent of one another. The amendments would eliminate carrier domination but not destroy system associations per se or affirmatively promote the standard organizations. Employees would determine their own form of association through free elections. Though temporary progress had been made under the Emergency Act, a long-term solution required revision of the 1926 statute. He pointed to the breakdown of grievance machinery, declaring that the war experience conclusively proved the effectiveness of national adjustment boards. Refraining from discussing the competence of the existing Board of Mediation, he urged a reduction in its membership in anticipation of a lower case-load.[43]

The labor organizations enthusiastically supported Eastman's proposals except on the closed shop. They asked that their definition of "company union" be inserted and that the denial of carrier interference and financial support be limited to such organizations. Eastman vigorously opposed protecting closed shop agreements, declaring,

Within recent years, the practice of tying up men's jobs with labor union membership has crept into the railroad industry which theretofore was singularly clean in this respect. . . . If genuine freedom of choice is to be the basis of labor relations under the Railway Labor Act, as it should be, then the yellow-dog contract, and its corollary, the closed shop, and the so-called "percentage" contract have no place in the picture.[44]

---

[41] *To Amend the Railway Labor Act,* 73d Cong., 2d sess., Sen., Hearings before Comm. on Interstate Commerce on S. 3266 (April 10–19, 1934), pp. 1–9, hereafter cited as Sen. Hearings, *To Amend the Railway Labor Act.*

[42] *Ibid.,* p. 10.   [43] *Ibid.,* pp. 12–25.   [44] *Ibid.,* pp. 27–39, 157.

The railroads, speaking through M. W. Clement, vice-president of the Pennsylvania, did not directly oppose the bill, rather suggesting amendments, several crippling in effect. Experience under the Act, he admitted, revealed two defects, failure to observe its "spirit" and to establish grievance machinery with final authority. Clement, however, asked for amendments to prevent the bill from superseding existing agreements, that is, company union "contracts," and to permit carriers to continue financial contributions. Language was suggested which might permit minority bargaining in face of the majority rule. He opposed the representation provisions for breeding jurisdictional disputes and preventing contact between "management and men." All penalties would be stricken out. He, of course, objected to making the closed shop legal. National adjustment boards would create delays and prevent local settlement. Instead the carriers proposed regional and system boards with referees, final awards, and enforcement in the courts, an offer first made at the hearings. Eastman regarded it as an expedient to forestall national boards and pointed to a number of legal loopholes.[45]

Winslow, though admitting weaknesses in the 1926 statute, opposed assuming jurisdiction in representation cases on the ground that losing parties would harbor grievances embarrassing to the board's mediation, suggesting instead *ad hoc* committees of three. In view of the expected reduction in case-load he did not object to lessening the number of members.[46]

The committee "considered" S. 3266 for more than a month. Dill was "not overly interested" in its enactment, informing Eastman that it was not on the President's "must" list. This intention was followed by the familiar salvo on the White House from the Coördinator and the labor committee.[47] On May 21st, accordingly, the committee reported favorably on Eastman's amendments with a stinging dissent by Senator Daniel O. Hastings of Delaware, arguing that they would deprive employers of liberties, abrogate contracts, upset satisfactory relationships, foment strife, and impair railroad service.[48]

The testimony in the hearings before the House Commerce Committee paralleled that presented to the Senate Committee, exceptions being an Eastman amendment and objections by the organizations as a whole, the Trainmen, and the Teamsters, to outlawing the closed shop. In view of the majority rule the Coördinator suggested "that

[45] *Ibid.*, pp. 55–78, 154.
[46] *Ibid.*, pp. 133–44.
[47] Eastman to Roosevelt, Apr. 27, May 4, 1934, White House, O.F. No. 31, Railroads.
[48] *Board to Settle Disputes between Carriers and Their Employees*, 73d Cong., 2d sess., Sen., Rep. No. 1065 (May 21, 1934).

nothing in this Act shall be construed to prevent an individual employee from presenting any grievance to the management in person or by an individual representative of his choice." "Majority" would apply to all employees rather than merely those voting. "If an organization cannot secure the backing of an actual majority of any class or craft, it will not have the elements of strength needed for collective bargaining. . . . As a practical matter I do not believe that serious difficulties will arise."[49] The union security argument followed familiar lines: it would enforce discipline, aid in fulfilling contracts, and eliminate "free riders." In addition, precedents were cited from other industries and the concurrent Wagner bill. The Trainmen were determined to preserve their "percentage" contracts.[50]

They conducted a vigorous campaign, informing Senator Couzens that they would do what they could to kill the bill rather than have it passed in the Senate form.[51] Eastman observed that the organizations, with this exception, had opposed linking jobs to membership throughout a "long and honorable history." He continued, "I can find no basis upon which to denounce the closed shop principle for company unions and at the same time give the blessing of Congress to such agreements when made by a national organization."[52] He pointed out that defeating the amendments in their entirety would perpetuate the *status quo,* namely, illegalization under the Bankruptcy and Emergency Acts.[53] At the same time the carriers urged deferring action (the hour of congressional adjournment approached) in the hope that they might agree with the unions on a joint legislative program. The labor leaders, however, rebuffed their overtures, while Eastman pointed to the railroads' failure to take such opportunities in the past.[54]

The organizations through Representative Robert Crosser of Ohio persuaded the committee on June 9th to accept the closed shop guarantee. Plans were laid to bring the measure out under a suspension of the rules prohibiting amendments and requiring a vote for or against the bill in its entirety.[55]

The prospect in mid-June was that the President's lukewarmness combined with the covert opposition of the Democratic leadership

---

[49] Eastman to Rayburn, May 28, 1934, FCT, National Archives, No. 026–408–2.

[50] *Railway Labor Act Amendments,* House Hearings, pp. 87, 94–106, 116, 118.

[51] Railroad Trainmen, Lodge 28, to Senators Dickinson and Murphy and Rep. Thurston, May 25, 1934, John Carson to Eastman, May 31, 1934, FCT, National Archives, No. 026–408–2.

[52] Eastman to Dill, *op. cit.,* June 1, 1934.

[53] Eastman to Carson, *op. cit.,* June 1, 1934.

[54] R. V. Fletcher to Eastman, *op. cit.,* May 29, 1934, Eastman to Fletcher, June 2, 1934.

[55] William P. Cole, Jr., to Eastman, *op. cit.,* June 9, 1934; Sen. Hearings, *To Amend the Railway Labor Act,* 73d Cong., 2d sess., H.R., Rep. No. 1944 (June 11, 1934), pp. 1, 14–16.

would permit adjournment before the bill came to a vote. Senator Robinson, in fact, submitted a "must" list to minority leader Charles L. McNary without the amendments to the Act.[56] Both the labor lobby and the Coördinator fully appreciated the danger. On June 13th, accordingly, Harrison wrote Robinson, " . . . the President personally assured us that he favored the enactment of this legislation and would ask the leaders of the Democratic Party to see that it was passed," and at the same time implored Roosevelt to put pressure upon the Senator.[57] On the following day Eastman and Secretary Perkins jointly petitioned the President to step in: "A host of strike threats and other labor difficulties will arise this summer demanding presidential intervention" unless orderly representation and grievance machinery be created. If the Administration were to wait for the carriers and unions to agree, there would be no issue. "It is therefore respectfully urged that the leaders in both the Senate and the House be requested to take the necessary action. . . ."[58]

On June 15th the House after cursory discussion passed its committee's bill without a roll call.[59] In the Senate the fate of S. 3266 remained in doubt until the moment of adjournment. Congress stayed in session longer than planned because the members, in the amendments to the Act and the railroad retirement bill, "insisted in doing more for labor than proposed in President Roosevelt's program."[60] The organization lobby mobilized the Republican Progressives, Senators La Follette and Couzens, as well as Democratic Senators Wheeler and Dill.

On June 18th the measure began a "descent into political oblivion," since neither Dill nor La Follette could get the floor and Hastings threatened a filibuster.[61] Robinson, in "a frank statement," declared that S. 3266 would meet persistent opposition and indefinitely postpone adjournment. Both he and the President, despite approval of its substance, therefore felt that it should go over. Wheeler, insisting upon a vote, declared, "the question is whether or not we will allow the Pennsylvania Railroad . . . in the closing hours . . . to block legislation which is so badly needed."[62] Hastings thereupon launched his filibuster but gave up after only an hour for lack of support. A roll call on consideration went 78 to 2 in favor, only Hastings and Senator Peter Norbeck of South Dakota voting in the negative. In view of this demonstration,

[56] *Cong. Record*, LXXVIII, pt. x, 12395.

[57] Harrison to Robinson and Roosevelt, June 13, 1934, White House, O.F. No. 31-B, Railroads, FCT.

[58] Perkins and Eastman to Roosevelt, *op. cit.*, June 14, 1934.

[59] *Cong. Record*, LXXVIII, pt. x, 11713–15, 11720.

[60] *New York Times*, June 19, 1934.

[61] *Ibid.*, June 18, 1934.

[62] *Cong. Record*, LXXVIII, pt. x, 12366–67.

Robinson shifted his position and the Senate, after rejecting an attempt by Wheeler to protect the closed shop, passed S. 3266 without a vote.[63]

Crosser immediately urged the House to accept the Senate bill, arguing that the substantial differences between the two chambers barred a conference agreement in time. The Trainmen, despite their threats, agreed to this solution. S. 3266 was then passed by voice vote in the evening of June 18th, almost simultaneously with the railroad retirement bill, as Congress adjourned.[64] The President signed the amendments to the Railway Labor Act on June 21, 1934.[65]

In these two statutes the standard organizations declared that they had "won the most impressive legislative victory in the history of the labor movement," a boast with some merit.[66] Harrison, who had led the lobbying, observed that

the amended Railway Labor Act ... removes the last remnant of employer influence over the right of employees to self-determination in use of the economic power to better their conditions. I think it is generally conceded that the ... Act in its amended form gives to railway employees all the protection in the exercise of their rights to organize that the law can possibly accord them.[67]

Dill remarked that he had never witnessed "such an impressive demonstration of the influence of organized labor," while the Amalgamated Clothing Workers, bitter over the defeat of the Wagner bill, observed that at least "one large group of workers ... understood the use of their organized political as well as industrial power."[68] *Railway Age,* organ of the carriers, denounced the Administration for its transportation policies, finding the amendments not least objectionable among them.[69] The press generally, observing that reign of silence which it reserves for railroad labor matters, took no position.

The amendments climaxed half a century of government intervention on the railroads. The new National Mediation Board was to declare, "the present law is the most advanced form of Government regulation of labor relations that we have in this country. . . . These principles and methods, built up through years of experimentation, provide a model labor policy, based on equal rights and equitable responsibilities."[70] The company union and the yellow-dog contract were soon to be eliminated.

---

[63] *Ibid.*, 12370–402.

[64] *Ibid.*, 12553–55.

[65] *New York Times*, June 22, 1934.

[66] *Railway Clerk*, XXXIII (1934), 25.

[67] "Railway Labor Act," *American Federationist*, XLI (1934), 1056.

[68] *Labor*, June 26, 1934; *Railroad Telegrapher*, LI (1934), 499.

[69] XCVI (1934), 941.

[70] *First Annual Report of the National Mediation Board* (Washington: 1935), p. 1.

In the context of the early New Deal the railway legislation is both a facet of the dominant tendency and a deviation from it. The Administration sought to encourage recovery through policies proposed by business and it is no coincidence that the Recovery and Emergency Transportation Acts took effect on the same day. In both a desire for balance on the part of Congress and the Administration and, perhaps more important, an aroused union movement wrote in safeguards for the right to organize. The railroad organizations, stronger and more effective politically, won far more than an amorphous Sec. 7(a). In both cases, however, the New Deal embarked upon a collective bargaining policy hesitantly and the White House supported it only under pressure. The job of the railway lobby, of course, was made easier by the fact that Eastman was the key administrative figure, since their joint efforts alone assured success in 1934. Wagner and the AFL, on the other hand, had to wait for the elections of that fall and the collapse of NRA. The amendments were significant not only to railway workers but also, George Harrison noted, "as a precedent in the extension of these same rights and privileges to employees of other industries. I don't see how the next Congress can refuse the demand of the American Federation of Labor for more specific legislation to implement the labor sections of the National Industrial Recovery Act."[71]

---

[71] "Railway Labor Act," *American Federationist*, XLI (1934), 1053.

V. POLICY EMERGES: THE 1934
WAGNER BILL

ALTHOUGH the railway unions achieved their legislative objectives in 1934, the road proved longer for the Federation. The conflict of interpretation over Sec. 7(a) was joined immediately after its enactment. The AFL argued that Congress intended workers to join independent organizations. "Trade unions are the obvious agencies through which . . . employees can act collectively."[1] Hence employer practices restricting this "chosen instrument" were illegal. The unions therefore undertook an organizational drive exceeding any since World War I, effective in many industries, particularly coal, textiles, steel, and clothing.[2]

Employers, on the other hand, denied that 7(a) outlawed restrictive practices. The NAM contended that the law was unchanged except for prohibiting the employer to require that the worker join a company union or refrain from joining an organization of his choice. NAM counsel advised its members that the Act permitted: individual bargaining; company unionism; refusal to bargain with alleged employee representatives; questioning prospective workmen on union affiliation; denial of leave to engage in union activities; barring company premises to unionists; advising employees not to join; individual, company union and trade union bargaining within the same plant; and inducements to join company unions. The closed shop was alleged to be illegal and it was hinted that 7(a) itself was unconstitutional.[3]

As a matter of policy, however, employers selected the company union as best designed to frustrate the AFL interpretation since it was employer controlled and yet appeared to be "collective" bargaining. They therefore launched a broad program of company unionism, notably in the heavy industries. Of 653 manufacturing and mining companies surveyed in November 1933, for example, 400 established plans under NIRA.[4]

A head-on clash was inevitable and the NRA codes provided the arena. Compelled to decide whether their labor provisions would be collectively bargained or be fixed unilaterally by employers, Recovery Administrator Hugh Johnson declared on June 19th that they need

---

[1] *American Federationist*, XL (1933), 677.

[2] Lewis L. Lorwin and Arthur Wubnig, *Labor Relations Boards* (Washington: 1935), p. 51.

[3] *Ibid.*, pp. 50–51; *Violations of Free Speech and Rights of Labor*, 76th Cong., 1st sess., Sen., Hearings before Subcomm. on Edu. and Labor pursuant to S. Res. 266, pt. 35, pp. 14253–58, hereafter cited as *La Follette Comm. Hearings*.

[4] *La Follette Comm. Hearings*, 14269; National Industrial Conference Board, *Individual and Collective Bargaining under the N.I.R.A.* (New York: 1933), pp. 13, 17, 24.

not be jointly determined. The AFL-dominated Labor Advisory Board at once voiced protest. When the Iron and Steel Institute brought in a draft affirming the open shop and incorporating a company union a bitter conflict with the Labor Board ensued which was settled only through intervention of the President. He ruled that the code should contain only the language of 7(a).[5]

On July 28th the Automobile Chamber of Commerce proposed the open shop and a "merit" clause. On this occasion the board eliminated only the former, the code granting employers the "right to select, retain, or advance employees on the basis of individual merit, without regard to their membership or nonmembership in any organization."[6] In bituminous coal, where the miners conducted a summer-long strike, segments of the industry made proposals ranging from acceptance of collective bargaining to the most extreme rejection. The President, however, approved the agreement signed on September 21st pursuant to Sec. 7(b) as part of the code, thereby reëstablishing union conditions over virtually the whole industry as well as the position of the UMW.[7]

While NRA struggled to cross the treacherous waters of 7(a) interpretation, a mounting wave of strikes threatened recovery. Man-days lost, under 603,000 monthly in the first half of 1933, spurted to 1,375,000 in July and 2,378,000 in August with the upturn in business and the organizational drives.[8] Since existing machinery proved inadequate the NRA Industrial and Labor Advisory Boards together proposed, and the President on August 5th approved, the creation of a National Labor Board. He issued no order granting it authority. The boards, however, proposed that NLB consider and adjust differences over interpretation of the President's Reëmployment Agreement,[9] establish regional agencies, and that employers and employees withhold "disturbing action" pending its decisions. Roosevelt named Wagner Chairman for the public, Dr. Leo Wolman, of the Labor Advisory Board, William Green, and John L. Lewis for labor, and Walter C. Teagle, Chairman of the Industrial Board, Gerard Swope of General Electric, and Louis E. Kirstein of Filene's for industry. Dr. William M. Leiserson was appointed Executive Secretary, with Professor Milton Handler the General Counsel. The board liberally interpreted its power to permit mediation and, failing agreement, the issuance of "decisions."[10]

---

[5] Lorwin and Wubnig, *op. cit.,* pp. 54–59; Raymond S. Rubinow, *Section 7(a): Its History, Interpretation and Administration,* Office of National Recovery Administration, Division of Review, Work Materials No. 45, pt. E (Washington: 1936), pp. 57–59.

[6] Lorwin and Wubnig, *op. cit.,* pp. 65–68.   [7] *Ibid.,* pp. 69–73.

[8] "Industrial Disputes," *Monthly Labor Review,* XXXVII (1933), 869.

[9] A blanket code, incorporating 7(a), designed to hasten the process of bringing industries under NRA.

[10] Rubinow, *op. cit.,* pp. 156–57; Lorwin and Wubnig, *op. cit.,* pp. 93–95.

NLB met its first major test with conspicuous success, a recognition strike in the early fall by the Hosiery Workers in the mills at Reading, Pa. The settlement, the "Reading Formula," provided for a return to work without discrimination, bargaining on wages and hours, a secret ballot election by the board to determine representatives, and NLB arbitration of disputes over interpretation of the agreement. In the voting thirty-seven of the forty-five mills selected the union and the employers complied with the settlement. This set a pattern for many other disputes, including the captive mines case, in the following three months. It appeared that an interpretation of 7(a) had been institutionalized.[11]

This success proved illusory, however, when employers turned on NLB at the end of 1933, exposing its inability to consummate agreements or enforce decisions. In October several companies refused to appear at hearings and on November 1st the NAM publicly declared that "the policies of the National Labor Board tend to prevent the prompt and peaceful settlement of industrial disputes. . . ."[12] The following month Weirton Steel refused to permit an election under board auspices and conducted a company union ballot instead. With equal impunity the Budd Manufacturing Company rejected a decision. The effects were felt immediately in the attitude of employers generally.[13]

On December 16th, therefore, the President issued an executive order retroactively ratifying NLB activities and authorizing it to adjust by mediation or arbitration disputes which "tend to impede the purposes of the National Industrial Recovery Act."[14] Despite these powers and more strikes, operations remained on dead center as a consequence of industry's refusal to coöperate. Hence, Roosevelt in February 1934 issued two further orders empowering NLB upon the request of employees to conduct representation elections under the majority rule. If the employer interfered or refused to deal with the representatives selected, the board might make recommendations to the Attorney General or the Compliance Division of NRA.[15] A cleavage of interpretation between NLB and NRA became manifest when, on February 3d, Johnson and his General Counsel, Richberg, in effect repudiated majority rule in favor of the right of minorities and individuals to bargain separately. The breach became irretrievable on February 27th, the board referring

---

[11] Lorwin and Wubnig, *op. cit.*, pp. 95–102. Suggestion of the election, the heart of the formula, is credited to Swope. Frances Perkins, "Eight Years as Madame Secretary," *Fortune*, XXIV (1941), 79.

[12] *New York Times,* Nov. 2, 1933.

[13] Lorwin and Wubnig, *op. cit.*, pp. 102–06.

[14] Exec. Order No. 6511, Dec. 16, 1933.

[15] Exec. Orders No. 6580, Feb. 1, No. 6612-A, Feb. 23, 1934.

the Weirton case to the Department of Justice and two days later asserting the majority principle in the Denver Tramway case. The failure of
the board was underlined on March 1st, when its chairman introduced
his Labor Disputes bill into Congress.[16]

The crisis in the auto industry destroyed NLB. The AFL had organized over 50,000 workers, employers countering with company unions.
In March 1934, the United Automobile Workers presented demands
for elections, recognition, and bargaining which the industry rejected.
When NLB intervention proved fruitless, Johnson assumed direction
and, with Roosevelt's imprimatur, worked out the automobile settlement
of March 25th. In essence it provided that employers bargain with
groups (individuals, company unions, trade unions) pro rata to their
membership; coercion from any source was prohibited; and a tripartite
Automobile Labor Board was created independent of NLB to consider
discrimination, when lists of union members were supplied, and representation cases. These terms, emanating from so high a source, were at
loggerheads with NLB policies and the executive orders and undermined
the board.[17]

During its short life, however, NLB evolved a "common law" of industrial relations in interpreting 7(a) that was to have a profound effect
upon legislative and administrative policy.[18] Its decisions gave specific
meaning to the four principles set forth in Chapter II. The first, the
right of employees to associate and designate representatives, was of
course, embodied in the statute and needed no elucidation.

The second, the injunction not to interfere with the exercise of these
rights, was construed to prohibit a variety of discriminatory practices
and the company union. The board ruled that union membership might
not be an employer's basis for discharging, laying off, demoting, depriving of seniority, or reinstating employees, or of transferring work
from an organized to a nonunion plant. His rights to hire and fire and
conduct his business, however, were unimpaired when the purpose was
nondiscriminatory.[19] It was often difficult to draw the line because the
antiunion employer covered his motives. Hence the board gave weight
to three factors: a history of hostility to unionism, previous threats of

---

[16] Lorwin and Wubnig, *op. cit.*, pp. 108–11.

[17] *Ibid.*, pp. 112–13. According to Frances Perkins, the President regretted his participation almost immediately afterward. *The Roosevelt I Knew* (New York: 1946), p. 304.

[18] Analyses of NLB cases and of its successor, the first National Labor Relations
Board, are found in Lorwin and Wubnig, *op. cit.*, chaps. vi and vii; Twentieth
Century Fund, *Labor and the Government* (New York: 1935), chap. x; William H.
Spencer, *Collective Bargaining under Section 7(a) of the National Industrial Recovery
Act* (Chicago: 1935), chaps. iii–vii; Rubinow, *op. cit.*, chaps. v and vi; and D. O.
Bowman, *Public Control of Labor Relations* (New York: 1942), pp. 48–50.

[19] *Decisions of the National Labor Board* (Washington: 1934), I, General Cigar *and
Cigar Makers*, 71, hereafter cited as *Decisions*.

dismissal, and the records of affected employees prior to the action.[20] Workers discharged discriminatorily were reinstated with seniority and, in one case, with back pay.[21] Strikers were considered employees and were to be reinstated without prejudice—even if necessary to dislodge those hired during the walkout.[22] The fact of discharge was not conclusive evidence itself of prejudice and, if nonunion as well as union employees were let out, the employer's action was sustained.[23] Since the Act outlawed yellow-dog contracts, the board refused to countenance them.[24]

A company union dominated by the employer constituted "interference, restraint, or coercion." The controlling standards were whether he initiated and imposed the plan and controlled its operations. The employees' desires were decisive and determinable under the "Reading Formula." Despite union protests, the alleged company union was placed on the ballot and, when chosen in a free election, was held lawful.[25] Plans whose inception antedated the Act did not by that fact become valid, since it conferred rights superior to a historical relationship.[26]

In regard to the third principle, representation, the board laid down far-reaching rules of procedure. In selecting spokesmen "of their own choosing" employees were not limited to fellow-workers but might elect anyone they wished, including an "outside" organization.[27] Since the purpose of the election was to determine the identity and authority of the employees' representatives, it was their concern exclusively.[28] The board conducted an election during a strike if the employer denied the authority of the spokesmen or if a substantial number of workmen so petitioned. Eligibility to vote was restricted to employees, and, in case of a strike, the pay roll preceding the stoppage was used. Both strikers and nonstrikers on the list were eligible, but not those hired during the shutdown. Care was taken to identify voters, insure secrecy, count ballots before watchers, hold elections off company premises, and bar electioneering near polling places. Where a trade union and company union competed both appeared on the ballot; where a company union did not run, the employees chose either the former or no union.[29] Representa-

[20] *Ibid.*, II, Jersey City and Lyndhurst Bus *and* Railroad Trainmen, 48; Tubize Chatilion *and* Rayon Workers, 64; Birtman Electric *and* Electrical Workers, 43.

[21] *Ibid.*, II, C. F. Smith *and* Teamsters, 56; I, United Air Lines *and* Behncke, 81.

[22] *Ibid.*, I, Roth & Co. *and* Ladies Garment Workers, 75.

[23] *Ibid.*, I, Bassett Furniture *and* Carpenters and Joiners, 93.

[24] *Ibid.*, II, Chicago Motor Coach *and* Amalgamated Street Railway Employees, 74.

[25] *Ibid.*, I, National Lock *and* Federal Labor Union, 15; Federal Knitting Mills *and* Textile Workers, 69.

[26] *Ibid.*, I, Republic Steel *and* Red Ore Local, 88.

[27] *Ibid.*, I, Berkeley Woolen Mills *and* Textile Workers, 5.

[28] *Ibid.*, I, B/J Aircraft *and* Aeronautical Workers, 55.

[29] Lorwin and Wubnig, *op. cit.*, pp. 157–61.

tives elected by a majority of those voting bargained for all the workers in the unit.[30] The majority rule obtained even when the union asked to represent only its own members or a minority.[31] On the intricate question of appropriate unit, NLB only ruled that the employer might not determine it and that a union might not represent an improper segment of an operation.[32]

The fourth principle, the employer's duty to bargain, the board stated as a duality of obligation, of the workers to offer adjustment prior to a strike and of the employer to confer and bargain in good faith with freely chosen employee representatives.[33] The terminal point was, of course, the agreement.[34] Although the law did not require its reduction to writing, NLB so recommended.[35]

The board dealt gingerly with the status of the closed shop under 7(a). The NAM argued that it was illegal under clause (1), granting employees the right to select representatives of their own choosing. The AFL amendment to (2) had sought to prevent such an interpretation, but since the first was unchanged, an inconsistency remained.[36] The board refrained from ruling directly on this question in its 7(a) decisions, but moved toward sanctioning the closed shop in two arbitration cases.[37]

The board's immediate achievement in these decisions was empty since industry refused compliance and the White House followed an ambivalent policy. By the end of 1933, therefore, Wagner was convinced of the need to write these principles into a permanent law outside the NRA structure. The AFL, similarly, called for amendments to the Recovery Act "in order to make real and vital the intent and purpose of the labor sections."[38] Hence the Senator, the board, and the Federation joined forces to prepare legislation. They did not seek the approval of the White House and, in fact, the President expressed no interest.[39] Johnson and Richberg, representing so divergent a viewpoint, were not invited, while the Department of Labor was asked.

[30] *Decisions,* I, Denver Tramway *and* Amalgamated Street Railway Employees, 64.
[31] Lorwin and Wubnig, *op. cit.,* 195.
[32] *Decisions,* I, National Lock, 15; II, Gordon Baking *and* Bakery Drivers, 53.
[33] *Ibid.,* I, National Lock, 15.
[34] *Ibid.,* I, Hall Baking *and* Bakery Drivers, 83.
[35] *Ibid.,* I, Pierson Mfg. *and* Garment Workers, 53.
[36] Cf. Paul F. Brissenden, "Genesis and Import of the Collective-Bargaining Provisions of the Recovery Act," *Economic Essays in Honor of Wesley Clair Mitchell* (New York: 1935), pp. 48–51, 60–61.
[37] *Decisions,* II, Peoples Pharmacies *and* Employee Pharmacists, 36; Lorwin and Wubnig, *op. cit.,* 200–01.
[38] AFL, *Weekly News Service,* Jan. 20, 1934.
[39] Emery of the NAM wrote on Jan. 17, "There is evidence that, in the highest quarters, there is unwillingness to support legislation of this character." *La Follette Comm. Hearings,* pt. 17, p. 7547.

At the first conference in January in the Senator's office, Green, Lewis, Henry Warrum, counsel for the miners, and Department of Labor Solicitor Charles E. Wyzanski, Jr., joined with Wagner and his legislative secretary, Leon H. Keyserling, in agreeing to cover substantively: the right to organize and bargain, bargaining unit, "outside" representation, elections, majority rule, duty to bargain, the closed shop, the company union, and the right to strike. Procedurally they decided to create a board with authority to investigate with the subpoena, conciliate, arbitrate, and issue findings that were enforced.[40]

The AFL leaders then withdrew from detailed participation and February was consumed in preparing the bill. Wagner, following his customary practice, insisted that the drafting be done in his office and placed Keyserling in charge. He, in turn, obtained technical assistance from the NLB staff—Leiserson, Handler, William G. Rice, Jr., and Benedict Wolf. When shaped the draft declared that economic concentration rendered the individual worker helpless and that failure to recognize the right to associate and bargain produced strife with consequent injury to commerce and the general welfare. Employers with one or more workers were covered, with strikers receiving its benefits. The right to organize and bargain collectively was affirmed. It was an unfair practice for an employer to interfere with that right; to refuse to recognize and deal with representatives of his employees; influence, participate in, or contribute financial support to a company union; or discriminate for membership or nonmembership in a labor organization. The closed shop, however, was lawful provided the contract did not exceed one year, the union represented a majority, membership was open, and it was not based on an unfair practice. Unfair practices were misdemeanors subject to fines of five hundred dollars per day and restraining orders of the district courts. Representatives selected by a majority of those entitled to vote, or by more than half of those voting—provided they were 40 per cent of those eligible—were exclusive representatives. An independent tripartite National Labor Board was created to engage in mediation and arbitration. It would also issue cease and desist orders in unfair practice cases that burdened commerce and would direct affirmative action to redress injustices, both enforceable in the district courts. In representation cases it would determine appropriate unit, conduct elections, and certify representatives, but majority rule was not explicitly stated. NLB would issue subpoenas and regulations. The U. S. Conciliation Service in the Department of Labor received a statutory base, while the right to strike was affirmed.[41]

---

[40] Proposals for National Labor Board, Jan. 31, 1934, Keyserling papers; Disputes Act, n.d., Wyzanski papers.

[41] Draft Bill, Feb. 26, 1934, Wyzanski papers.

The Department, of Labor took exception to several provisions. It regarded the economic concentration argument as legally gratuitous, certain to arouse employer resentment, and urged that NLB be placed in the department. Jurisdiction over all unfair practices that burdened commerce was of doubtful constitutionality and would weigh the board down with inconsequential discrimination cases. Wyzanski urged restricting jurisdiction to *labor disputes* that obstructed commerce, since the Supreme Court in antitrust cases had found them within the ambit of federal regulation. Making an unfair practice a crime was extreme and would impose difficulties in obtaining convictions from juries. The department deplored the absence of the majority rule, since a minority union might by a closed shop impose membership upon an unwilling majority. It censured tripartism as poorly adapted to a board enforcing rights, preferring an all-public agency with quasi-judicial functions alone.[42]

On March 1st Wagner introduced the Labor Disputes bill, S. 2926, into the Senate. Workers, he declared, deserved the rights of association and bargaining already enjoyed by employers as set forth in 7(a). It, however, had broken down in the face of restrictive practices, particularly the company union, while a cloud hung over the status of the closed shop. Seventy per cent of NLB's cases involved union recognition, employer unwillingness to deal with employee representatives.[43]

Title I declared that economic concentration had destroyed the balance of bargaining power between employer and employee and rendered the individual worker helpless to exercise liberty of contract, a major cause of strife. To remove obstructions to commerce, encourage uniform labor standards, and provide for the general welfare, the policy of Congress was to eliminate obstacles to the organization of labor, encourage equality of bargaining power, and provide agencies for the settlement of disputes. The department's suggestion to delete this statement was overruled since the Supreme Court had recently upheld statutes by reference to congressional intent as expressed in the declaration of policy.[44]

In the definitions in Sec. 3 an "employer" was a person with one or more employees—save only governments, carriers subject to the Railway Labor Act, and labor organizations—covering virtually all businesses

---

[42] Wagner, favorably impressed with NLB's success with mediation, was the principal supporter of tripartism. Labor Disputes Act, Feb. 19, Wyzanski to the Secretary, Feb. 26, Wyzanski memo., Feb. 27, 1934, Wyzanski papers; Comments by Department, Feb. 28, 1934, Keyserling papers.

[43] *Cong. Record*, LXXVIII, pt. iv, 3443–46. The same day Representative Connery introduced an identical measure as H.R. 8423. *Ibid.*, 3576.

[44] Analysis of Bill Suggested by Wagner, n.d., Keyserling papers.

in commerce. Persons ceasing work as a consequence of a dispute or an unfair practice were "employees," replacements, however, not being so protected. "Representative" would mean "any individual or labor organization," shielding the outside union. "Labor organization" included both independent and company unions. Employer-sponsored organizations administering pension, welfare, and recreational plans were excluded provided that they did not impinge upon bargaining.

Sec. 4 asserted the right of employees "to organize and join labor organizations, and to engage in concerted activities, either in labor organizations or otherwise, for the purposes of organizing and bargaining collectively through representatives of their own choosing or for other purposes of mutual aid or protection." This language strengthened 7(a) by removing any ambiguity over the right of organization in unions.

These rights were linked to Sec. 5, which forbade an employer to engage in unfair practices. The first was to impair these benefits by "interference, influence, restraint, favor, coercion, or lockout, or by any other means." The second was "to refuse to recognize and/or deal with representatives of his employees, or to fail to exert every reasonable effort to make and maintain agreements with such representatives." The third was "to initiate, participate in, supervise, or influence the formation, constitution, by-laws, other governing rules, operations, policies, or elections of any labor organization." Fourth was a prohibition against financial support of such an association. Taken together they would illegalize the company union when employer dominated and not per se. The fifth was failure to notify employees that contracts in conflict with the act were void. The final practice was discrimination in the terms of employment to encourage membership or nonmembership in a labor organization. A proviso protected the closed shop on condition that the labor organization was not based on an unfair practice and represented a majority and that the term of the contract did not exceed one year.

The district courts received jurisdiction by Sec. 6 to restrain a practice that "burdens or affects commerce." At exclusive instance of the board U. S. district attorneys would bring suits.

Title II created an independent tripartite National Labor Board of seven, three public, two employer, and two labor representatives, appointed by the President and confirmed by the Senate. Nonpartisan members would serve five years and the others one year. Sec. 204 empowered the board to proffer its services as conciliator or mediator, leaving unclear whether this was confined to unfair practice and representation questions or extended as well to contract disputes.

Sec. 205 gave the board authority to prevent an unfair practice that "burdens or affects commerce or obstructs the free flow of commerce." Despite Wyzanski's caution, existence of a dispute would not be a precondition for jurisdiction. When information "from any source whatsoever" alleged that a person committed such a practice, the board served a complaint with notice of hearing. The latter was not subject to the rules of evidence. If the board sustained the complaint, it issued findings of fact and an order like those of the Federal Trade Commission. "The order may require such person to cease and desist from such unfair labor practice, or to take affirmative action, or to pay damages, or to reinstate employees, or to perform any other acts that will achieve substantial justice under the circumstances." If an employer failed to comply, the board might petition a district court for enforcement. Similarly, a person aggrieved by an order might obtain review in the same tribunal.

Sec. 206 empowered NLB to act as arbitrator in disputes voluntarily submitted, awards to be final and binding. Either side or the board might ask the courts to enforce or vacate the decision.

Authority to determine representatives was given by Sec. 207. NLB might conduct elections or use other means to ascertain workers' preferences. Despite the department's criticism, majority rule was not asserted, being left to the discretion of the board. NLB decided who would vote on the basis of "employer unit, craft unit, plant unit, or other appropriate grouping." It might certify names of individuals or organizations as representatives. Except for the nimbus of doubt covering the majority principle, Sec. 207 codified NLB decisions. Sec. 208 granted powers to subpoena witnesses and documents and issue regulations.

Title III granted the Conciliation Service in the Department of Labor full statutory support for the first time since its inception in 1913. This gave legal recognition to the existing agency and its policies without clarifying the potential conflict between Service and board over mediation and arbitration. Sec. 303 declared that "nothing in this Act shall be construed so as to interfere with or impede or diminish in any way the right to strike." Sec. 305 was the usual separability clause saving the remainder of the statute in case any provision was held invalid.

To gain criticism, Wagner submitted the bill to a group of experts who, with one exception, favored it as a whole, objecting only to particulars. Ludwell Denny of the Scripps-Howard Newspapers and Professor John A. Fitch of the New York School of Social Work opposed excluding unions from coverage when acting as employers as discrimination against their employees. Fitch also argued that the duty to bargain could not be stated legally. Denny urged amending the closed shop proviso to eliminate restrictions on union membership. Louis B.

Boudin, the labor attorney, feared for the status of minorities in face of the implied majority principle and the board's authority to determine units, suggesting an amendment permitting employees to petition for separate units. Leiserson and Denny objected to the tripartite arrangement in view of its enforcement function. Leiserson continued this argument to ask for elimination of mediation and arbitration and removal of the hiatus with the Conciliation Service. Boudin and Mary van Kleeck of the Russell Sage Foundation feared weakening of the right to strike. She, in fact, opposed S. 2926 on the ground that it was impossible to equalize bargaining power and that government intervention would lead eventually to regulation of unions.[45]

In addition, Wagner sounded out several businessmen. Ernest G. Draper of Hills Brothers Co. endorsed it without qualification. G. S. Anderson, employer member of the Bituminous Code Authority, on the other hand, was opposed, observing that "it will not be possible to put it through the channels of industry . . . without at least the moral support of liberal, or 'left-wing,' management. As it stands, the deficiencies of both commission and omission must inevitably alienate that support."[46]

At that moment the NAM was busy mobilizing industry to fight the bill by preparing for trade association, business and company union representatives to testify, for press statements and radio broadcasts, for a demonstration in Washington, and for pressure on the White House.[47] Supporting associations sent circulars to their members, urging them to wire congressmen. The steel companies distributed similar brochures to suppliers, customers, and employees.[48] On March 20th an NAM committee asked the President to kill the measure, a visit preceded by many wires reflecting their viewpoint.[49]

The press responded more quickly to this bill than it had in 1933, at least fifteen newspapers commenting in March. The overwhelming majority, twelve, remarked unfavorably.[50] Only two spoke sympatheti-

[45] Denny, Fitch, Boudin, Leiserson, Van Kleeck to Wagner, Feb.–March 1934, Keyserling papers.

[46] Draper, Anderson to Wagner, *op. cit.*, March 8, 13, 1934. The views of Ralph E. Flanders may have been representative of liberal businessmen. The Wagner bill, he thought, "went much too far and . . . weighted the scales in favor of the labor unions. . . . At the time I felt that a forced development of collective bargaining would raise problems for the nation which it would be difficult to solve." Senator Flanders to the writer, May 10, 1949.

[47] *La Follette Comm. Hearings,* pt. 35, 14055 ff.

[48] Wagner collected a large number of these documents. Keyserling papers. Cf. also *New York Times,* March 4, 15, 19, 24, 1934.

[49] J. P. Selvage to McIntyre, McIntyre to Roosevelt, March 19, 1934, White House, O.F. No. 716, NLRB.

[50] *Baltimore Sun,* March 3, *Chicago Daily News,* March 14, *Detroit Free Press,* March 30, *Minneapolis Journal,* March 20, *New York Evening Sun,* March 16, *New York*

cally of the bill,[51] while the *Washington Star* was noncommittal. Party loyalties dissolved in the opposition as Democratic papers joined in the attack. The sponsors of S. 2926 therefore learned that they would have to contend with a hostile press.

The hearings before the Senate Committee on Labor called forth a full-dress debate. Those supporting S. 2926 were representatives of NLB led by Wagner, the AFL and its constituent unions, the railroad brotherhoods, government experts, specialists from the universities, and the Socialist Party. The opposition consisted of employer associations, individual employers, company unions, particularly from steel, university officials, and the Communist union movement. Administration spokesmen were either ambivalent (Secretary Perkins) or conspicuously absent (General Johnson).[52]

The proponents argued, first, that 7(a) suffered from such ambiguity and weakness that the board had been unable to enforce it in face of employer resistance. S. 2926, drafted out of this experience of shortcoming, gave clarity to the law and teeth to NLB. Professor Paul H. Douglas observed that "the legal powers of the National Labor Board to prevent . . . discrimination, to hold . . . neutral elections and to compel unwilling employers to abide by the result, were shadowy and uncertain." The result, inevitably, was that the board "with the best will in the world was forced into the assumption of responsibility without power."[53]

The second justification was that the bill would redress the balance of bargaining power between employees and employers arising from economic concentration. NRA, offering inducements to businessmen to band together, tipped the scales more unevenly. Unless labor won the right to organize into unions, employers would use their superiority to impose onerous conditions.[54]

Third, effectuating the purposes of 7(a) required regulation of the company-dominated union. The industry program to fasten these organizations upon employees flouted freedom of association as laid down in the statute. The bill, however, prohibited only those controlled by the employer; an unaffiliated union selected by workers would be permitted. The same was the case with employee welfare associations which did not bargain.[55]

Journal of Commerce, March 3, *Philadelphia Public Ledger,* March 4, *Providence Journal,* March 26, *St. Louis Post-Dispatch,* March 4, *San Francisco Argonaut,* March 23, *Wall St. Journal,* March 3, *Washington Post,* March 5, 1934.

[51] *Philadelphia Record,* March 3, *Springfield Daily News,* March 5, 1934.

[52] *To Create a National Labor Board,* 73d Cong., 2d sess., Sen., Hearings before Comm. on Edu. and Labor on S. 2926 (March 14–Apr. 19, 1934), *passim,* hereafter cited as *National Labor Board,* Sen. Hearings.

[53] *Ibid.,* pp. 8, 10, 37, 69, 185, 208.

[54] *Ibid.,* pp. 8, 17, 68, 140, 171, 206, 209.

[55] *Ibid.,* pp. 9, 12, 73, 76–79, 83, 143, 169.

The bill, fourth, would foster economic recovery and stability. Unless it was enacted, Green reasoned, Congress must expect a loss of public confidence in NRA. A major cause of the depression, he argued, was a low level of wages in relation to profits prior to 1930. NIRA sought to counter this by increasing mass purchasing power and distributing the national income more equitably, in large part by 7(a). Higher wages through bargaining could not be achieved, however, unless that provision was given substance. Eleanor Herrick warned that "only by . . . equitable distribution of the national wealth can this country avoid another complete collapse of the industrial system."[56]

Fifth, an administrative tribunal with flexible procedures was justified on the ground that the problems required expert and expeditious handling. Experience proved the courts inadequate for this purpose, in part because their proceedings were involved. To be effective, moreover, the board required full enforcement powers as well as access to vital information. Although many disputes might be resolved by mediation, it would work only if the parties knew that the board had real authority.[57] Finally, the proponents contended that the bill was constitutional without submitting a sustaining argument.[58]

The supporters of S. 2926 were not without differences, essentially over administrative issues. Miss Perkins urged placing the board in the Department of Labor though not to be responsible to her in rendering decisions. Board spokesmen, on the other hand, argued for an independent agency to gain the confidence of employers and the public since the department's purpose was to promote the welfare of wage earners. The Secretary, Leiserson, and Otto S. Beyer sought to protect the Conciliation Service's mediation authority. Finally, Leiserson and Beyer objected to tripartism. Wagner and Green, on the contrary, desired partisan representation to facilitate mediation.[59]

The viewpoint of NRA was less favorable though somewhat equivocal. Johnson, in an open letter, declared that "the government should not favor any particular form of organization." Employers were entitled to initiate company unions, but should not "finance, foster, nor direct what the men do." Control over employment was "so potent a force" that freedom of choice could not exist where management maintained dominance over employee organizations once established. Wagner with oracular insight interpreted these remarks as an endorsement of S. 2926.[60]

The industry opponents of the bill began by attacking the measure

---

[56] *Ibid.*, pp. 8, 12, 71, 120, 167, 180.
[57] *Ibid.*, pp. 11, 30, 36, 185.
[58] *Ibid.*, pp. 109–10.
[59] *Ibid.*, pp. 21–25, 32, 111, 229–30, 236.
[60] *New York Times*, Apr. 10, 1934.

as unconstitutional. The commerce clause did not sanction federal regulation of labor relations since, as the Supreme Court had held repeatedly, production was not commerce and jurisdiction over employment relations flowing therefrom was the exclusive prerogative of the states.[61]

Second, they contended that the company union should not be outlawed. Management did not interfere in the election of representatives, while joint conferences were defended as genuine collective bargaining. In view of the objective of promoting coöperative relations participation of both workers and employers in company unions was proper. By intervening the government would upset satisfactory relationships, some dating to the beginning of the century. Company union spokesmen described themselves as the real representatives of employees. Workmen, they charged, would lose pensions, insurance, and other benefits under S. 2926.[62]

Third, the bill would create an AFL monopoly by closing the door on other forms of organization, compelling the majority of workers to conform to the unionized ten per cent. The closed shop, it was charged, would be forced upon unwilling workmen in defiance of their wishes and constitutional prerogatives. Industry, particularly small businessmen, would be helpless in face of the labor colossus. While granting the AFL great power, S. 2926 imposed no corresponding responsibilities despite the fact that many leaders were racketeers, agitators, and Communists. Furthermore, the Federation's craft structure was not adaptable to mass production industries.[63]

Fourth, the bill would undermine economic recovery, defeating the purpose of NRA. It would encourage unions to call strikes with consequent loss of production and employment.[64]

Finally, industry charged the procedures were arbitrary, destroying constitutional rights. The same administrative agency would decide both facts and law without proper judicial review. It would flout the rules of evidence and pry into private affairs. It would act simultaneously as prosecuting attorney and judge, while tripartism would foster partisan rather than judicial decisions.[65]

---

[61] Sen. Hearings, *National Labor Board,* pp. 341, 501–02, 651.

[62] *Ibid.,* pp. 354–61, 666, 674, 732–52. An Ohio farmer wrote Wagner: "I have been asked by some of the employees of the steel mills in Youngstown to write to you regarding the stand of the steel workers on your bill which is creating such a furore among steel men. They claim some of the mill workers will soon be sent to Washington to testify against the passage of your bill but they also say the men sent DO NOT represent the wishes of the men as they have been given no opportunity to express themselves." J. A. Shafer to Wagner, March 22, 1934, Keyserling papers.

[63] Sen. Hearings, *National Labor Board,* pp. 536, 618, 619, 645, 651, 726, 752, 755.

[64] *Ibid.,* pp. 502, 618, 638, 643, 648, 651, 731.

[65] *Ibid.,* pp. 341, 366, 383, 502, 612, 764.

The Communist Trade Union Unity League joined the NAM against the bill, but for different reasons. Marxist analysis formulated an irremediable struggle between capitalist and working classes, the government serving as the instrument of the dominant class. Hence there could be no identity of interest as S. 2926 presupposed. In capitalist America government intervention in labor relations was *ipso facto* a means to oppress the workers and deprive them of the right to strike. The bill's real purpose, TUUL charged, was to further the Administration's plan, as embodied in NRA, to salvage capitalism, depress labor standards, and promote company unionism.[66]

The hearings concluded, the fate of the bill rested with contending forces. The unfavorable considerations began, of course, with industry's unqualified opposition. Halting economic rehabilitation under NRA depended on the coöperation of business, a factor fully recognized by the Administration. The President's concessions in the automobile settlement, furthermore, constituted a blow from which the 1934 bill never recovered. Employers exploited it in pointing to its inconsistency with the bill, flouting NLB, promoting company unions, and refusing to recognize unions. A final unfavorable factor was fear that so controversial a measure would drag a weary Congress through the Washington summer. The President and the Democratic leadership were anxious to call a halt to the 73d's extraordinary output before the fall elections, while business also urged a respite.[67]

The fundamental condition favorable to enactment was an ominous strike situation at a time when the government had no adequate disputes machinery. The National Labor Board's collapse left workers no alternative but economic action, while the auto settlement epitomized the Administration's unwillingness to assist them. AFL organizational activities were successful in some industries, while in others, notably steel, auto, and West Coast longshoring, militant "rank-and-file" movements arose.[68] In the spring of 1934, therefore, a series of "head-busting" strikes occurred. Employees of Toledo's Electric Autolite Co. refused to submit their demand for recognition to the new Automobile Board, climaxing sporadic walkouts protesting the March 25th terms. Troops were called in, a number of people were killed, and a general strike threatened. A bitterly contested trucking dispute in Minneapolis was cut from the same

[66] *Ibid.*, pp. 972–93.

[67] *New York Times*, March 28, May 27, 1934; *New Republic*, LXXIX (1934), 67–68; *Kiplinger Washington Letter*, Apr. 14, 1934; *Public Papers and Addresses of Franklin D. Roosevelt*, ed. by Samuel I. Rosenman (New York: 1938), III, 300.

[68] Roy Howard reported confidentially to Roosevelt that the leaders of the steel and Toledo auto groups, at least, were not Communists. They were rather restive workmen who were dissatisfied with AFL conservatism. Howard to Louis Howe, July 3, 1934, White House, O.F. No. 407-B, Labor: Strikes.

cloth. In May the great San Francisco dockside strike began what was
to become, after military intervention, one of the few general strikes in
American labor history. Other disputes in a formative stage promised
trouble for the summer and fall. In March the insurgents in steel formulated demands in an atmosphere recalling 1919. Textile workers suffered
a cut in take-home that brought their wages under the code, a major
grievance in the strike for recognition that began on Labor Day. Rum-
blings were heard as well from coal, iron ore, copper, and shoes.[69] The
year, in fact, yielded the heaviest strike-load in over a decade—reaching
a peak during the spring and summer—and the outstanding characteristics were the number of very large cases and the importance of recognition among their causes.[70]

A second factor was an impatience on the part of the President and
several cabinet members with what they regarded as industry's flouting
of 7(a), particularly by the steel companies.[71] A final consideration was
AFL pressure, although its significance at this stage can be exaggerated.

The revision of S. 2926 which Chairman Walsh of the Senate Committee undertook was conditioned by these pressures and by his own
views. Though granting the need for a statute, his predilections led him
to propose drastic changes in the bill. To assist with the drafting, he
enlisted Wyzanski, who brought along the concepts formulated in the
department. Their alterations included eliminating the economic analysis in the declaration of policy, restricting coverage, paring the scope
of the unfair practices, removing the duty to bargain, placing the board
in the department, protecting the Conciliation Service, and restricting
jurisdiction to disputes that burdened commerce.[72]

To stave off fundamental changes, Wagner proposed modifications of
his own. He denatured the policy declaration without eliminating a
statement of the relationship between labor and commerce. The unfair
practices were revised to permit an employer to initiate a company union
and were made reciprocal in prohibiting employees from interfering
with employers in self-organization and collective bargaining. The closed

---

[69] Lorwin and Wubnig, *op. cit.*, pp. 114–15, 416, 420; *New York Times,* March 28,
May 14, 25, 26, 27, 1934.

[70] Twentieth Century Fund, *op. cit.*, pp. 126–27; "Industrial Disputes," *Monthly
Labor Review,* XXXIX (1934), 1140.

[71] *New York Herald Tribune,* May 26, 1934.

[72] Wyzanski interview; Draft Bill, Apr. 18, 1934, Wyzanski papers. The cleavage between Walsh and Wagner may be expressed in this fashion: The former believed that
the government should only protect the civil right of association, placing the right to
join a union upon a basis like that of joining a lodge. Wagner, however, went further
in urging that the national interest called for the encouragement of collective bargaining as a balance wheel in the economy, the spread of unionism being a necessary condition thereto. Cf. Wyzanski's review of Bowman, *op. cit., Yale Law Journal,* LII
(1942), 182–83.

shop proviso would allow the states to outlaw union security regardless of the statute. The right of minorities or individuals to present grievances was asserted, the procedures were relaxed, and the right to strike was made to conform to the language of the Thirteenth Amendment.[73] The NRA, in a measure drafted by Richberg, proposed elimination of the declaration of policy, substantive unfair practices for employees, a "merit" clause in the closed shop proviso, protection of employers from the "coercion" of their employees, the unqualified right to hire and fire, and employer petitions for elections.[74]

The committee reins, however, were firmly in Walsh's hands. A Republican effort to make further concessions to industry failed and nine of the eleven members present, six Democrats and three Republicans, voted for the Walsh bill.[75] On May 25th at an off-the-record press conference the President expressed concern over strikes and "autocratic" employers. When asked whether he wished legislation enacted during the current session, he declared, "I would like to have it very much. I think it would be helpful."[76]

The Senate Committee the following day reported Walsh's National Industrial Adjustment bill, a new title to avoid the overtones conveyed by "disputes."[77] The concentration of economic power argument was stricken out of the declaration of policy. Sec. 2 delimited coverage by defining "employer" to include no one with fewer than ten employees, although labor organizations were included when acting as employers. A striker was not an "employee" unless the stoppage was caused by an unfair practice and he did not obtain another job. The bill's benefits did not extend to farm laborers, domestic servants, and those working for relatives. "Unfair practice," a new term, was limited to those enumerated, circumscribing the board's discretion.

The proscribed practices in Sec. 3 provided first, that it would be illegal for an employer by "interference or coercion" to impair the right of employees to form and join organizations, select representatives, and engage in concerted activities. The committee changed the language of 7(a) by removing "restraint." Second, it would also be unlawful for employees to interfere with or coerce employers in the enjoyment of equivalent rights. Third, employers must not interfere with, dominate, or contribute financial support to "the administration" of a labor organ-

[73] Analysis of Bill Suggested by Wagner, n.d., Keyserling papers; Analysis of Revised Bill Compared with Perkins' Suggestions, Apr. 20, 1934, Wyzanski papers.

[74] Richberg to Perkins, Apr. 24, 1934, National Archives, NRA, No. 3705; Memo. on Richberg Bill, n.d., Keyserling papers.

[75] *New York Herald Tribune*, May 27, 1934.

[76] *Roosevelt Public Papers*, III, 260–62.

[77] *To Create a National Industrial Adjustment Board*, 73d Cong., 2d sess., Sen., Comm. on Edu. and Labor, Rep. No. 1184 (May 26, 1934).

ization, remaining free to initiate company unions. A proviso permitted them to pay representatives for working time lost, subject to rules of the Department of Labor. Finally, employers must not discriminate in the terms of employment to encourage or discourage membership. The proviso permitted an employer to make a closed shop agreement on condition that only those seeking employment were required to join and that the majority of employees approved it. Employers, however, were explicitly relieved of any obligation to sign such contracts. Several unfair practices of the Wagner bill, particularly the duty to bargain, were omitted.

Sec. 4 created a five-man National Industrial Adjustment Board within the Department of Labor. Three public members, serving five-year terms, would control the administrative machinery, while rotating partisan panels would supply an additional member from each side. Under Sec. 8 it would prevent unfair practices leading to labor disputes affecting commerce. NIAB would be notified of an alleged practice only by the Secretary after the Conciliation Service had failed in its efforts and might not initiate hearings itself. It would issue cease and desist orders and require affirmative action to redress an injustice, although reinstatement and back pay were not explicitly mentioned.

Sec. 10 authorized the board to use either majority rule or proportional representation in elections. The employer might discuss grievances with individuals or groups of employees. The board under Sec. 13 must report annually to Congress. Title III of the Wagner bill dealing with the Conciliation Service was eliminated. Sec. 14 replaced the old protection of the right to strike with a prohibition on requiring an employee to render labor without his consent and on the issuance of injunctions to compel such service.

The committee emphasized that the substantive features of the bill merely codified policies already determined by Congress and defended its constitutionality. Disputes resulting from restraints upon the right to organize obstructed commerce, and it declared such basic industries as automobiles, coal, and steel were clearly in commerce.

The Walsh bill momentarily obtained the support of virtually all the key government figures: the President, the Department of Labor, NRA, the Senate Committee, and Wagner.[78] It was the only measure of its kind in the New Deal era to receive such unanimous endorsement. That so many divergent views were temporarily reconciled indicates that the bill had different meanings for each and that little was needed to pry them loose from it.

The press, however, proved less enthusiastic. Of seventeen papers that

---

[78] *New York Herald Tribune,* May 24, 26, 1934; *New York Times,* May 26, 1934.

commented on NIAB, thirteen were unfavorable.[79] Only three expressed a measure of approval of the bill, while the *Washington Star* continued to refrain from taking a position.[80] The fact that NIAB was substituted for the Wagner bill introduced a note of confusion into the reaction. J. David Stern's *Philadelphia Record* and *New York Evening Post* refused to support the bill because they felt it inadequate, while the remaining opposition papers regarded it as objectionably strong. Only the *Washington Daily News* fully endorsed the measure, inasmuch as the *Cleveland Plain Dealer* was lukewarm, while the *Journal of Commerce* favored it as the lesser of two evils.

The reaction of both labor and industry to the Adjustment bill was less than friendly. The AFL took no public attitude, while the American Civil Liberties Union attacked it as "a sham and a fraud."[81] The NAM denounced the report for "its injustice, its invalidity, and its impolity," and the Chamber of Commerce, though admitting it to be an improvement over its predecessor, remained strongly opposed.[82] On June 5th the auto executives called at the White House to request the *coup de grâce.*[83]

---

[79] *Akron Beacon-Journal,* June 16, *Baltimore Sun,* June 12, *Chicago Journal of Commerce,* May 31, *Cincinnati Enquirer,* June 13, *Los Angeles Times,* June 11, *Minneapolis Tribune,* June 2, *New York Evening Post,* May 31, *New York Herald Tribune,* June 4, *Philadelphia Inquirer,* June 8, *Philadelphia Record,* May 27, *Pittsburgh Post-Gazette,* June 5, *Wall St. Journal,* May 29, *Washington Post,* May 26, 1934.

[80] *Cleveland Plain Dealer,* June 10, *New York Journal of Commerce,* May 28, *Washington Daily News,* May 28, *Washington Star,* May 27, 1934.

[81] *Amalgamated Journal,* XXXV (June 14, 1934); H. F. Ward to Wagner, June 5, 1934, Keyserling papers.

[82] *New York Times,* May 31, 1934. The Chamber proposed crippling amendments to the Administration. Chamber of Commerce Amendments, n.d., Wyzanski papers.

[83] *New York Herald Tribune,* June 6, 1934.

VI. THE PRESIDENT HESITATES: PUBLIC RESOLUTION NO. 44

IN VIEW of the unfavorable response of industry, labor, and the press to the National Industrial Adjustment bill, there was no hope of putting it through both houses of Congress and conference in the spring of 1934 without prolonged and acrimonious debate. Members, moreover, suffering from the biennial ailment of "election itch," as the *New York Times* put it, wanted to go home and the President was equally anxious to get them out of Washington. Had events steered the charted course, therefore, S. 2926 would have been laid quietly to rest. The situation in the steel industry, however, dictated otherwise.[1]

Under the stimulus of Sec. 7(a) the moribund craft-minded Amalgamated Association of Iron, Steel, and Tin Workers, AFL, reluctantly accepted an influx of members, while the steel companies promoted company unionism. A group of militant labor leaders, consolidated as the rank-and-file committee on March 25th, determined to press for union reorganization on industrial lines (President Tighe was described as "too damn conservative to be an Irishman") and for recognition by the industry. At the convention of April 17th they won a program calling for presentation of bargaining demands on May 21st and, failing acceptance, an industry-wide strike in mid-June. In creating the deadlines these leaders overplayed their hand, since they lacked organization, membership, funds, experienced leadership, and outside support for a walkout. The industry, aware of these weaknesses, rejected the demands, proposing instead a board similar to that in the auto industry. Hoping for the government to bail them out, the rank-and-filers went to Washington where they were passed gingerly between the Labor Board, Department of Labor, NRA, and the White House. General Johnson without success tried to persuade the union militants to accept the steel industry's plan.[2]

An Amalgamated convention met in Pittsburgh on June 14th, two days before the strike date, with both factions searching for a way out without loss of face. The industry, on the other hand, made strike preparations—purchasing munitions, stringing barbed wire, hiring extra employees, and conducting elections to show worker sentiment against the walkout.[3] The AFL determined to forestall a showdown lest it wreck

[1] Lewis L. Lorwin and Arthur Wubnig, *Labor Relations Boards* (Washington: 1935), p. 335.
[2] Robert R. R. Brooks, *As Steel Goes, . . . Unionism in a Basic Industry* (New Haven: 1940), chap. iii.
[3] *New York Times,* June 15, 16, 1934; Lorwin and Wubnig, *op. cit.,* p. 335.

the Amalgamated and delay unionization of steel. Hence, Green saw Roosevelt and was informed that legislation was underway to permit creation of a steel labor board.[4]

On June 15th Green addressed the convention, insisting that the strike be called off in return for the following program. First, the President would appoint an impartial board to investigate and adjust complaints, to mediate and propose voluntary arbitration, and to determine discrimination and discharge cases in violation of 7(a). Second, the board would conduct representation elections. Finally, disputes over wages, hours, and conditions might be referred to it for adjustment. After Green's assurance that the President would accept this formula, the convention adopted it with hardly a dissenting voice.[5]

The steel crisis demonstrated to Roosevelt the government's helplessness without machinery and convinced him of the need for legislation. At the same time, however, he wanted a noncontroversial bill that would move through both houses quickly, preferably with Republican support. The adverse reaction to the Walsh report made it unacceptable. The formula was a brief enabling statute granting the President authority to create boards with details to be supplied later by executive order.[6]

Wyzanski and Richberg were instructed to draft such a bill. On June 11th the former prepared a measure authorizing the President to establish a National Labor Board in the Department of Labor. It would interpret 7(a), ask the Secretary for conciliators and, with her permission, appoint boards of mediation, select arbitrators, act as a board of arbitration, and determine representatives. In the last it would conduct elections within appropriate units and certify representatives. In 7(a) cases the board would have essentially the procedural powers of the Walsh bill, while the right to strike was affirmed.[7] Richberg's draft empowered the President to create boards to investigate controversies, determine their merits, act as arbitrators, and provide means for designating representatives including the secret ballot. There was an affirmation of the right to organize without interference. Neither employees nor employers were obligated to bargain and no person was required to render labor without his consent. Penalties were provided for violations.[8]

On June 12th the President called a White House conference of the

[4] Brooks, *op. cit.,* p. 66.

[5] *Amalgamated Journal,* XXXV (June 21, 1934), 1–2; *Iron Age,* CXXXIII (June 21, 1934), 70.

[6] *Public Papers and Addresses of Franklin D. Roosevelt,* ed. by Samuel I. Rosenman (New York: 1938), III, 300; Richberg to McIntyre, June 13, 1934, National Archives, NRA, No. 3705; Wyzanski, Keyserling interviews.

[7] Wyzanski's Proposal, June 11, 1934, Wyzanski papers.

[8] Richberg's Proposal, June 11, 1934, Wyzanski papers.

majority leaders, Senator Robinson and Representative Joseph W. Byrns, Walsh, Wagner, Miss Perkins, Wyzanski, and Richberg. With the memoranda before him Roosevelt dictated Public Resolution No. 44 in essentially the form in which it was introduced. By Sec. 1, to effectuate the Recovery Act, "the President is authorized to establish a Board or Boards authorized and directed to investigate issues, facts, practices or activities of employers or employees in any controversies." Such boards, by Sec. 2, were "empowered when it shall appear in the public interest to provide for and supervise the taking of a secret ballot of any of the employees of an employer, to determine by what person or persons or organization they desire to be represented in order to insure the right of employees to organize and to select their representatives for the purpose of collective bargaining as provided in Section 7(a) of the Industrial Recovery Act." In conducting elections they would have power to subpoena documents and witnesses and might invoke the circuit courts for enforcement as provided in the Federal Trade Commission Act. Sec. 3 declared that "any such Board, with the approval of the President, may prescribe such rules and regulations as may be necessary to carry out the provisions of this resolution." The fourth imposed penalties up to $1,000 or imprisonment not to exceed one year or both for violations.[9] Upon leaving the White House, Robinson informed the press that "additional information" was sought (Republican leaders were being sounded out) and that an early adjournment of Congress was possible.[10]

The President submitted his resolution to Congress on June 13th, seeking Republican support. Although the minority leaders hesitated to identify their party with labor legislation, they were as eager as the Administration for the recess. Hence they agreed to give the resolution favorable consideration after wiring "back home," as the *New York Times* put it, to find out where business stood.[11]

At a caucus of Senate Republicans on June 14th, minority leader Charles L. McNary of Oregon appointed a committee, consisting of Davis of Pennsylvania, Couzens of Michigan, Walcott of Connecticut, Goldsborough of Maryland, and Steiwer of Oregon, to amend the resolution in line with industry's ideas. On the following day it proposed six amendments. The last words of Sec. 1, stating among the purposes that of preventing impairment of NIRA, were deleted lest the President gain authority to change the Act itself. In Sec. 2 "organization" was

---

[9] As dictated by the President, June 12th, redictated by the President, June 12, 1934, Wyzanski papers.

[10] *New York Times,* June 13, 1934.

[11] 73d Cong., 2d sess., Sen. Jt. Res. 143 and H.R. Jt. Res. 375, June 13, 1934; *New York Times,* June 13, 14, 15, 1934.

erased, so that only "persons" might be designated as representatives. Sec. 3, the issuance of regulations, was amended by adding "assure freedom from coercion in all elections." The penalty provisions in Sec. 4 were restricted by requiring that violations be "willfully and knowingly committed." A Sec. 5 would terminate the resolution and the boards when NIRA expired, or sooner if Congress or the President declared the emergency at an end. A Sec. 6 proposed to bar the President or the boards from imposing the closed shop by regulation. Although suggested, protection for proportional representation was not inserted since they anticipated Roosevelt's insistence on it in practice.[12] The caucus adopted the amendments on June 15th, and the Administration concurred except for retention of "organization" in Sec. 2 and elimination of the closed shop provision.[13]

The Republican progressives—La Follette, Norris, Gerald P. Nye of North Dakota, and Bronson Cutting of New Mexico—had no sympathy for the Administration's agreement with their party, a view which Democrat Edward P. Costigan of Colorado shared. They felt that the nation faced a strike crisis which required the full and, if necessary, prolonged attention of Congress to enact a measure approximating the Wagner bill. Hence they determined to force consideration of S. 2926. Wagner, informed of this intention, did not disapprove.[14]

The resolution was introduced into both houses on June 15th by the majority leaders and was railroaded through the lower chamber in record time with virtually no debate. When Byrns on the following day demanded immediate passage to permit adjournment that very night, Representative C. E. Mapes of Michigan declared that "not half a dozen members of the House of Representatives have had an opportunity to read the resolution." Nevertheless, the measure was passed without a roll call.[15]

In the Senate similar tactics proved less successful. Robinson defended the resolution as the minimum required to bridge the gap between the 73d and 74th Congresses. In referring it to the Labor Committee, the majority and minority leaders insisted upon an immediate report to permit consideration no later than the following day. Walsh, in fact, brought it back in little more than an hour with two amendments. The

---

[12] *New York Times*, June 15, 1934; *Cong. Record,* LXXVIII, pt. xi, 4.

[13] With regard to the former, Roosevelt declared: "There seems to be a very small minority that does not understand plain English. . . . Section 7(a) says that the workers can choose representatives. Now if they want to choose the Ahkoond of Swat they have a perfect right to do so. If they want to choose the Royal Geographic Society, they can do that. If they want to choose a union of any kind, they can do that. . . . That has to be made absolutely clear in this legislation." *Roosevelt Public Papers,* III, 301.

[14] *New York Times*, June 16, 1934; *Cong. Record,* LXXVIII, pt. xi, 12027–29, 12044.

[15] *Cong. Record,* pp. 12120–22.

first concerned the expenses of the boards, while the second, to Sec. 3, added the words "with reference to the investigations authorized in Section 1." The latter was suggested by Senator Borah to limit the boards' authority to issue regulations exclusively to investigations, thereby laying to rest employer concern lest the closed shop be imposed.[16] These changes were adopted without a vote.

Wagner then rose to support the resolution, a position reached on the eve of debate. Without illusion as to its efficacy, he nevertheless did not feel that the Walsh bill merited a fight. In addition, a number of Democrats, facing reëlection, hesitated to vote on so controversial a measure. Finally, Wagner recognized that it was impossible to push a bill satisfactory to him through both houses and conference so late in the session. The resolution, he therefore declared, is "backed by the wisdom and judgment of the President." This Congress had enacted most comprehensive changes in the economic life of the nation. "Perhaps it may be a good thing to allow these reforms to encounter an additional period of trial and error, so that the processes of education may catch up with the social progress that has been inaugurated." That was Roosevelt's view, and Wagner continued, "I am prepared to go along with him. No one is in a better position than he to weigh the program in its entirety, and no one is more determined than he that we are but commencing a new deal that will in proper time be pushed forward to its ultimate conclusions."[17]

La Follette, speaking for the progressives, then moved that S. 2926 as reported by the committee and strengthened by Wagner's own amendments be substituted. He painted an ominous picture of the industrial strife which would jeopardize economic recovery. Despite weariness with the session and threats of filibuster, he was prepared to remain in Washington all summer; Norris and Nye echoed his views. Cutting declared, "The New Deal is being strangled in the house of its friends." Wagner, under the prodding of Senator Huey P. Long of Louisiana, thereupon asked La Follette to withdraw the motion. If that were not done, he pointed out, he would have to vote against the bill. "We will fight for it next year," he promised. La Follette had no alternative but to acquiesce.[18]

La Follette then moved to add a Sec. 6 providing that "nothing in this resolution shall prevent or impede or diminish in any way the right of employees to strike or engage in other concerted activities." Walsh

[16] 73d Cong., 2d sess., Sen., Comm. on Edu. and Labor, Rep. No. 1447; *Cong. Record,* LXXVIII, pt. xi, 11647, 12016–17.

[17] *Ibid.,* pp. 12017–18.

[18] Wagner Amendments, n.d., Wyzanski papers; *Cong. Record,* LXXVIII, pt. xi, 12044, 12052.

argucd that it was unnccessary since the boards' authority would be severely limited, the committee, in fact, having rejected such language. La Follette, while inclined to agree, pointed to the concern of some labor people and noted that there would be no harm in the double safeguard. The roll was called—the sole occasion during the debate—and the amendment was adopted 82 to 3. Only Senators Barbour of New Jersey, Hastings of Delaware, and Bailey of North Carolina were opposed, and they recalled their votes later to make it unanimous.[19]

Passage was then consummated in routine fashion. Robinson's motion to accept the House bill with the Senate amendments was adopted, and Byrns got the House to agree to the upper chamber's revisions. The President fixed his signature to Public Resolution No. 44 on June 19, 1934, as Congress adjourned.[20]

Although the AFL did not openly oppose the resolution, there was bitterness against the Administration for killing the Wagner bill. This was compounded by the delays attending consideration of the amendments to the Railway Labor Act. AFL and brotherhood leaders, convening in Washington on June 17th, discussed political revolt in November to repay those who "double-crossed" labor. Green declared,

> Labor firmly believed that the enactment of the Wagner Disputes Act was necessary if the working people of the Nation were to be accorded the enjoyment of the right to organize and bargain collectively as provided for in Section 7(a). . . . The submission of a compromise Wagner bill is a keen disappointment to Labor. . . . Labor can neither approve nor endorse the so-called compromise Wagner bill.[21]

Industry, on the other hand, maintained a discreet public silence. The vice-president in charge of industrial relations of the U. S. Steel Corporation, however, wrote privately,

> I view the passage of the joint resolution with equanimity. It means that temporary measures that cannot last more than a year will be substituted for the permanent legislation proposed. . . . I do not believe there will ever be given as good a chance for the passage of the Wagner Act as exists now, and the trade is a mighty good compromise. I have read carefully the joint resolution, and my personal opinion is that it is not going to bother us very much.[22]

---

[19] *Cong. Record,* LXXVIII, pt. xi, pp. 12044–46; *New York Times,* June 17, 1934.

[20] *Cong. Record,* LXXVII, pt. xi, 12041, 12052, 12236–37, 12453.

[21] *Amalgamated Journal,* XXXV (June 21, 1934); *New York Times,* June 18, 1934. A dissenting labor view was that of Charlton Ogburn, General Counsel of the AFL, who wrote, "The President's substitute is an advantage to us and . . . we have much more to gain than to lose under it." He argued that vagueness of the boards' power would give labor a broad arena; there were no restrictions on the right to strike; the AFL might influence the rules and regulations; and board members need not be feared since fair-minded men would side with labor, witness Taft on the War Labor Board. Ogburn to Green, June 16, 1934, Shishkin papers.

[22] *National Labor Relations Board,* 74th Cong., 1st sess., H.R., Comm. on Labor, Rep. No. 969 (May 20, 1935).

As was to be expected, the resolution was more favorably received than its predecessors by the eight newspapers that commented editorially. Four were friendly, the *Cleveland Plain Dealer, Danbury News-Times, Jamestown Post,* and *Washington Post,* while an equal number took the other side, the *Baltimore Sun, Charlotte Observer, New York Evening Post,* and *Philadelphia Evening Bulletin.* Again, there was an element of confusion in that the opposition papers differed in their motivation; the *New York Post* felt that the legislation was inadequate while the others feared that it went too far.[23]

Passage of the resolution completed only half the job since an executive order was needed to place it in operation. The Department of Labor therefore prepared a draft, which, at the President's suggestion, Wagner and Richberg approved on June 20th. On the following day they submitted to Roosevelt the order creating the National Labor Relations Board of three public members. It would be "in" the department, though not subject to the Secretary's review of decisions. It would make investigations, order and hold elections, hear discharge and discrimination cases, and issue regulations. It might recommend to the President that existing boards be given added authority and that new boards be created. NLB was abolished and minor employees were absorbed. NLRB's jurisdiction would be exclusive, but it would report administratively to the President through the Secretary. At the suggestion of the Department of Justice, the language was changed to place the board "in connection with the Department" on the ground that an executive agency might not be expanded without legislative authority. On June 29, 1934, the President created the National Labor Relations Board by executive order.[24]

In conclusion, the theme of the 1934 legislative effort was division and confusion. The struggle between labor and industry left the meaning of Sec. 7(a) unresolved and Resolution No. 44 was hardly designed to add clarity. The President, wedded to NRA as his basic recovery policy, refused to jeopardize its success with a statute that business opposed. The floundering from one crisis to another revealed that he had not formulated a collective bargaining policy. Johnson and Richberg emerged as the principal conservative voices within the Administration, while the internecine cleavage between Wagner and NLB on the one

[23] *Baltimore Sun,* June 15, *Cleveland Plain Dealer,* June 17, *New York Evening Post,* June 15, *Philadelphia Evening Bulletin,* June 14, and *Washington Post,* June 18, 1934. A contemporary press survey cited the *Charlotte Observer, Danbury News-Times,* and *Jamestown Post. United States News,* July 2, 1934.

[24] Summary of Exec. Order, June 20, 1934; Perkins, Wagner, Richberg, Wyzanski to Roosevelt, June 21, 1934, Wyzanski papers; J. Crawford Biggs to Roosevelt, June 22, 1934, White House, O.F. No. 716, NLRB; Exec. Order No. 6073, June 29, 1934.

hand and the Department of Labor on the other had been widened by the latter's victory in the executive order. The rift bore not only upon the narrow question of location of the board, but, more important, upon its function and independence. The responsibility for drafting the original resolution was shared by Roosevelt, Richberg, and Wyzanski, while the amendments were provided by the Republican leadership and La Follette. The press was now thoroughly aroused; the fact that of twenty-seven papers commenting on the Wagner bill and NIAB only five were favorable prefigured the role it would thereafter play.

Yet the AFL was now firmly committed to legislation, voluntarism, like last year's bonnet, being cast into discard. NLB laid the foundation in its decisions, the basic form of the statute was worked out, and the three-month contest over S. 2926 had educated Congress and the public. Finally, Wagner believed that only a battle and not the war had been lost, and was determined to fulfill the promise he made during the debate.

VII. WAGNER TRIES AGAIN:
THE NATIONAL LABOR RELATIONS BILL

THE National Labor Relations Board created under Public Resolution No. 44 came to have a large influence upon the shaping of legislative policy. This derived in substantial measure from the men chosen as members: Dean Lloyd K. Garrison of the Wisconsin Law School, Chairman; Professor Harry A. Millis of the University of Chicago; and Edwin A. Smith, Commissioner of Labor and Industries of Massachusetts. When the Chairman resigned in mid-term he was replaced by the Philadelphia attorney Francis Biddle. The board had authority to investigate disputes involving Sec. 7(a) or affecting commerce, to order elections, conduct hearings and issue findings of fact in cases of alleged breach of the statute, issue regulations subject to presidential approval, arbitrate in disputes voluntarily submitted, and subpoena in election cases. Aside from imposing penalties for deliberate violations of regulations, its only enforcement power was to refer noncompliance cases to NRA for removal of the Blue Eagle or to the Department of Justice for such action as the Attorney General deemed appropriate.[1]

The vague directive to establish the board "in connection with the Labor Department" was worked out in an arrangement reached by Garrison and Miss Perkins on July 16, 1934, by which NLRB consulted her on major appointments but retained control over decisions, hiring, firing, and funds. At the time he resigned, however, relations were strained by an unsuccessful and devious attempt by the department to give the Secretary unfettered authority over NLRB.[2] The board carried over seventeen regional offices of NLB, hoping through them and the industrial boards to erect a unified structure of interpretation of 7(a), itself serving as the "Supreme Court." Roosevelt thwarted this aspiration in part in January, 1935, by removing the coal, newspaper, and auto boards from its jurisdiction. NLRB, following this conception of function, emphasized the adjudication of rights rather than the adjustment of differences, breaking with the policy of its predecessor. Although tripartite panels were employed, the board enjoined them against mediating settlements that did not conform with its principles. As a consequence the quasi-judicial function became paramount, dependent agencies applying decisions to their cases. Although willing to serve as arbitrator, it seldom acted in this capacity.[3]

---

[1] Exec. Order No. 6763, June 29, 1934.

[2] H. K. Gilbert, The United States Department of Labor in the New Deal Period (unpublished Ph.D. thesis, Wisconsin, 1942), p. 160; Garrison interview.

[3] Lewis L. Lorwin and Arthur Wubnig, *Labor Relations Boards* (Washington: 1935), chap. xi.

In its decisions NLRB carved the details into the rough slab of "common law" passed on by NLB. In the area of employer interference the board primarily concerned itself with the company union, discriminatory practices, and hostile statements. About thirty per cent of its decisions involved company unions, which it did not hold unlawful per se but only when the employer intervened in their initiation, sponsorship, support, elections, by-laws, and other affairs. An election did not of itself constitute freedom of choice unless the employees were permitted to vote on whether they wanted the company union in the first place.[4] In extreme cases of coercion, or where the company union did not bargain, the board denied it a place on the ballot.[5] In less drastic situations it was permitted to participate on equal terms with the trade union.[6]

Discrimination based on union membership took the form of discharge, layoff, demotion, transfer, forced resignation, and division of work; and like NLB, the board restricted the employer's right to hire and fire only insofar as his motive was animus against unionists. It ordered a discharged employee's reinstatement only in face of substantial evidence of discrimination; in other cases, however, it frequently recommended the same redress. Where a strike was caused by the employer's violation of 7(a), NLRB returned the workers to their jobs without prejudice. Where there was no such breach, strikers had no legal claim to restoration.[7] The board's existence created a special practice—discharge or demotion for complaining to or testifying before NLRB—which was, of course, held unlawful.[8]

The board inaugurated examination of the employer's statements to his employees for evidence of intimidation, venturing into the area of freedom of speech. When during a controversy an employer called workmen into his office and in coercive fashion examined them on union activities, the board ruled that he exceeded permissible conduct.[9]

In designating representatives, NLRB, like its predecessor, considered an election the most satisfactory and democratic device for determining employee preferences. It ordered an election if there were contending

---

[4] *Decisions of the National Labor Relations Board* (Washington: 1935), I, Firestone Tire *and* Rubber Workers, 173; B. F. Goodrich *and* Rubber Workers, 181.

[5] *Ibid.*, I, Danbury and Bethel Fur *and* Fur Workers, 195; Davidson Transfer *and* Teamsters, 55; Ely & Walker Dry Goods *and* Wholesale Workers, 94; North Carolina Granite *and* Granite Cutters, 89.

[6] *Ibid.*, I, Kohler *and* Federated Labor Union, 72. In this case the company union, which had been found to be dominated, won the election.

[7] *Ibid.*, I, E. F. Caldwell *and* Lighting Equipment Workers, 12; Century Electric *and* Employees, 79; Eagle Rubber *and* Rubber Workers, 155; Fischer Press *and* Printing Pressmen, 84; International Furniture *and* Upholsterers, 63.

[8] *Ibid.*, I, New York Rapid Transit *and* Street Railway Employees, 192; Zenith Radio *and* Radio Workers, 202.

[9] *Ibid.*, I, Carl Pick Mfg. *and* Auto Workers, 161.

organizations or if a substantial body of employees asked for one.[10] The board, however, refused to do so where the employer already dealt with a trade union or a craft sought to carve itself out of an established larger unit.[11]

The board, notably in the Houde case, affirmed majority rule as the touchstone of collective bargaining:

> When a person, committee or organization has been designated by the majority of employees in a plant or other appropriate unit for collective bargaining, it is the right of the representatives so designated to be treated by the employer as the exclusive bargaining agency of all the employees in the unit, and the employer's duty to make every reasonable effort, when requested, to arrive with this representative at a collective agreement covering terms of employment of all such employees, without thereby denying to any employee or group of employees the right to present grievances, to confer with their employer, or to associate themselves and to act for mutual aid or protection. . . . We believe it [majority rule] to be the keystone of any sound, workable system of industrial relationship by collective bargaining.[12]

The board, however, found no pat answer to the closely linked question of appropriate unit. It demarcated boundaries therefore with flexibility on such standards as the nature and growth of unions, effective bargaining in the particular case or industry, eligibility to membership in the organization, community of interest, geographical convenience, occupational differences, functional or departmental coherence, and the history of bargaining. Insofar as possible the board avoided entering into jurisdictional disputes between unions on the ground that 7(a) granted no authority in such cases and that the labor movement alone could supply the machinery. Where the employer made a closed shop with a union to which his employees did not belong and thereupon dismissed nonmembers, the board held interference with self-organization.[13] The NLRB permitted the carving out of a craft unit where there was such a history or where skilled workmen had peculiar problems.[14]

As had NLB, the board held that the right of employees to bargain laid a correlative duty upon the employer; without one the other was sterile. The obligation entailed negotiating in good faith with freely chosen representatives, matching proposals with counterproposals, and making reasonable efforts to reach an agreement for a definite period

[10] *Ibid.*, I, Davidson Transfer, 55; Firestone Tire, 173; B. F. Goodrich, 181; Kohler, 72.

[11] *Ibid.*, I, Omaha and Council Bluffs Railway *and* Street Railway Employees, 190; United Dry Docks *and* Mechanic Welders, 150.

[12] *Ibid.*, I, Houde Engineering *and* Auto Workers, 35. Richberg commented that NLRB here assumed the robes of the bench by "expanding the simple language of Section 7(a) in the traditional manner of great judges writing their social and economic convictions into the one word 'liberty'." *The Rainbow* (Garden City, N.Y.: 1936), p. 150.

[13] *Decisions*, I, Hildinger-Bishop *and* Projectionists, 127.

[14] *Ibid.*, I, Street Railway Commissioners of Detroit *and* Street Railway Employees, 123; United Dry Docks, 150; II, Indiana Brass *and* Metal Polishers, 127.

of time. Empty declarations of willingness to confer, offers to adjust individual complaints, or assent to only a limited number of minor demands without an understanding as to duration failed to constitute good faith. The subject matter of bargaining included wages, hours, and basic working conditions and might not be confined to such questions as toilet facilities, ventilation, and slippery stairs.[15] Collaterally, once the parties reached an agreement, neither might terminate it unilaterally during its life. Reducing it to writing, though not required, was recommended as consistent with business practice, common sense, and the purpose of the statute. If the employer refused, the board might, in the light of other circumstances of his conduct, consider it denial of the employees' right to bargain.[16] The NLRB required that a "runaway" employer offer reëmployment to workers who lost jobs as a consequence of his removal.[17]

The board's decisions on the closed shop were as cautious as NLB's. It assumed that 7(a) did not impair a closed shop contract with a bona fide labor organization. Discharges based on such an agreement with a company union were invalid, while those flowing from a contract with an independent union were sustained.[18]

These decisions had little immediate value since they could not be enforced against a determined and resourceful employer—the NLRB possessed responsibility without authority. Removal of the Blue Eagle was an inequitable penalty, crippling some businessmen and not affecting others. The Attorney General, in addition, revealed a disinclination to take any action. His department insisted upon a complete record before proceeding to court and, without the subpoena, the board was helpless to obtain the facts on either the issues or commerce. These procedures, moreover, fostered delay, an advantage to the antiunion employer since a discharged employee or a new unstable union required prompt remedies. Even in election cases, where the board could issue orders, an employer might refuse to yield his pay roll and tie the case up in the courts. The statistics were overwhelming: judgments were not obtained in any of the thirty-three noncompliance cases referred to the department between July 1, 1934, and March 1, 1935. Biddle observed that "the machinery under which we are trying to enforce the law makes inevitable the breakdown of legal enforcement."[19]

[15] *Ibid.*, I, Houde Engineering, 35.

[16] *Ibid.*, I, Ely and Walker, 94; National Analine and Chemical *and* Chemical Workers, 114.

[17] *Ibid.*, I, Maujer Parlor Frame *and* Furniture Workers, 20.

[18] *Ibid.*, I, Tamaqua Underwear *and* Clothing Workers, 10; II, Bennett Shoe *and* Reynolds, 29.

[19] *National Labor Relations Board*, 74th Cong., 1st sess., Sen., Hearings before Comm. on Edu. and Labor on S. 1958 (March 11–Apr. 2, 1935), pp. 36–38, 92–93, 192.

The congressional elections of November, 1934, were no less influential than the board in laying the foundation for the enactment of comprehensive legislation the following year. The brake exercised by anticipation of an electoral test was swept away. As the results came in, the *New York Times* declared, "The President and his New Deal . . . won the most overwhelming victory in the history of American politics."[20] The majorities the Democrats brought into the 74th Congress were 45 in the Senate and 219 in the House. The election for practical purposes eliminated the right-wing of the Republican Party. Hence the legislature was prepared to entertain more progressive measures. The realignment of the two chambers was equally significant. In the 73d the House had been the more progressive body, but in its successor the Senate occupied that position, a factor weighed in planning legislative strategy.

Wagner, determined to win permanent legislation in this favorable political climate, directed Keyserling to revise the bill in the fall of 1934. He, in turn, worked closely with the legal staff of the board, General Counsel Calvert Magruder, Philip Levy, and P. G. Phillips. Although the AFL was content to leave the preparation in their hands, they constantly consulted it and received many suggestions through its counsel, Charlton Ogburn. As a consequence of earlier differences, they excluded the Department of Labor except for peripheral matters. Wagner and his advisers did not seek the advice of NRA, nor did he approach the White House until the bill was ready for introduction.[21]

The draftsmen found their task eased by what went before: the 1934 Wagner bill, National Industrial Adjustment bill, and Resolution No. 44, the 1934 hearings, and the experience of NLB and NLRB. They sought to recast the measure in a simple conceptual pattern. First, they established the board as a "Supreme Court" to eliminate the confusion under 7(a) resulting from diversity of interpretation by a multiplicity of agencies. Hence, emphasis was on the enforcement of rights rather than the adjustment of differences; exclusion of partisan members; removal of the agency from the Department of Labor to avoid proximity to mediation; and uniformity of interpretation and application through exclusive jurisdiction and maximization of coverage. Second, they broadened administrative discretion by employing general enabling language. This flexibility applied to such areas as the unfair practices, determination of appropriate unit, and restitution to the worker for losses suffered. The other side of the coin was avoiding court intervention except where indispensable. Third, they devoted scrupulous attention to constitutionality in view of the growing number of cases in 1934 and 1935 in which the Supreme Court held social legislation invalid. Fourth, assertion of the lawful status of the outside labor organization confronted

---

[20] Nov. 7, 1934.   [21] Keyserling, Levy, Wyzanski interviews.

the reluctance of many employers to deal with others than their own employees. Finally, NLRB's compliance difficulties required a scheme combining enforcing teeth, reasonable speed, and safeguards of the rights of employers within due process. To forestall charges of inequitable methods, the draftsmen took precautions to base procedures upon precedents of other quasi-judicial agencies that the courts had approved.

The AFL did not agree with all these premises, and suggested several provisions that were rejected. An attempt to confine the board's authority to determine appropriate unit on the basis of plant, craft, or classification, thereby eliminating reference to employer and other units, revealed concern with the growing industrial union issue. The Federation desired to make employer refusal to bargain an unfair practice, and went further in grievance cases in requiring both employers and employees to confer within ten days. The AFL suggested explicit language for the unfair practices, particularly with regard to company unions and discrimination. The statute would require that all labor contracts incorporate the general rights of employees and the proscribed practices. Once agreements were reached, employers would be obligated to abide by their terms without reciprocal responsibilities for unions. The Federation asked that complainants themselves have authority to seek enforcement, while the circuit courts would give priority to NLRB cases. Violations would be misdemeanors subject to severe penalties, each day of noncompliance constituting a separate offense. The AFL, however, raised no objection to making the NLRB an all-public body and was willing to lodge it outside the department.[22]

Despite the fact that many of its suggestions were not incorporated, the Federation firmly supported the measure, in fact, sought no other so earnestly. On February 11, 1935, the Executive Council called upon Roosevelt to enlist his aid in converting the principles of 7(a) into "substantive legislation." "We . . . are urging the enactment of an industrial disputes measure which will assure to all wage earners the right to membership in free trade-unions and representation through persons of their own choosing and will implement these rights."[23]

This and a similar effort by Wagner to gain the President's support prior to the bill's introduction proved unavailing. Despite his determination to exploit the election by pressing for a broad program of reform in 1935, Roosevelt declined to back this measure. This response may have been influenced by the fact that neither the Department of Labor nor NRA gave evidence of enthusiasm.[24]

---

[22] Ogburn Draft Bill, n.d., Ogburn to Wagner, Feb. 4, 19, 1935, Keyserling papers.
[23] Green to Roosevelt, White House, O.F. 142, AFL.
[24] Raymond Moley, *After Seven Years* (New York: 1939), p. 304; *New York Times,* Jan. 15, 1935; William P. Mangold, "On the Labor Front," *New Republic,* LXXXI (1935), 333.

Wagner, nevertheless, on February 21st introduced the National Labor Relations bill, S. 1958, into the Senate. A week later Connery sponsored the measure in the House as H.R. 6288.[25]

The declaration of policy in Sec. 1 argued that equality of bargaining power was unattainable unless the organization of employers was balanced with "free exercise by employees of the right to bargain collectively through representatives of their own choosing." Absence of this equality led to disequilibrium between the rate of wages and industrial expansion. As a consequence economic stability was impaired and depressions were aggravated with detrimental effects upon commerce. Further, denial of the right to bargain caused strikes and therefore obstructions to commerce. The policy of the United States was to remove these impediments and promote the general welfare by encouraging collective bargaining and protecting the freedom of the worker in self-organization and designation of representatives of his own choosing. This provision revised the declaration of the 1934 Wagner bill and went beyond that of the Walsh measure.

The declaration had a twofold purpose: to voice an economic philosophy and to lay a constitutional foundation for the Act. The first was, in effect, a restatement of the struggle between the haves and the have-nots. Industrial concentration, the declaration argued, destroyed the worker's bargaining power, leaving him with an inadequate share of the national wealth. A redistribution of income by collective bargaining would raise those at the bottom and remove inequalities within the wage structure. This would benefit society as a whole by creating mass purchasing power to fill in the troughs in the business cycle. Further, the Act would remove a prime cause of industrial conflict, the right to associate, and establish a mechanism in collective bargaining for eliminating other causes of strife.[26]

The constitutional argument was that deterrents to mass purchasing power have a detrimental effect upon, and that strikes obstruct, interstate commerce. This theory rested on the power of Congress to regulate or prevent activity which, if unrestrained, would affect or burden commerce. Hence constitutionality depended upon court findings as to the effect on commerce of the subjects of the regulation. The draftsmen anticipated that the declaration of policy would be given great weight by the Supreme Court. Hence, they felt it imperative to make the statement precise.[27]

[25] *Cong. Record*, LXXIX, pt. iii, 2368–72, 2783.

[26] Leon H. Keyserling, "Why the Wagner Act?" *The Wagner Act: After Ten Years*, ed. by Louis G. Silverberg (Washington: 1945), pp. 8–12; Joseph Rosenfarb, *The National Labor Policy and How It Works* (New York: 1940), chap. ii.

[27] *National Labor Relations Board, Comparison of S. 2926 and S. 1958 and Proposed*

The definitions in Sec. 2 began with "person," which would include "individuals, partnerships, associations, corporations, legal representatives, trustees, trustees in bankruptcy, or receivers." This virtually copied the language of the Walsh report and paralleled that of the 1934 Wagner bill. Its significance lay in part in its use in the term that followed. "Employer" would cover "any person acting in the interest of an employer, directly or indirectly," excluding only federal, state, and subsidiary governments, persons subject to the Railway Labor Act, and labor organizations. This was the form of the old Wagner bill except that the latter specifically included an employer of one or more employees, S. 1958 achieving this effect without surplusage. The Walsh bill differed in excluding those with fewer than ten and by including unions when acting as employers. A purpose of the definition was to hold employers accountable for the acts of their agents, for example, foremen or detective agencies. Concerns with few employees were included because the board heard many cases involving them, particularly in the motion picture and trucking industries. Otherwise the act might discriminate against these employees and encourage evasion by creating small units. To cover labor organizations, the draftsmen reasoned, would endanger the purpose of the Act by subjecting unions to the restraints from which the measure specifically aimed to free them. The sweeping character of the definition was motivated by a desire to impose no limitations upon the board's jurisdiction beyond the constitutional inhibitions of the commerce clause. The courts, therefore, through a specific showing of commerce in individual cases, would determine how far the board might go in applying the act.[28]

"Employee" would cover "any" employee, not be limited to those of a particular employer, and "any individual whose work has ceased as a consequence of, or in connection with, any current labor dispute or because of any unfair labor practice, and who has not obtained any other regular and substantially equivalent employment." Agricultural laborers, domestic servants, and employees of a parent or spouse were excluded. This definition prevented employers from distinguishing between bargaining with their own employees and outside organizations. Under this language, as well, the board might include professionals

Amendments, 74th Cong., 1st sess., Sen., Comm. on Edu. and Labor (Washington: 1935), pp. 15–18, hereafter cited as *Comparison,* Sen. Labor Comm. This document contains (pp. 15–43) the best guide to the meaning of the Wagner Act in the sense of court construction of statutory "intent." Drafted by Magruder and Levy at the request of Senator Walsh, it was printed "for the use of the Committee on Education and Labor." So far as is known, it was not generally circulated and has received no attention in the literature.
[28] *Ibid.,* pp. 18–19; Rosenfarb, *op. cit.,* pp. 51–60.

and supervisors. The National Industrial Adjustment bill had considered strikers as employees only if the cessation was a consequence of a labor dispute connected with an unfair practice. There would have to be a strike or threatened strike before a worker discriminatorily discharged could get to the board, putting a premium on conflict. S. 1958 granted him this right merely if work ceased because of an unfair practice. The draftsmen also removed a feature of the committee bill that excluded individuals whose work stopped in connection with a current dispute; that is, men striking for economic reasons were denied the benefits of the Act, for example, elections, while out. The qualification of "substantially equivalent" employment protected strikers who obtained "regular" undesirable jobs out of necessity and wanted the old ones back. Under S. 1958, however, the employer remained free to refuse to rehire strikers or to take on replacements during a stoppage so long as his purpose was not discriminatory.[29]

"Representative" was "any individual or labor organization." This, the language of the old Wagner bill, differed from the Walsh report, which required that the representative be designated by the employees and extended the term to include employer representatives. The former was dropped as redundant, while the latter became unnecessary by the exclusion from Sec. 8 of employee unfair practices. The status of the outside union was again asserted.[30]

"Labor organization" covered "any organization of any kind, or any agency or employee representation committee or plan in which employees participate and which exists for the purpose, in whole or in part, of dealing with employers concerning grievances, labor disputes, wages, rates of pay, or hours of employment." The definition covered company unions, despite AFL objections, to meet the specific objectives of the Act. If they were not so included, employer domination would become legal. S. 1958 differed from both earlier versions by including grievance settlement as an objective of labor organizations, since many company unions had this purpose.[31]

The definition of "commerce" was identical with that in both 1934 drafts:

trade or commerce, or any transportation or communication relating thereto, among the several States, or between the District of Columbia or any Territory of the United States and any State or other Territory, or between any foreign country and any State, Territory, or the District of Columbia, or within the District of Columbia or any Territory, or between points in the same State but through any other State or any Territory or the District of Columbia or any foreign country.

---

[29] *Comparison,* Sen. Labor Comm., pp. 19–22.
[30] *Ibid.,* p. 22.
[31] *Ibid.,* pp. 22–23.

"Affecting commerce," a term omitted from both earlier versions, meant:

in commerce, or burdening or affecting commerce, or obstructing the free flow of commerce, or having led or tending to lead to a labor dispute that might burden or affect commerce or obstruct the free flow of commerce.

Its purposes were to broaden jurisdiction under the commerce clause and to avoid repeating the same phrases in the bill.[32]

Another new definition, "labor dispute," was:

any controversy concerning terms, tenure or conditions of employment, or concerning the association or representation of persons in negotiating, fixing, maintaining, changing, or seeking to arrange terms or conditions of employment, regardless of whether the disputants stand in the proximate relation of employer and employee.

It was inserted because of repeated use in the bill and since, in some instances, it was a jurisdictional precondition. The definition was lifted from Sec. 13(c) of the Norris-LaGuardia Act and again protected the outside organization.[33]

The board was styled National Labor Relations Board to provide continuity with the existing agency. National Industrial Adjustment Board would be misleading in view of the emphasis upon adjudication rather than mediation.[34]

Sec. 3 created NLRB as an independent body of three members appointed by the President and confirmed by the Senate for five-year terms The 1934 Walsh and Wagner bills proposed a tripartite board, while the former placed it in the Department of Labor. The Secretary was denied jurisdiction over the NLRB to give it stature with the public, attract high quality men, prevent contact with the adjustment functions of the Conciliation Service, avoid the charge that its purpose was to promote the welfare of wage earners, eliminate budgetary and personnel controls of the department, and conform with precedents of other quasi-judicial agencies, ICC, FTC, SEC, and NMB. The draftsmen excluded partisan members to avoid compromise and inconsistency in decisions.[35]

Secs. 4 and 5 set forth the organization of the agency. In Sec. 6 the board gained authority to issue rules and regulations. The committee bill requirement that they be "reasonable" was stricken out to avoid a ground for controversy.[36]

Sec. 7 presented a general affirmation of the rights of workers, taken verbatim from the Recovery Act. "Employees shall have the right to self-organization, to form, join, or assist labor organizations, to bargain

[32] *Ibid.*, p. 23.
[33] *Ibid.*
[34] *Ibid*
[35] *Ibid.*, pp. 23–24.
[36] *Ibid.*, p. 25.

collectively through representatives of their own choosing, and to engage in concerted activities, for the purpose of collective bargaining or
other mutual aid or protection." This was more explicit than the earlier
Wagner bill, while the Walsh draft eliminated the statement altogether.
The language of 7(a) was used because it was already the subject of
administrative and judicial construction and would not require extended reinterpretation.[37] It laid the basis for what immediately followed.

The first clause of Sec. 8 made it an unfair practice for an employer
"to interfere with, restrain, or coerce employees in the exercise of the
rights guaranteed in Section 7." This blanket prohibition was intended
to perform a general policing function like Sec. 7(a). It would bar practices not specifically outlawed later, such as espionage, blacklisting,
agreements in violation of the act, hostile statements, and strikebreaking. It would also permit the board to prevent activities for which the
old agency's experience provided no precedent. The other unfair practices would not restrict its scope since they were not exclusive in application.[38]

The second proscribed practice, dealing with the company union,
denied the right of an employer "to dominate or interfere with the
formation or administration of any labor organization or contribute
financial or other support to it." A proviso qualified this by declaring
that, subject to board regulations, "an employer shall not be prohibited
from permitting employees to confer with him during working hours
without loss of time or pay." The term "company union" was avoided
since the purpose was not to eradicate it as such but rather to eliminate
employer domination. This differed from the NIAB, which permitted
employers to particiate in their "formation." While the draftsmen had
no desire to bar management from suggesting to employees that they
organize, they were determined that the employer not engage in critical
initiating activities, such as writing constitutions and bylaws and elect-
ing officers. The proviso protected individuals and minorities in face
of the majority rule and was to be taken in conjunction with 9(a).[39]

The third practice illegalized employer activities "by discrimination
in regard to hire or tenure of employment or any term or condition of
employment to encourage or discourage membership in any labor organization." This went beyond the yellow-dog contract clause of 7(a) in
undermining all forms of discrimination, such as hiring, discharging,
laying off, demoting, refusing to reinstate strikers, or establishing wage

[37] NLRA, Legislative History, William H. Davis, n.d., Levy papers.
[38] *Comparison*, Sen. Labor Comm., pp. 26–27.
[39] *Ibid.*, pp. 26–27.

and hour differentials. A proviso protecting the closed shop contract, however, declared,

that nothing in this Act . . . or in any other statute of the United States, shall preclude an employer from making an agreement with a labor organization (not established, maintained, or assisted by any action defined in this Act as an unfair labor practice) to require as a condition of employment membership therein, if such labor organization is the representative of the majority of the employees in the appropriate collective bargaining unit covered by such agreement when made.

The draftsmen here preserved the legal *status quo* on the closed shop, removing the hiatus in 7(a). Union security contracts were not legalized by this language; it simply prevented them from becoming unlawful under this and other laws of the United States. The common law in the states was undisturbed where it prohibited such agreements, and those jurisdictions were free to ban the closed shop in the future. Unlike the Walsh bill, the proviso covered both new and old employees. The latter needed this protection or strikes for the closed shop would be prohibited and enjoinable in the courts.[40]

The fourth unfair practice made it unlawful for an employer "to discharge or otherwise discriminate against an employee because he has filed charges or given testimony under this Act." The NLRB found need for this provision in its cases and the purpose was apparent.

The absence of refusal to bargain in good faith as an unfair practice in Sec. 8, unlike the 1934 Wagner bill, was of great significance. The draftsmen agreed that the right of employees to bargain was meaningless without a reciprocal obligation on the employer. Hence the Labor Board and the AFL urged such a provision, the former going so far as to consider a requirement that the agreement be reduced to writing. Wagner and Keyserling, however, were concerned about the difficulties of casting the duty in statutory language. They omitted it in hope that the board would establish the obligation on a common law basis as its predecessors had under similar circumstances.[41] The first clause took care of the final practice in the 1934 measure, that the employer notify his workmen that agreements in violation of the Act were invalid. The draftsmen struck out the Walsh bill's unfair practice for employees, interference with employers in designating representatives for bargaining. They saw no practical need for it in the existing market place and felt that it contradicted the bill's purpose, equalization of bargaining power. It might, in addition, serve as an opening wedge for restrictions upon unions.[42]

[40] *Ibid.*, pp. 28–29.
[41] P. Levy and P. G. Phillips, Proposed Wagner Bill, n.d., Levy papers; Ogburn Draft Bill, n.d., Keyserling papers; Keyserling interview.
[42] *Comparison*, Sen. Labor Comm., p. 26.

By Sec. 9(a) representatives designated "by the majority of the employees in a unit appropriate for such purposes, shall be the exclusive representatives of all the employees in such unit for the purposes of collective bargaining." Both 1934 measures left the question of majority rule as against proportional representation to the discretion of the board. The purpose here was to establish the former conclusively. The experience of the Auto Board convinced the draftsmen that pluralism provoked confusion and strife, defeating collective bargaining. Precedents in political life, labor relations, and employer associations were multifarious. A proviso, however, declared "that any individual employee or group of employees shall have the right at any time to present grievances to their employer through representatives of their own choosing." The Walsh report authorized the employer to discuss grievances directly with his employees, while S. 1958 recast the language from the standpoint of the workers. Minorities were given this protection in light of the majority rule.[43]

Sec. 9(b) empowered the board to determine whether "in order to effectuate the policies of this act, the unit appropriate for the purposes of collective bargaining shall be the employer unit, craft unit, plant unit, or other unit." This paralleled both earlier bills except for inserting the purpose of the statute as a standard for the courts in reviewing orders in unfair practice cases based on the results of elections. The adjectives modifying unit would permit the NLRB to sanction industrial unions despite the criticism of the AFL leaders. None of the draftsmen, however, foresaw the cleavage in the union movement that appeared later in 1935. They were rather exercised by jurisdictional difficulties that would arise even without the CIO. They could find no acceptable alternative to lodging authority over unit with the board. Giving it to the employer, they believed, would invite violations of the act, while employees might use it to defeat the majority principle and, by the creation of small units, impede the employer in running his plant.[44]

When a representation question affecting commerce arose, the board might under 9(c) "investigate such controversy and certify to the parties ... the names or names of the representatives that have been designated or selected." It would hold a hearing and might "take a secret ballot of employees, or utilize any other suitable method to ascertain such representatives." Similar language appeared in both earlier versions. The term "representatives," defined by Sec. 2 as either individuals or labor organizations, again asserted the status of the outside union.

The board by Sec. 10(a) would "prevent any person from engaging

---

[43] *Ibid.*, p. 30.
[44] *Ibid.*; Keyserling, Levy interviews.

in any unfair labor practice . . . affecting commerce." This authority
was exclusive and not affected by other means that had been or might
be established. Neither 1934 draft contained such a provision. It realized
the board's aspiration to become a "Supreme Court" by establishing
uniformity of interpretation and by avoiding conflicts of jurisdiction
with other agencies. The draftsmen erased the Walsh bill's requirement
that an unfair practice lead to a dispute affecting commerce on the
theory that a controversy was not necessary under the commerce clause.
They, instead, relied on the constitutional underpinning of Sec. 1. In
10(b) the board gained discretion to defer the exercise of its jurisdiction
when other means of adjustment were available. In such cases, however,
it might intervene at any stage to effectuate the Act and to foster uniform
interpretation.[45]

Sec. 10(c) to (j) outlined procedure in unfair practice cases. When a
charge was brought or the board on its initiative believed a person
engaged in such a practice, it might issue a complaint with notice of
hearing. The board or its agent might conduct the proceeding and the
charges might be amended at any time prior to the order. The rules
of evidence would not control the hearings. If the board concluded
that the person did act unfairly, it should "state its findings of fact"
and should "issue and cause to be served on such person an order requiring such person to cease and desist from unfair labor practice, and
to take such affirmative action, including restitution, as will effectuate
the policies of this Act." If the complaint was unfounded, the board
issued findings and an order of dissolution. Upon failure to comply,
the agency would petition the circuit court for enforcement. That tribunal might grant temporary relief, a restraining order, or a final decree
enforcing, modifying, or setting aside in whole or in part the board's
directive. The court might not consider objections not raised before
the NLRB except under extraordinary circumstances. "The findings
of the board as to the facts, if supported by evidence, shall be conclusive." The court's jurisdiction was exclusive and its decree final except
for appeal to the Supreme Court. A person aggrieved by a board order
might obtain review in the circuit court under parallel procedures.

These processes resembled those in the 1934 Wagner bill, differing
in that the latter spelled out the restitution a person guilty of an unfair
practice would make and invoked the district courts. The Walsh measure required that the complaint be certified by the Secretary of Labor
after exhausting the adjustment facilities of the Conciliation Service.
The draftsmen here drew on precedents from administrative statutes approved by the courts. The Federal Trade Commission Act proved most

---

[45] *Ibid.,* pp. 31–32.

suggestive, other sources including the Packers and Stockyards Act, Securities and Exchange Act, Grain Futures Act, Clayton Act, Interstate Commerce Act, and Communications Act. They considered exception to the rules of evidence vital to avoid a maze of legal form. This was, furthermore, an essential component of the administrative process, as the experience of many quasi-judicial agencies attested. A safeguard was provided by making the board's conduct subject to judicial check under due process. The broad term "restitution" covered a host of remedies; express language might limit the agency's discretion and risk an inappropriate corrective. Direct appeal to the circuit courts was introduced in the interest of expedition. Temporary restraining orders would prevent continuance of an unfair practice from inflicting irreparable damage on an employee or a labor organization. Avoiding review of findings of fact would forestall delays and was a general practice with administrative tribunals.[46]

Sec. 11 gave the district courts jurisdiction to prevent and restrain unfair practices affecting commerce. U. S. district attorneys at the sole request of the board would institute proceedings and the courts might issue temporary restraining orders. This provision appeared in the original Wagner bill but not in the committee version. It provided an alternative enforcement procedure in unusual situations, for example, where the board was overburdened, circumstances required immediate action, or the circuits were on vacation. The draftsmen maintained the exclusive initiative of the NLRB despite AFL insistence that complainants themselves be permitted to bring actions.[47]

Sec. 12 authorized the board to arbitrate disputes voluntarily submitted with provision for court enforcement of awards. This section paralleled the 1934 bills. There was little basis for the retention of the arbitration function in view of the purging of other provisions concerned with the conduct of bargaining as distinguished from its establishment and the fact that the NLRB had seldom engaged in arbitration.

By Sec. 13 NLRB gained access to necessary information. Board members could issue subpoenas requiring the testimony of witnesses and production of evidence. In case of refusal to obey, the district courts issued orders and treated failure to comply as contempt. No person would be excused from testifying on the ground of self-incrimination. On the other hand, he might not be prosecuted for matters on which he was compelled to bear witness after claiming this privilege. These procedures followed both earlier versions and the precedent of other administrative agencies. Persons who wilfully impeded an agent of the

[46] *Ibid.*, pp. 32–37.
[47] *Ibid.*, pp. 37–38; Ogburn to Wagner, Feb. 19, 1935.

board were in Sec. 14 subject to fine and/or imprisonment. This feature appeared in both 1934 measures as well as in Resolution No. 44.

Sec. 15 declared that "nothing in this Act shall be construed so as to interfere with or impede or diminish in any way the right to strike." This, the language of the old Wagner bill, paralleled the La Follette amendment to the Public Resolution, while the Walsh bill merely restated the Thirteenth Amendment. The purpose was to ease any fears the unions might harbor that the bill would permit compulsory arbitration. The application of Sec. 15, however, was remote since the measure did not inhibit economic action, in fact, protected strikers.

The Act would by Sec. 16 prevail if conflict developed with other federal statutes, again affirming the "Supreme Court" concept. The usual separability provision appeared in Sec. 17, and the title in Sec. 18, National Labor Relations Act.

Anticipated reactions were voiced upon the introduction of S. 1958. The AFL issued an enthusiastic endorsement, while the NAM denounced it. Secretary Perkins, describing the measure as "very interesting," significantly withheld comment.[48] The press, however, attacked the bill. The *Boston Herald* called it "a closed shop bill," while the *New York Sun* predicted that it would promote "rule by unionism" and spawn conflict. The *New York Times* and *Philadelphia Inquirer* pointed out that the bill directly conflicted with the President's automobile settlement and would undermine what they regarded as the impressive achievement of the Auto Board. The *Inquirer* added that it "would tend to destroy the rights of workers and to reëstablish medievalism in industry." The *Washington Post* failed to see how the measure would provide "a practical working relationship between management and labor."[49]

Meanwhile, both sides prepared themselves for the crucial Senate hearings that lay ahead.

---

[48] *New York Times,* Feb. 22, 1935.

[49] *Boston Herald,* Feb. 24, *Chicago Journal of Commerce,* Feb. 22, *New York Evening Sun,* Feb. 22, *New York Times,* Feb. 22, *Philadelphia Inquirer,* Feb. 18, *Washington Post,* Feb. 23, 1935.

VIII. ORDER OF BATTLE

IN LAYING his strategy for the National Labor Relations bill Senator Wagner played to strength rather than weakness. In light of the 1934 elections, he took the offensive in the Senate, assuming that victory there would carry the House as well. The opposition reached the same conclusion despite the effect of the elections on the relationship between the chambers. The result was a lopsidedness in the legislative history of S. 1958. The great debate on the Wagner Act took place before the Senate Labor Committee, leaving little to be said on the floor or in the House. The argument before the committee, between March 11th and April 2, 1935, was detailed and penetrating with all-out marshaling of forces and the full attention of the nation's press.[1]

The roll call paralleled that of the year before. The author of the measure, the NLRB, the union movement, industrial relations experts, religious leaders, and a handful of businessmen appeared in support. The opposition comprised the business community in virtually solid phalanx, the company unions, an academic official, and the Communists. Secretary Perkins was the only Administration spokesman to testify, ambivalently.

The argument advanced by the supporters of the bill, though paralleling that made in 1934, was more inclusive and detailed, being based on an additional year of experience. The central contention was that the principles enunciated in Sec. 7(a) failed in practice because of the breakdown of enforcement. Wagner argued that it was flouted at the points where observance was most essential, for example, recognition of representatives, and that the Public Resolution was inadequate. The sharp increase in strikes under NRA represented in large part employer unwillingness to accept its collective bargaining provisions. Biddle revealed the statistics of noncompliance: in the 86 cases of violations of 7(a) between July 1, 1934, and March 1, 1935, employers refused 52 times to abide by board directives. Neither removal of the Blue Eagle nor the efforts of the Department of Justice were effective. This failure, he felt, went beyond the board's status to undermine the bargaining process throughout the country. NLRB had assumed responsibility without authority. He stressed particularly the need for the subpoena, final authority to hold elections, and speedy enforcement. This last the Wagner bill itself did not meet effectively in deference to due process.[2]

The concentration of economic power, they argued, gave the employer

---

[1] Keyserling interview; *National Labor Relations Board*, 74th Cong., 1st sess., Sen., Hearings before Comm. on Edu. and Labor on S. 1958 (March 11–April 2, 1935), hereafter cited as *National Labor Relations Board*, Sen. Hearings.
[2] *Ibid.*, pp. 94–98, 153.

a favored bargaining position over the worker that could be redressed only if employees gained freedom to organize and bargain collectively. Green felt that this was the bill's fundamental purpose, while Garrison described it as "a matter of simple justice." Wagner saw S. 1958 as one of several efforts to establish balance in the economy by congressional action in the face of the integration of wealth and power. The first with contemporary significance was the antitrust legislation, which sought to protect worker, small businessman, and consumer against unregulated monopolies. Not only had it failed to achieve its purpose, but the courts turned the statutes against labor. After World War I combination continued unabated, while the Recovery Act speeded the process and gave it government sanction. Labor now asked for the same consideration. "In order that the strong may not take advantage of the weak," he maintained, "every group must be equally strong." Millis described the characteristics of the labor market as they affected the individual workman. Alone, he was ignorant of the conditions of other workers in the industry, had no savings, feared being fired or other discrimination if he pressed his grievance, was threatened by job competition from the unemployed, and his "contract" might be changed without notice at the will of the employer. Smith argued that 7(a) had little effect upon checking economic imbalance. Increased membership in unions was concentrated in those industries already partly organized—coal, the garment trades, and textiles—while most mass production concerns remained non-union. Meanwhile, he declared that company unions had sprung up like "weeds."[3]

Wagner argued that S. 1958 involved no novel principles but simply affirmed and extended concepts already established in the law. He demonstrated the sources of the unfair practices in congressional policy—the railway legislation and the Norris-LaGuardia Act.[4]

The proponents advanced the mass purchasing power theory, arguing that both recovery and long-term prosperity depended upon a higher level of wages and a more even distribution of the national income. Collective bargaining, they believed, promoted these ends. The collapse of America's foreign trade, Ogburn reasoned, threw the country back upon its domestic market, requiring a compensatory increase in local consumption to take up the slack. Experience indicated that employers did not grant higher wages voluntarily. Garrison added that the government could feasibly set wage minima by statute only and that a general system of bargaining, preferably industry-wide, was needed for the middle and upper groups. NRA, Biddle pointed out, had little effect

[3] *Ibid.*, pp. 102, 126, 173, 159–160.
[4] *Ibid.*, pp. 38–40.

upon real wages since rising prices offset higher wage rates. Millis, the only economist to take this position, supported the theory in part. The smaller the share of national income going to labor, he reasoned, the larger the segment to savings and investment in either productive capacity or speculation with increased risk of "industrial miscarriage." In a sound economy additions and replacements in capital go hand in hand with a rise in the capacity to consume. Unbalanced distribution of the national income had been a major cause of the 1929 collapse and redress was vital to long-term recovery. He cautioned, however, that the doctrine might be overdone, that dollars distributed as profits and interest might also be spent, and that businessmen needed such an incentive to assume risks and afford employment.[5]

The history of government intervention on the railroads was pointed to as an experiential proving ground. "Why," Leiserson queried, "should we have this effort . . . to discover America all over again, and go through the same fight and strife that the railroads went through thirty years ago?"[6] The Railway Labor Act and its 1934 amendments, he believed, paralleled the Wagner bill and demonstrated its practicability. "We learn from experience the only way we will ever have peace on the railroad is to say that the . . . employees have the same right to associate themselves and act through a body that the investors in railroads have." Since unions do not tell stockholders who shall represent them, a law is not needed for their protection, but "employers should not be permitted to interfere when investors of labor want to set up similar entities to these corporations."[7]

"I am for it [S. 1958]," Garrison began, "as a safety measure, because I regard organized labor in this country as our chief bulwark against Communism and other revolutionary movements." Give workers a means of expressing and redressing their economic grievances and they have no inducement to overthrow the social system. Millis added that revolutionary unions as frequently arose from employer opposition to labor's right to organize and bargain as from radical theory.[8]

The eradication of company-dominated unions, it was argued, preconditioned the establishment of collective bargaining, since they by nature negated freedom of association. Inasmuch as the employer prohibited his employees to act jointly with those of other companies in the industry on issues that were regional, industry-wide, or national in scope, company union representatives were not informed in dealing with management. The requirement of being employees subjected them to the

[5] *Ibid.*, pp. 152, 125–26, 76–78, 175–76.
[6] *Ibid.*, p. 871.
[7] *Ibid.*, pp. 884–85.
[8] *Ibid.*, pp. 125, 179.

job control of the employer, undermining their effectiveness. Collective bargaining was negated when one side depended for financial support upon the other. Direct employer intervention to provide constitutions, bylaws, and internal management obstructed free association and the formulation of honest demands. Discriminatory practices threatened employees who refused to participate and favored those who sought to get into the employer's good graces. The history of company unionism was evidence of its antiunion character, namely, its correlation with periods of trade union growth. Wagner, for example, declared that sixty-nine per cent of the plans in existence in 1935 were created under 7(a). This was particularly true of the mass production industries where large companies predominated and inequality of bargaining power was most marked. Workers voted convincingly for trade unions over company unions in free labor board elections, indicating their preferences. Leiserson observed, "If the employer can have something to say about who the sales agent shall be we would be in the position of the customer dictating who should be the sales agent of the fellows who have goods to sell." S. 1958, however, did not forbid employees of one company voluntarily to refuse to join the AFL, nor did it affect welfare and recreation plans established by employers if their purpose was not discriminatory.[9]

Majority rule, the supporters contended, was the only fair and workable principle for selecting representatives. Those who contest it, Wagner declared, "are in truth avoiding the duty to bargain collectively by creating conditions which make collective agreements impossible." Proportional representation fragmentized and destroyed unions, creating jealousy, friction, and division within the plant. Millis observed that employers proposed it as a short-term device to break unions and could not afford its permanent risks to production. Precedents in economic and political life were legion. The War Labor Board, the railway boards, and most of the 7(a) agencies applied it. American political democracy, as well, observed the majority rule. The NAM and the Chamber of Commerce employed it in their internal affairs. Company-dominated unions, similarly, operated under the same rule.[10]

The right of employees to self-organization, the proponents argued, was empty without a reciprocal obligation upon the employer to bargain

---

[9] *Ibid.*, pp. 39–43, 109–14, 128–31, 163–71, 882, 40, 109, 164, 165, 873.

[10] *Ibid.*, pp. 43–46, 81, 127, 180–82. Garrison, largely responsible for the Houde decision, declared, "I am tired of hearing theoretical arguments about the rights of the minority. I have never yet seen a case in which these arguments were advanced by a *bona fide* minority group genuinely concerned with negotiating a collective agreement applying to all. . . . The minority, in fact, are benefited by placing upon the employer the duty to bargain exclusively with the majority, for it is only under such circumstances that better terms for the employees, including the minority, are at all likely to be obtained." "7-A and the Future," *Survey Graphic,* XXIV (1935), 56–57.

with their representatives. There was little value in employee associations, Wagner pointed out, if used solely for "Saturday night dances and Sunday afternoon picnics." Although the bill did not explicitly state the duty to bargain because of the difficulty of reducing it to statutory language, "such a duty is clearly implicit in the bill." The NLRB went beyond the Senator and introduced an amendment for this purpose. Although the proponents felt it incumbent upon the employer to negotiate, they concurred that he could not be compelled to agree. As William H. Davis put it, "You can lead a horse to water, but you cannot make him drink."[11]

The employer charge that the bill would promote the closed shop was declared to be without foundation. Wagner argued that S. 1958 did not compel anyone to join a union, since the proviso to 8(3) merely preserved the existing situation with regard to union security. Millis declared that the related argument that coercion and interference by unions should be outlawed was based on "poor analysis." Unions engaged in coercion in the forms of physical violence, threats of violence, opprobrious names, and the closed union shop. State and municipal law, he thought, abundantly covered the first three. Many states, in addition, outlawed the closed shop and S. 1958 deferred to them. He predicted that this institution would cease to be an issue when employers accepted unions and collective bargaining as had been the case in England. The Railroad Trainmen endorsed the closed shop proviso in light of their experience under the Railway Labor Act.[12]

A final supporting argument was a defense of the bill's constitutionality. There were, Wagner and Milton Handler pointed out, two basic questions: first, does regulation of employer-employee relations by Congress violate due process? and, second, can federal jurisdiction be sustained under the commerce clause? In answer to the first they relied upon the Supreme Court's decision in the railway clerks case upholding an act guaranteeing freedom of association, prohibiting the company-dominated union, and preventing employers from requiring membership or nonmembership in a union.[13] They reasoned that this case covered the first three unfair practices under due process and that the fourth was equitable on its face. This decision was not relevant to commerce, however, since it involved an interstate railway. The argument here was that strikes caused by unfair practices burdened commerce and that Congress had authority to regulate or remove such obstructions. The court held, for example, that refusal of workmen to process stone

[11] *National Labor Relations Board*, Sen. Hearings, pp. 43, 79, 136–37, 716.

[12] *Ibid.*, pp. 41, 179–80, 199. Cf. chap. iv.

[13] *Texas & New Orleans R. R. Co. v. Brotherhood of Railway & Steamship Clerks* (1930), 281 U.S., 548.

shipped from another state affected commerce and that it was within the power of the legislature to prohibit this conduct under the antitrust laws.[14] By extension, S. 1958 applied to any business in which a strike or boycott of employees would be subject to these statutes. Other cases showed judicial recognition that prices, and by the same reasoning wages, as well as general business conditions, affected commerce.[15]

The bill's advocates disagreed over several features, starting with the question of the relationship of NLRB to the Department of Labor. Miss Perkins urged that the board be placed under her authority with control over personnel and funds, but suggested a clause stating that "the Secretary of Labor has no right to review, modify, or change the judicial decisions of the Labor Relations Board." Her argument was that a proliferation of independent agencies burdened the President, functions—particularly conciliation—would be duplicated, the department could perform services for the board, such as research and statistics, and administrative symmetry and good sense called for unification of labor activities. The Executive Order of June 29, 1934, furthermore, was a precedent. The AFL, changing its views, supported her position. Green declared, "Labor is a bit sentimental, because it feels that the Department of Labor is set up for labor." The Federation's advocacy, however, was *pro forma*. It did not lobby seriously in its behalf.[16]

Wagner and the board spokesmen, on the other hand, insisted that the agency stand alone. Pointing to the distinction between judicial and adjustment functions, they warned against mixing them by placing the NLRB alongside the Conciliation Service. Independence and impartiality were essential to a quasi-judicial body to gain the confidence of industry and public. Along with this fact, Garrison emphasized, it was equally important for people to think that the board was independent. If the Secretary controlled personnel and budget, it would be charged that the agency promoted the aims of the department. There would, furthermore, be pressure to tailor decisions to the policies of the administration in power. Similar independent tribunals were precedents—the ICC, FTC, SEC, NMB, and others. A committee of experts for the Twentieth Century Fund concurred with this position.[17]

[14] *Bedford Cut Stone Co. v. Journeymen Stone Cutters Assn.* (1927), 275 U.S. 37.

[15] *National Labor Relations Board,* Sen. Hearings, pp. 52–55, 233–34.

[16] *Ibid.,* pp. 60–66, 114–15; Shishkin, Keyserling interviews.

[17] *National Labor Relations Board,* Sen. Hearings, pp. 39, 51–52, 85–90, 131–32, 171, 177, 706. Feelings had become embittered by this time. Cf., Levy to Keyserling, May 20, 1935, Keyserling papers. Writing a decade later Miss Perkins observed that "Wagner was opposed for reasons which, when viewed in retrospect, seem slightly humorous. . . . One sometimes wonders a little ruefully whether or not this Board would not have been better off under the more pedestrian supervision of the Department of Labor." *The Roosevelt I Knew* (New York: 1946), p. 242.

A difference also existed over the relationship of mediation and arbitration to the board's judicial functions. The AFL favored a tripartite agency in order to gain a voice in its operations. Lewis, for example, argued that men likely to be appointed would not have associates in the labor movement, hence subconsciously would favor employers. Even public-spirited individuals would welcome practical experience with collective bargaining supplied by partisans. The Twentieth Century Fund committee took issue with this view on the ground that a tripartite structure fostered adjustment. It is of "paramount importance," Davis declared, "that the functions of mediation . . . should be rigidly separated from the law enforcement function." Further, the committee urged changing the board's name since it was associated in the public mind with mediation and recommended eliminating the arbitration provision.[18]

In addition, Biddle, for the board with the support of the AFL, proposed to state the duty to bargain explicitly in view of the pressing problems of recognition that arose under 7(a). He admitted the logic of Wagner's reticence but felt that the prospective advantages justified the effort. Hence he suggested a fifth unfair practice for an employer "to refuse to bargain collectively with the representatives of his employees, subject to the provisions of Section 9(a) ."[19]

The AFL proposed several amendments characterized by concern over application of majority rule and a desire to retain procedural initiative in its own hands. Unions should be permitted to enter closed shop agreements even when not representing majorities, while the right of individuals to present grievances should be eliminated. The Federation, anxious to prevent delay in representation cases, proposed requiring that elections be held within thirty days. It would permit investigation of unfair practices only after a charge had been filed and not at the instance of NLRB, while unions themselves might institute proceedings in the district courts.[20]

The opposition to the bill was built upon the argument advanced the year before. No effort was made to soften the effect by amendment. The central argument was that the bill was unconstitutional, stated most effectively by James A. Emery, counsel for the NAM.[21] He charged, first, that S. 1958 rested on a subterfuge in undertaking to regulate local em-

---

[18] *National Labor Relations Board,* Sen. Hearings, pp. 106, 121, 197–98, 886, 706–10, 869–70, 59, 71–72.

[19] *Ibid.,* pp. 79–80, 136.

[20] *National Labor Relations Board, Comparison of S. 2926 and S. 1958 and Proposed Amendments,* 74th Cong., 1st sess., Sen., Comm. on Edu. and Labor, 10–11, hereafter cited as *Comparison,* Sen. Labor Comm.; NLRA, Legislative History, Ogburn, n.d., Levy papers.

[21] *National Labor Relations Board,* Sen. Hearings, pp. 243–64, 840–69, 238, 331–34, 465, 470.

ployment relations arising out of acts of production under the guise of removing obstructions to commerce. Jurisdiction over manufacturing and its labor conditions was reserved to the states and denied to Congress by the Tenth Amendment. For seventy-five years the Supreme Court held that manufacturing was not commerce and that one must end before the other began. Within the year, twenty district courts ruled without exception in NRA cases that the federal government had no commerce power over local production or services. If production lay outside its jurisdiction, he queried, how could Congress regulate employment relations arising therefrom?

Emery's second argument was that the bill violated due process. Amended complaints might be enforced against a person without proper notice or hearing, depriving him of liberty and property. An administrative body would take evidence without regard for established rules and upon it make findings of fact conclusive upon the reviewing court. Third, the board's "inquisitorial" powers over records and persons without judicial restraint violated the safeguard against unreasonable searches and seizures in the Fourth Amendment. Fourth, its authority to assess damages, require restitution, and make findings of fact binding upon the courts abrogated the guarantee of trial by jury in the Seventh Amendment. Finally, the judiciary clauses of the Constitution were infringed by yielding powers to an administrative agency that were reserved to the courts, namely, making final judgments on civil rights and the rights of persons and property, while enforcing them by proceedings in equity in the district courts.[22]

Industry charged as well that arbitrary board procedures deprived employers of rights not constitutional in origin. It would be complainant, prosecutor, and judge in the same case. It might use the subpoena for "persecution," making private records public. Unions might gain access to financial statements, turning them against the companies, while unscrupulous competitors might take over trade secrets. Sec. 8(4), by giving employees a "lease" on their jobs, encouraged abuse of the employer. Exception to the rules of evidence permitted decisions based upon hearsay. "The powers invested in such board," industry concluded, "are arbitrary and so broad that the board in reality takes on dictatorial powers."[23]

The opponents reasoned that there was no need for the bill since 7(a) and the Public Resolution adequately covered the law of collective bargaining. Harriman of the Chamber, concurrently supporting extension of the Recovery Act, urged deferral of the Wagner bill to give more opportunity to study industrial relations under 7(a).[24]

---

[22] *Ibid.*, pp. 463, 597.
[23] *Ibid.*, pp. 238, 846–47, 465, 511, 604, 614, 636, 672.
[24] *Ibid.*, pp. 463, 597.

S. 1958, industry charged, assumed an unalterable conflict between employee and employer which could not be changed or abated except through governmental intervention. Business, on the contrary, asserted an identity of interest between management and men. The measure would provoke strikes despite the declared purpose to diminish them. This would hamper recovery and reduce employment by creating uncertainty among businessmen, leaving them unwilling to assume risks.[25]

The measure, industry argued, would create a monopoly for the AFL and foster the closed shop. "Stripped of all camouflage," the American Mining Congress declared, "the bill is a deliberate attempt to fasten upon industry in this country a system of organized labor affiliated with the . . . American Federation of Labor." Government would assist this organization to gain control over all of labor, though it represented only a fraction of the nation's workers. The steel companies feared that a closed shop would be "imposed," although it was "un-American" and workmen themselves opposed it. Steel demonstrated the distaste of employees for unionism since only two per cent belonged to the Amalgamated Association as contrasted with an overwhelming majority in company unions. The auto manufacturers voiced their opposition to legislation that "deprives men of their inherent right to work regardless of the dictates of a labor organization."[26]

The bill, business contended, imposed responsibilities upon management without corresponding duties for unions, violating the principle of equality before the law. If labor practices were "unfair," they should be denied to both sides. "If this law is intended to give labor organizations such a far-reaching authority, it certainly should provide also for full responsibility of the individual labor organization." Only employers could be sued; unions would not be regarded as employers even when acting in that capacity; and, most important, union coercion of employees was lawful, while prohibited to employers. Hence they urged outlawing "coercion from any source," defined as union pressure to prevent a man from working who desired to do so.[27]

Industry charged that the bill, in effect, destroyed the company union, described as an effective, fair instrument. Many spokesmen testified that "existing satisfactory relationships" would be upset with detrimental results to operations. Bethlehem Steel, long engaged in sponsoring a plan, asserted it to be "the most practical method by which labor relationships may be carried on, not only from the standpoint of employees and employers but also from that of the public welfare." They defended it as an efficient system for disposing of complaints, as conforming with

---

[25] *Ibid.*, pp. 238, 345, 371, 379, 509, 605, 625, 673, 467–70, 499.

[26] *Ibid.*, pp. 278, 371, 510, 596, 614, 626, 670.

[27] *Ibid.*, pp. 238, 344, 362, 463–64, 493, 633, 673, 858.

employee wishes (as elections of representatives attested), and as being conducted without discrimination based on membership. While the trade union drew a line of battle between the classes, the company union assumed that "the best interests of labor can be served by having the employee and employer sit down together in a friendly and constructive atmosphere and, with a firsthand practical knowledge of their problems, work out a fair and equitable solution." The auto industry observed that S. 1958 conflicted with the President's settlement of March 25, 1934, protecting the company union.[28]

Business attacked the majority rule for denying the rights of minorities and, combined with board authority to determine unit, for leading to the closed shop. Fifty-one per cent could bargain away the rights of the remainder. If the larger group voted a closed shop, they charged, all the employees must join the union or be discharged. The NLRB, they feared, would gerrymander units to give the AFL majorities, imposing union membership on everyone.[29]

The Communist Party vigorously opposed any government interference in the conduct of labor relations. " 'Impartial government,' " it argued, "is a polite but dangerous fiction," since the political apparatus is the instrument of the ruling class, in the United States the capitalist class. The interests of workers and employers conflicted irreconcilably and a board therefore would decide differences in favor of those in control. "The Wagner board to be established by this bill will be a weapon to destroy the power which the workers have gained through their economic organizations by outlawing strikes, establishing compulsory arbitration, and increasing company unions." The bill was combed to find evidence for these conclusions. The statement of policy, declaring the purpose to prevent work stoppages that obstruct commerce, weakened the right to strike. The reservation of this right in Sec. 15 was a "sham," just as 7(a) proved a "fraud" in guaranteeing self-organization. The provisos of 8(2) and 9(a), preserving the rights of individuals to present grievances, protected the company union, while Wagner himself asserted that he did not seek to outlaw them per se. Compulsory arbitration inhered in the fact of government intervention in the organization process.[30]

The press joined the opposition to S. 1958. Walter Lippmann wrote, "If the bill were passed it could not be made to work. . . . It is preposter-

---

[28] *Ibid.*, pp. 336, 366–68, 371–72, 405–10, 490, 605.

[29] *Ibid.*, pp. 344, 379, 465, 604, 615–17, 635, 671.

[30] *Ibid.*, pp. 581–87, 811–14. In the early stages the American Civil Liberties Union opposed S. 1958 as leading to federal intervention in strikes on the side of the employer, later withdrawing its opposition. *New Republic*, LXXXI (1935), 312; AFL, *Weekly News Service*, June 8, 1935.

ous to put such a burden upon mortal men. . . . The bill should be scrapped."[31] Of seven papers commenting during March and April, only one supported it with enthusiasm, another giving it a reluctant nod. The *New York Herald Tribune* described it as an effort "to prolong and make permanent all the worst features of Section 7(a) . . . without at the same time attempting to meet any of the grave criticisms of that vague and blundering enactment." The *Indianapolis News* declared the bill unconstitutional and "a flagrant interference with personal liberty." The *St. Louis Post-Dispatch* feared that the rights of minorities would be trampled upon, while the *Washington Herald* called it a threat to recovery and a national "disgrace."[32]

At the same time the NAM undertook a campaign that the *United States News* called "the greatest ever conducted by industry regarding any Congressional measure."[33] The radio, newspapers, speeches, broadsides, and correspondence were employed to attack the bill. Manufacturers were asked to put pressure on suppliers and dealers and were themselves urged to join the "Come to Washington Idea." The NAM informed them, "Practically every employer in the United States would be directly affected if this bill becomes law." Letters were prepared asking congressmen to vote against the measure. The NAM Board of Directors urged Roosevelt to defer a Senate vote until after the Supreme Court handed down a decision in the Schechter case. Despite these efforts, the Association wrote its representatives as the hearings closed, "The campaign has not been sufficient."[34]

It had not been adequate in part because labor had also lobbied vigorously. On April 29th the AFL called into conference in Washington four hundred representatives of internationals, state federations, and city centrals. The purpose was to press the Administration and Congress for the AFL legislative program, the Thirty-Hour bill, the Guffey coal bill, extension of NRA, and, above all, the labor relations bill. A resolution addressed to the President began, "The time is not for words. Circumstances require immediate and determined action." Sec.

[31] *New York Herald Tribune,* March 28, 1935.

[32] The opposition papers were the *Indianapolis News,* Apr. 3, *New York Evening Sun,* Apr. 22, *New York Herald Tribune,* March 23, *St. Louis Post-Dispatch,* Apr. 22, *Washington Herald,* Apr. 27, 1935. J. David Stern's *New York Evening Post,* March 25, favored the legislation, while the *Washington News,* Apr. 12, felt its objectives were desirable but doubted that it was "wisely drawn in all particulars."

[33] Cited in *Violations of Free Speech and Rights of Labor,* 75th Cong., 3d sess., Sen., Hearings before Subcomm. on Edu. and Labor, pt. 18, 14199.

[34] *Ibid.,* 14175, 14199. A conference of the Chamber of Commerce, meeting in Washington on May 2, denounced the New Deal in its entirety including the Wagner bill, the first open break between the Chamber and the Administration. Business was now in full opposition to Roosevelt, and restraints that previously led him to hesitate about labor legislation were relaxed. *New York Times,* May 3, 1935.

7(a) had failed, the company union was becoming a noose throttling the windpipe of labor. "There are other legislative measures now before Congress of far-reaching importance to Labor, but of transcending importance to Labor's rights and to national recovery is the Wagner Labor Disputes Act." Special conventions had met in the past, but, the resolution continued, "none of these conferences were called upon to consider questions more vitally affecting Labor's rights than the one in which we are now participating."[35] Senator Walsh informed the cheering delegates that his Labor Committee had just voted to report S. 1958 and predicted its passage. The meeting over, the conferees broke into state groups and called upon Senators and Representatives for their support.[36]

---

[35] A. O. Wharton *et al.* to Roosevelt, May 3, 1935, White House, O.F. No. 466, NRA-Misc. The President passed copies to Democratic leaders of House and Senate without comment. Roosevelt to Doughton and Harrison, May 3, 1935, White House, O.F. No. 466, NRA-Misc.

[36] AFL, *Weekly News Service,* Apr. 20, May 4, 1935; *United Mine Workers Journal,* May 15, 1935; *New York Times,* Apr. 29, 30, May 2, 1935.

IX. THE BIRTH OF THE WAGNER ACT

IN THE DELIBERATIONS of the Senate Labor Committee Chairman Walsh reversed his 1934 position, delegating full responsibility to Wagner without asserting his own views. As a result, Wagner was asked to prepare the report and was again assisted by Keyserling. They regarded this as a key opportunity to break with the 1934 report and, more important, to state congressional intent for the guidance of the board and the courts.[1]

On May 2nd the committee without a dissenting voice reported S. 1958 with amendments, one of great importance. The committee accepted Biddle's suggestion of a fifth unfair practice on the obligation to bargain in the original language. In addition, the declaration of policy was rewritten without disturbing the basic ideas; unions when acting as employers were covered; the Department of Labor was protected against encroachment of an independent board upon its conciliation and statistical functions; the arbitration section was stricken out, the alternative procedure for enforcement in the district courts suffering the same fate; and the right of individuals and minorities to present grievances was strengthened by elimination of, "through representatives of their own choosing."[2]

"The compelling force of . . . experience," the committee declared, "demonstrating that the government's promise in Section 7(a) stands largely unfulfilled, makes unacceptable any further temporizing measures." The first objective was to remove a basic cause of strikes, perhaps twenty-five per cent of the total, involving the right to bargain. "Prudence," however, "forbids any attempt by the government to remove all the causes of labor disputes." A second purpose was to encourage equality of bargaining power. The depression demonstrated a disparity between consumption and production and the necessity to bring them into equilibrium by stimulating higher wages through collective bargaining. The committee found 7(a) in a state of collapse, criticizing its ambiguity and generality, diffusion of administrative responsibility, the disadvantages in linking enforcement to NRA, the helplessness of the NLRB in compliance, and the obstacles to elections. These defects were neither "intrinsic nor irremediable" and might be cured by S. 1958.[3]

The bill did not make all company unions unlawful but merely prevented interference by employers in their formation or operation. A variety of practices fell within the proscription: employer participation

---

[1] Levy interview; Keyserling to the writer, June 11, 1948.

[2] *National Labor Relations Board,* 74th Cong., 1st sess., Sen., Comm. on Edu. and Labor, Rep. No. 573 (May 2, 1935), pp. 6, 8, 12–13.

[3] *Ibid.,* pp. 1, 2, 3–6.

in framing constitutions and by-laws, approval prior to organizational changes, intervention in internal management or elections, supervision of agenda or procedure of meetings, and financial support. The committee named propaganda "absolutely false" which declared that the measure gave special legal sanction to or imposed the closed shop. The proviso to 8(3) simply preserved the *status quo*. The Biddle amendment, 8(5), was accepted because "experience has proved that neither obedience to law nor respect for law is encouraged by holding forth a right unaccompanied by fulfillment." It did not, however, compel agreement nor permit governmental supervision of contract terms. "It must be stressed that the duty to bargain collectively does not carry with it the duty to reach an agreement, because the essence of collective bargaining is that either party shall be free to decide whether proposals made to it are satisfactory." The committee found need to "establish a single paramount administrative . . . authority in connection with the development of the Federal American law regarding collective bargaining."[4]

The committee could discover no sound reason to apply the unfair practices to employees. No showing was made of practical need to prevent interference by workers or unions. The courts, on the other hand, had construed the word "coercion" to prohibit: a threat to strike, refusal to work on material of nonunion manufacture, picketing, and peaceful persuasion. To prohibit employees to engage in "coercive" acts would "raise in Federal law the ghosts of many much-criticized injunctions issued by courts of equity . . . which it was supposed Congress had laid low in the Norris-LaGuardia Act." Its introduction would overwhelm the board with countercharges and recriminations, preventing it from doing the job at hand.[5]

The constitutional argument followed that Wagner advanced during the hearings. The due process theory was based on the railway clerks case. Evidence for the effect of disputes upon commerce appeared in the estimate that the cost of strikes approximated one billion dollars annually, a fact judicially recognized. Failure to accept collective bargaining was a major cause of many of these stoppages. Since the courts, moreover, observed that unsound economic practices affect the volume and stability of commerce, congressional authority to prevent unfair practices should be exercised even where the threat of strife was not imminent.

While this bill of course does not intend to go beyond the constitutional power of Congress, as that power may be marked out by the courts, it seeks the full limit of that power in preventing these unfair labor practices. It seeks to prevent them, whether

[4] *Ibid.*, pp. 12, 15.
[5] *Ibid.*, p. 16.

they burden interstate commerce by causing strikes, or by occurring in the stream of interstate commerce, or by overturning the balance of economic forces upon which the full flow of commerce depends.[6]

The committee report discouraged the NAM. Emery wrote privately on May 10th, "The Wagner bill situation is more desperate. . . . If it comes to a vote it will undoubtedly pass." He continued to feel that opposition strength was concentrated in the Senate and that the major stand should be made there. As it was impossible to defeat S. 1958 as a whole, an attempt should be made to "divert" it by an amendment, the familiar "coercion from any source." This device, he hoped, would appeal to many Senators who would vote for the bill in its entirety. The AFL would then object so strenuously, Emery predicted, as to prefer no legislation at all.[7]

The idea of amendment appealed as well to the Department of Justice, which, through Senator Robinson, proposed a change in the board's litigation. Instead of NLRB attorneys handling enforcement proceedings in the courts, Sec. 4 would give the Attorney General authority "to appear for and represent the Board in any judicial proceeding to which the Board is a party." The purpose was twofold, to guard the department's jurisdiction over federal litigation and give it control over enforcement like that exercised under 7(a). The draftsmen opposed the change for these very reasons. "If authority to conduct the civil litigation of the Board were vested in the Attorney General and the district attorneys, . . . [they] would be the final arbiters as to when and how various civil proceedings should be prosecuted or defended, and whether they should be prosecuted or defended at all."[8] The proposal would, in other words, promote the diffusion of responsibility, conflict of interpretation, and delay they sought to avoid. Other administrative tribunals, ICC, FTC, and SEC, retained this authority themselves.[9] The Robinson amendments were vigorously opposed by Wagner and hence were not formally offered.

Robinson and Senator Pat Harrison, in fact, were cool to the bill in its entirety. They tried to defer consideration in hope that the session would terminate before it came to a vote. To this end they sought to enlist the support of the President; Wagner received a call to the White House. Urging Roosevelt not to intervene again, he asked that the Senators have the opportunity to be counted. Roosevelt, finding this

[6] *Ibid.*, p. 19.

[7] Emery to Homer D. Sayre, May 10, 1935, *Violations of Free Speech and Rights of Labor*, 75th Cong., 3d sess., Sen. Hearings before Subcomm. on Edu. and Labor, pt. 18, 14202.

[8] NLRA, Legislative History, Robinson Amendments, n.d., Levy papers.

[9] Levy to Keyserling, May 13, 1935, Levy papers.

request fair on its face, placed no impediment in the way of consideration. Wagner felt certain of passage once the bill reached the floor.[10]

On May 15th he presented S. 1958 to the Senate in a formal address.
The bill, he declared, "does not break with our traditions. It is the
next step in the logical unfolding of man's eternal quest for freedom."
The struggle for the political liberation of the common man, having
its inception in the American Revolution, was now extending to industry in the face of concentrated wealth and power. The right of workers
to associate emerged gradually in the nineteenth century despite the
doctrine of conspiracy. The effort to broaden the economic base of society in the antitrust laws was perverted by the courts, while integration
actually proceeded at an accelerated pace in this century. As a consequence, he argued, the worker's share of "the product created by manufacturing" declined from 51 per cent in 1849 to 36 per cent in 1933,
despite the growth of production; inevitable collapse arrived in 1929.
NRA sought to recover losses by permitting businessmen and workmen
to organize to help themselves. Industry succeeded, prices and profits
rose. Sec. 7(a), however, broke down, real wages dropped while unemployment did not improve. Wages, in fact, rose in proportion to profits
only in those sectors where collective bargaining existed. The conclusion, Wagner felt, was obvious and he accordingly turned to the familiar
justification for the bill presented to the committee.[11]

On the following day the Senate commenced debate, Walsh presenting
the committee revisions which were accepted without objection. Senator
Tydings of Maryland then brought out the NAM amendment, proposing that Sec. 7 read [additions italicized], "Employees shall have the
right to self-organization, to form, join, or assist labor organizations,
to bargain collectively through representatives of their own choosing,
and to engage in other concerted activities, for the purpose of collective
bargaining or other mutual aid or protection, *free from coercion or
intimidation from any source.*"[12] A wrong, he declared, was equally bad
whether the act of an employer or a union. The individual workman
would gain genuine freedom of association only if all forms of intimidation were outlawed. By omitting such language Congress would

[10] Levy interview.

[11] *Cong. Record*, LXXIX, pt. vii, 7565–73. The opposition was so much on the defensive that no one sought to reply. In fact, Senator Hastings, with a speech in his
pocket, quietly inserted it in the *Record*. *Ibid.*, pp. 7975–79.

[12] *Ibid.*, p. 7952. Tydings also offered an amendment to Sec. 8 making it an unfair
practice "for any person to coerce employees in the exercise of their rights guaranteed
in Section 7, or to coerce employees in their right to work or to join or not to join
any labor organization." *Ibid.*, p. 7954. Its language went far beyond the first and it
would, presumably, have been pressed if he could have gained support for the change
in Sec. 7.

encourage the use of force by unions. "Is not this still a country where a man can select, without coercion or intimidation, the kind of organization to which he shall belong?" Senator Couzens added that rivalries between unions led them to employ force upon workers and their families. Wagner replied that the Tydings amendment was sponsored by large employers and that workmen did not request or need such relief. State and municipal law already prohibited noxious activities, while "coercion" had been the subject of extreme judicial construction. "If we should adopt this amendment, it would practically nullify the Norris Anti-Injunction Act." Senator Barkley noted that the prime instrument of coercion, the right to fire, was in the hands of employers. Senator Norris declared that he would favor the amendment "if there did not recur to me what I have learned of the injunction question, . . . if I had not the ideas which are now back in my brain which were pounded into me during long and tedious debates." We are a nation governed by the judiciary. "One man sitting as a district judge can nullify, by a stroke of a pen, the acts of the President, the Senate, and the House of Representatives, even though their action be unanimous."[13]

The Administration leaders would have preferred to avoid a roll call. Tydings, however, insisted upon it and the amendment was rejected, fifty to twenty-one, a majority so impressive as to prevent further delay. The Senate then passed S. 1958 by a vote of sixty-three to twelve. Forty-nine Democrats, eight Republicans, one Farmer-Laborite, and one Progressive voted for the measure, while only four Democrats and eight Republicans opposed it. Twenty-three Senators did not go on record. The Democrats supported the bill overwhelmingly including the majority from the South. The Republicans divided evenly in the voting.[14]

The speed with which debate proceeded, the feebleness of the opposition, and the preponderance of the vote exceeded Wagner's expectations. There were two reasons for this. The bill was presented at the most favorable possible moment since 1935 was the apogee of the New Deal as a progressive domestic reform movement. The influence of labor was at its height and Senators who had little enthusiasm for S. 1958 feared to face the AFL at the polls with a negative vote on their records. The White House, moreover, no longer blocked the way. Second, many Senators, convinced that the bill was unconstitutional, shifted the onus of its defeat to the Supreme Court. While gaining labor's political support, they felt certain that the measure would not take effect since employers would withhold compliance until the court declared it void.

[13] *Ibid.*, pp. 7953–55, 7967–69.
[14] *Ibid.*, pp. 7973–74, 7980; *New York Times*, May 17, 1935. Emery's tactic of using an amendment broom so broad as to sweep up the votes of many Senators who would have favored the bill as a whole failed, of course, but not entirely. Nine Senators who did not oppose S. 1958 in the final roll call voted for the Tydings amendment.

In view of the large issues at stake, the "debate" in the Senate was a disappointment. This was due, first, to the fact that the bill had been discussed for more than a year in Congress, in the press, and over the radio and had been the subject of a flood of congressional mail. When the Senators entered the chamber they already knew how they would vote. Since this was recognized by both sides, neither sought needless debate. The second factor was that the opposition lacked a champion.[15]

The Senate action reverberated in the press; eighteen of twenty papers expressed opposition. The basic complaint was that the Senators disregarded their oaths of office by voting for an unconstitutional measure, although the *New York Times* admitted uncertainty on this point. For the rest, arguments followed the pattern: AFL "monopoly," "class warfare," imposition of the "closed shop," "one-sidedness," the "dangerous principle of majority rule," derangement of business and recovery, etc. The *Richmond News-Leader* hailed Virginia's Byrd for remaining faithful to the Constitution. The *Charlotte Observer* "relentlessly" upheld the democratic principle of "individual bargaining," then declared itself against majority rule. The *St. Louis Post-Dispatch* noted that the AFL position conflicted with the Gompers philosophy of voluntarism and that labor risked putting its neck in a governmental "noose."[16]

The hearings of the House Committee on Labor were only a pale reflection of those held by the Senate and the arguments were echoes.[17] Chairman Connery, in fact, delayed action by his committee until after Senate passage on May 16th. Three days later House leaders called at the White House and, although the President declined to state his views publicly, the way was cleared for consideration.[18]

Meanwhile, within the House Committee a storm was brewing. The AFL at the instance of Miss Perkins prevailed upon Connery to place the board in the department. Despite efforts by Wagner and the NLRB to undo this decision, Connery secured a majority to go along with him.[19]

---

[15] Basil Rauch, *The History of the New Deal* (New York: 1944), Chap. X; *New York Times*, May 17, 1935; *Business Week*, May 25, 1935, 5; *New Republic*, LXXXII (1935), 72, 99; Keyserling interview.

[16] *Akron Beacon-Journal*, May 18, *Boston Transcript*, May 17, *Charlotte Observer*, May 20, *Chicago Journal of Commerce*, May 18, *Cleveland Plain Dealer*, May 18, *Dallas Morning News*, May 18, *Detroit News*, May 18, *Indianapolis News*, May 17, *Kansas City Times*, May 18, *New York Evening Sun*, May 17, *New York Herald Tribune*, May 18, *New York Times*, May 17, *Philadelphia Bulletin*, May 23, *Philadelphia Inquirer*, May 18, *Richmond News-Leader*, May 16, *St. Louis Post-Dispatch*, May 17, *Wall St. Journal*, May 20, *Washington Herald*, May 28, 1935. The only papers to applaud the Senate were the *New York Evening Post*, May 18, and *Washington News*, May 17, 1935.

[17] *Labor Disputes Act*, 74th Cong., 1st sess., H.R., Hearings before Comm. on Labor on H.R. 6288 (March 13–Apr. 4, 1935).

[18] *New York Times*, May 18, 1935.

[19] Levy interview; H. K. Gilbert, The United States Department of Labor in the New Deal Period (unpublished Ph.D. thesis, Wisconsin, 1942), 170; Levy to Magruder, May 20, 1935, NLRA, Legislative History, Levy papers.

On May 20th the committee reported H.R. 7978 in the form passed by the Senate except for an amendment to Sec. 3(a). Instead of being established "as an independent agency in the executive branch of the Government," the board would be "created in the Department of Labor." Only Representative Vito Marcantonio dissented on this question. The majority gave no reason for the change beyond inclusion of a letter from the Secretary summarizing her viewpoint. The report did emphasize independence and dignity, hence eschewing any intention "to subject the Board to the jurisdiction of the Secretary of Labor in respect of its decisions, policies, budget, or personnel." Marcantonio, on the other hand, felt that control of the purse gave Miss Perkins full authority over operations and policies. This made an impartial independent quasi-judicial agency impossible, subjected the board to shifting political winds, contaminated it with conciliation, undermined its prestige and capacity to obtain high-level personnel, and deterred the department from its appointed task, promoting the welfare of wage earners.[20]

These legislative events and the imminent Supreme Court decision in the NRA case pressed Roosevelt to take a position on S. 1958. If he failed to take a stand, he might later feel constrained to veto the measure in face of an overwhelming congressional majority or accept it reluctantly without having taken a hand in its formulation. Accordingly, Roosevelt called Wagner, Miss Perkins, Richberg, Assistant Attorney General Harold M. Stephens, Green, Hillman, and Lewis to the White House on May 24th. Despite continuing pressure by industry, Roosevelt agreed to back S. 1958 subject to the ironing out of differences between Stephens and Richberg on one hand and Wagner on the other. After the conference the press learned that Roosevelt, after fifteen months of consideration, had endorsed the National Labor Relations bill.[21]

The differences at the conference were so sharp that Wagner could not have accepted the views of the Department of Justice and NRA without radical revision of his bill. Stephens, in fact, did no more than make comments—eschewing a "legal opinion"—in setting down his and

---

[20] *National Labor Relations Board,* 74th Cong., 1st sess., H.R., Rep. No. 969 to accompany H.R. 7978 (May 20, 1935), pp. 9–12, 24–27, 29–30. Marcantonio not only strongly supported the substantive features of the measure but proposed that its benefits be extended to agricultural laborers, since no group more desperately needed the right to organize.

[21] *New York Times,* May 25, 1935. At this time New York bankers through Wetmore Hodges and Marriner S. Eccles sought the President's influence to insert drastic amendments. There is no evidence that Roosevelt was impressed. Hodges to McIntyre, May 27, Roosevelt to McIntyre, May 29, Perkins to McIntyre, June 18, 1935, White House, O.F. No. 407, Labor.

Richberg's suggestions. He criticized the statement of the purchasing power theory as being of dubious reference to the commerce clause. He was particularly concerned about the prerogatives of the Department of Justice in litigation, feeling that the board invited criticism by acting as both prosecutor and judge and by retaining exclusive jurisdiction. The power to determine appropriate unit, Richberg warned, would evoke complications, since employees had heretofore selected their own units and an unsympathetic tribunal might use the authority discriminatorily. Stephens felt that exempting the board from the rules of evidence went too far since the courts, in any case, would grant such authority within a "proper" area and the parties might be deprived of rights in such matters as cross-examination. The language in which the obligation to bargain was cast appeared to force employers to make contracts, infringing the basic legal concept that persons cannot be compelled to agree. He asked that the duty also be imposed upon employees and be limited to making "reasonable efforts" and affording "proper opportunity for collective bargaining."[22]

With only the week end intervening after the President's endorsement of the Wagner bill as well as NRA extension the Supreme Court delivered the Schechter decision on May 27th, knocking out Title I of the Recovery Act, including 7(a), and questioning the power of Congress to regulate commerce.[23] A unanimous court through Chief Justice Hughes ruled that the Act was an invalid delegation of legislative power and an unconstitutional regulation of intrastate transactions with only an indirect effect upon interstate commerce.[24] The first was unrelated to the Wagner bill since it entailed no surrender of congressional authority, but the ruling on commerce was of utmost significance.

The Schechter brothers, convicted of violating the poultry code, argued that the law contravened the Constitution. The brothers purchased chickens raised in other states in New York City markets and transported them to Brooklyn for slaughter and final local sale. The court held that the transactions were outside the "current" or "flow" of interstate commerce, hence not subject to the regulatory power of

[22] Stephens to Wagner, May 27, 1935, Keyserling papers. The board opposed imposing a duty to bargain on employees for these reasons: (1) it existed in fact since the board could not hold that an employer had failed to bargain unless the employees had first come forward with their demands; (2) it would restrict the right to strike; and (3) the case of the union that did not exhaust collective bargaining was rare. NLRA, Legislative History, Should there be a duty on employees to bargain collectively? n.d., Levy papers.

[23] *A. L. A. Schechter Poultry Corp. v. United States* (1935), 295 U.S. 495.

[24] Justice Cardozo rendered a separate concurring opinion for himself and Justice Stone dealing with delegation. On commerce, he said, "little can be added to the opinion of the Court."

Congress. The poultry came to "a permanent rest" within the state of New York. Of course, the court observed, "the power of Congress extends not only to the regulation of transactions which are part of interstate commerce, but to the protection of that commerce from injury. It matters not that the injury may be due to the conduct of those engaged in intrastate operations." In other words, Congress may regulate actions which, though purely intrastate themselves, *affect* interstate commerce. That power may be invoked, however, only when the effect is direct. "If the commerce clause were construed to reach all enterprises and transactions which could be said to have an indirect effect upon interstate commerce, the federal authority would embrace practically all the activities of the people and the authority of the State over its domestic concerns would exist only by sufferance of the federal government." The NRA attempt to fix hours and wages in this intrastate business was an invalid exercise of the commerce power over transactions with only an indirect effect upon interstate commerce. If wages and hours might be determined, as the government argued, because of a relationship to cost and indirect effects upon commerce, a similar control might be exercised over other elements of cost, such as the number of employees, rents, and advertising.

It is not the province of the Court to consider the economic advantages or disadvantages of . . . a centralized system. It is sufficient to say that the Federal Constitution does not provide for it. Our growth and development have called for wide use of the commerce power of the federal government in its control over the expanded activities of interstate commerce, and in protecting that commerce from burdens, interferences, and conspiracies to restrain and monopolize it. But the authority of the federal government may not be pushed to such an extreme as to destroy the distinction, which the commerce clause itself establishes, between commerce "among the several States" and the internal concerns of a State. . . .

The press felt that the decision clearly invalidated the Wagner bill. The Schechter case, the *New York Herald Tribune* forecast, had buried S. 1958. "This bill," the *Wall St. Journal* declared, "asks something that Congress cannot give."[25] The *New York Times* cautiously observed that, "certainly the least that can be said is that the Wagner bill, once enacted, would be contested in the courts."[26] Even the pro-NLRA *Philadelphia Record* admitted that enforcement of the right to bargain collectively "would be an 'interference' with intrastate commerce." It asked, nevertheless, that the bill be passed and that the Constitution be amended.[27]

---

[25] *Herald Tribune*, May 28, 31, 1935. Similar constitutional obituaries appeared in the *Indianapolis News*, May 30, *Philadelphia Inquirer*, June 3, *Charlotte Observer*, June 4, *New York Evening Sun*, June 7, *Portland Oregonian*, May 28, *Wall St. Journal*, June 8, 1935.
[26] June 1, 1935.
[27] May 29, 1935.

The immediate effect of the decision upon the New Deal as a whole was drastic. The comprehensive program of social and economic reform before Congress was held in abeyance as that body recessed; silence fell over the White House; and the AFL was fearful that legislation on the verge of enactment would be snatched away. On June 4th, however, Roosevelt announced his decision: the New Deal program including S. 1958 would proceed, if necessary, in defiance of the court.[28]

No less than the President, Wagner was determined that his bill be enacted. He and his advisers, in fact, were convinced that the ruling on commerce did not fundamentally challenge its constitutionality, and on May 30th Wagner issued a public statement.[29] In the decision "the door was not closed to federal regulation of employment conditions related to goods that are intended for subsequent interstate shipment or that are in the flow of commerce." Even if limited to these areas alone, the bill would have ample room, but the ruling opened another and more important jurisdiction. "The court has made it abundantly clear in a long series of decisions that the issue of whether a practice 'directly' affects interstate commerce, and thus is subject to federal regulation, depends more upon the nature of the practice than upon the area of activity of the business in which the practice occurs." An old-age insurance statute for railway workers on a clearly interstate instrumentality, for example, was held invalid on the ground that retirement had no appreciable effect on the flow of goods. Conversely, the courts sustained antitrust injunctions involving businesses no more in commerce than that of the Schechter brothers because strikes interrupted interstate transactions. In this case the regulation was over wages and hours, subjects S. 1958 did not presume to determine. "It is clear that the Schechter decision limits federal supervision of wages and hours in situations where federal efforts to maintain industrial peace, and thus to prevent interference with the physical flow of goods, would be sustained."[30]

Wagner, however, felt that some changes were necessary and instructed Keyserling, Magruder, and Levy to prepare them. They submitted amendments to the declaration of policy to make a showing by explicit language of the direct relationship between industrial disputes and commerce, of emphasizing this by reversing the order of paragraphs, and of basing authority exclusively on the commerce clause by striking

---

[28] *New York Times*, May 28, 29, June 5, 1935.

[29] Wagner, Keyserling, Magruder, and Levy believed at this juncture that there was room for the bill within the Schechter opinion. Even Richberg, who opposed the measure, did not attack it on constitutional grounds, while Wyzanski felt that it would be sustained to the limit of the regulatory power of Congress over commerce. Keyserling, Levy, Wyzanski interviews.

[30] *New York Times*, May 30, 1935.

out reference to the "general welfare." In addition, they altered the definitions of "commerce" and "affecting commerce" to attain the same objectives.[31] The President approved the revisions and instructed Connery to press for immediate enactment with their inclusion. On June 5th he gained permission of the House to recommit the bill for this purpose.[32]

The committee on June 10th made its second report, incorporating the Senator's amendments. Sec. 1, now styled "findings and policy" rather than "declaration of policy," began,

> The denial by employers of the right of employees to organize and the refusal by employers to accept the procedure of collective bargaining lead to strikes and other forms of industrial strife or unrest, which have the intent or the necessary effect of burdening or obstructing interstate and foreign commerce by (a) impairing the efficiency, safety, or operation of the instrumentalities of commerce; (b) occurring in the current of commerce; (c) materially affecting, restraining, or controlling the flow of raw materials or manufactured or processed goods from or into the channels of commerce, or the prices of such materials or goods in commerce; or (d) causing diminution of employment and wages in such volume as substantially to impair or disrupt the market for goods flowing from or into the channels of commerce.[33]

The provision went on to the subject of inequality of bargaining power and demonstrated its relationship to commerce. By removing sources of unrest, fostering friendly adjustment of disputes, and restoring equality of bargaining power commerce would be safeguarded from injury. The policy of the United States therefore was to encourage collective bargaining and freedom of association. Sec. 3 was amended to permit the President to remove NLRB members after notice and hearing for neglect of duty or malfeasance but for no other reason.[34] The committee did not change its previous determination to place the board in the Department of Labor.

Connery, anxious for immediate consideration, sought a special rule from the Rules Committee, where he encountered Republican resistance and coolness on the part of many Democrats. Nevertheless, with apparent White House assistance, he won a rule on June 18th providing for three hours of debate and unrestricted amendments.[35]

---

[31] Keyserling, Levy interviews.

[32] *New York Times,* June 5, 1935; *Cong. Record,* LXXIX, pt. viii, 8727, ix, 9688.

[33] *National Labor Relations Board,* 74th Cong., 1st sess., H.R., Rep. No. 1147 (June 10, 1935), p. 1.

[34] *Ibid.,* p. 14. On the day of the Schecter case the Supreme Court issued a decision in *Rathbun v. United States* (1935), 295 U.S. 602, holding that the President might not remove a member of the Federal Trade Commission except for causes stated in the statute since the commission was quasi-judicial. The Wagner bill was amended in light of the Rathbun case.

[35] *New York Times,* June 19, 1935. Rules Committee Chairman O'Connor informed

On June 19th, the House opposition struck at the bill on the grounds of constitutionality. The federal government, they charged, sought to destroy the distinction the Supreme Court had always made between production and commerce. "I know the difference," Representative R. F. Rich of Pennsylvania declared, "between regulating the relations between employer and employee in carrying on interstate communication on a railroad or a telephone company or a ship, and undertaking to regulate the employment relations of the parties who are engaged in building engines or making telephones or putting a ship together." They described the committee amendments as "circumventing" the Constitution as read by the court in the Schechter case. Law-abiding citizens, Representative Howard Smith of Virginia warned, would live with an invalid statute for two years before the tribunal could issue a ruling. Honest sponsors would withhold this bill until they had obtained a constitutional amendment granting Congress authority to act. Smith joined Eugene Cox of Georgia in denouncing the measure for stripping the states of residual police powers and subverting state sovereignty.[36]

"Surely," Rich warned, "no Member of this House who has regard for the oath which he took to support the Constitution can fail to have a doubt as to the validity of this legislation. If he does have such a doubt, then he ought to resolve it before he acts." Congress could not in good faith pass the question to the courts. "We are agents with limited powers, and the Court gives every reasonable presumption to the constitutionality of what we do, because it believes that we have settled our own doubts."[37]

Representative C. V. Truax of Ohio replied, "We see the same old faces that oppose all progressive humanitarian legislation. . . . What are you going to do with this sacred old Constitution? You cannot eat it, you cannot wear it, and you cannot sleep in it." Connery advanced the familiar argument that labor disputes are subject to the commerce power of Congress. The statute itself, Marcantonio pointed out, would not be unconstitutional but each case would be examined on its merits. The court would ask, "Does the application of the law in this case violate the interstate commerce definition as handed down in the Schechter case?"[38]

Rich then turned his fire on the bill itself: The AFL was favored; the closed shop was imposed; the fundamental American right to work

Steve Early that it would take a little time "to sell" the bill, and Early accordingly suggested to the President that he might "turn on the heat." Early to Roosevelt, June 8, 1935, White House, O.F. No. 407, Labor.
[36] *Cong. Record*, LXXIX, pt. ix, 9688, 9694.
[37] *Ibid.*, p. 9689.
[38] *Ibid.*, pp. 9698, 9714.

or not to work was violated; Communist unions won protection; employers must hire incompetents and malcontents; union coercion was permitted but denied to employers. "We are faced with a condition and not a theory," Truax replied. With the Recovery Act invalid the need for the Wagner bill was even greater to abate the threat of strikes over the right to associate and bargain.[39]

The House then considered the committee amendments, adopting the new findings and policy, the revised definitions, and the removal of board members without discussion. Two committee members, Ramspeck and Marcantonio, vigorously attacked the plan to place the agency in the Department of Labor. The former argued that independence was essential to the NLRB's effectiveness and that the validity of the statute hinged upon it. The Rathbun case demonstrated the court's recognition of the distinction between quasi-judicial and executive agencies, while the Schechter case showed that legislative powers could not be delegated to the President. Connery replied that Roosevelt had approved the amendment. The House then voted to make the NLRB an independent agency, 130 to 48.[40]

The opposition thereupon presented amendments seeking objectives that Tydings strove for in the Senate. They prohibited favoring a particular union or form of employee organization, denied "coercion from any source," regulated union activities as a qualification for enjoying the benefits of the Act, eliminated the closed shop proviso, permitted employer contributions to labor organizations, and required board adherence to the rules of evidence. The House rejected them without a roll call. An amendment by Representative Biermann of Iowa, defining a strike in conflict with an agreement as a "violation of the spirit of this act," however, was approved, 115 to 109. Connery's insistence upon a recount after Administration stalwarts were summoned buried the proposal 140 to 107.[41]

Marcantonio described the conditions among farm workers and asked that the definitions be amended to cover them. "If the industrial workers are entitled to protection, then by the same token the agricultural workers are entitled to the same protection." Connery, despite personal sympathy with the amendment, declared that "just now I believe in biting off one mouthful at a time." Representatives from rural districts who otherwise would vote for the bill were certain to oppose it in this form. The House consequently rejected the amendment.[42]

Ramspeck then asked that a proviso be added to Sec. 9(b) to give the

[39] *Ibid.*, pp. 9710, 9713, 9715.
[40] *Ibid.*, pp. 9717–25.
[41] *Ibid.*, pp. 9718, 9721, 9726, 9727, 9729, 9730.
[42] *Ibid.*, p. 9720.

board authority to determine appropriate unit only on condition "that no unit shall include the employees of more than one employer." The amendment aimed directly at textiles, since representatives from North Carolina who otherwise would vote for the bill were concerned about the unit power in relation to that industry which was organized in the North and nonunion in the South. They feared that the board would declare the whole country an appropriate unit and compel southern employers to accept unions.[43]

Neither the National Labor Board nor the National Labor Relations Board, in fact, had ever certified a unit larger than one employer, although the latter felt that such a contingency might arise in the future.[44] Representative Wood of Missouri opposed the proviso, declaring that it would undermine established association bargaining in such industries as coal and construction. Ramspeck replied that employees might continue to agree to bargain on a multiemployer basis; only the board would be barred from ordering it. The House then adopted the proviso, 127 to 87.[45]

Concern with appropriate unit was not confined to employers. The craft leaders of the AFL, harassed by emerging industrial unionism that was later to erupt into the CIO, were similarly distraught lest an unsympathetic board join these forces against them. The NLRB, for example, might decide that drivers working for a brewery were part of a unit comprising all its employees, hence presenting the Brewery Workers rather than the Teamsters with a majority. The drafting of Sec. 9(b), Wagner wrote, "gave us more trouble than any other," and neither he nor the board derived much satisfaction from it. Their defense, in fact, was of a necessary evil, Biddle stating, "to lodge the power . . . with the employer would invite abuse and gerrymandering. . . . If the employees themselves could make the decision . . . they could defeat the practical significance of the majority rule; and by breaking off into small groups, could make it impossible for the employer to run his plant." Even though giving the power to the NLRB entailed a similar danger of gerrymandering, "that is the risk you must run in all democratic governments."[46]

On May 25th the *Brewery Worker* published an editorial declaring that industrial unions would be "the immediate beneficiaries" of the Wagner bill.

---

[43] *Ibid.*, p. 9727; *Proposed Amendments to the National Labor Relations Act*, 76th Cong., 1st sess., H.R., Hearings before Comm. on Labor (Feb.–July 1939), pp. 683, 1075.
[44] Magruder, House Amendments to S. 1958, n.d., Keyserling papers.
[45] *Cong. Record*, LXXIX, pt. ix, 9727–28.
[46] Wagner to Tobin, June 14, 1935, Levy papers; Sen. Hearings, *National Labor Relations Board*, pp. 82–83.

As far as the Brewery Workers are concerned, nothing better could happen than the Wagner bill becoming the law of the land. Of course the craft unions and A. F. of L. in working for its enactment do not yet realize that in sponsoring the bill they are saying goodbye to their prerogatives of attacking an industrial union whenever they see fit.

Dan Tobin, President of the Teamsters, circulated this editorial among the members of the Executive Council, all of whom, except Lewis, expressed grave concern. T. A. Rickert of the Garment Workers, for example, wrote Tobin that the bill will "injure organizations like your own and possibly mine." Hence on June 6th Wagner appeared before the council in Washington to assure the members that S. 1958 would not destroy craft organizations, that AFL jurisdictional conflicts would continue to be resolved by the unions themselves rather than by the NLRB, that the power to fix unit had to be lodged somewhere and there was no alternative but to leave it to the board, and that board members would not be labor-baiters because their appointments must be approved by the Senate. Although the council's fears were not stilled completely and were, in fact, to break forth into an assault upon the board several years later, the members were constrained to keep them under the surface at this time. As a result the AFL continued its un-deviating public support for the bill without asking for changes in 9(b).[47]

The Ramspeck proviso adopted, Connery proposed a new Sec. 14 to read, "Nothing in this act shall abridge the freedom of speech or the press as guaranteed in the first amendment of the Constitution." It originated in a desire by publishers to avoid recognition of the Newspaper Guild. They put pressure on the White House, Louis Howe asking Connery to insert new language. The change, drafted by attorneys at the NLRB, innocuously restated the First Amendment and the House adopted it in perfunctory fashion.[48]

The bill then passed without a roll call, a Republican attempt to require a count being defeated. On the following day, June 20th, the Senate voted to disagree with the House amendments and S. 1958 went to conference.[49] At this time industry sought to introduce amendments through Secretary of Commerce Roper. In the interest of "friendly and sympathetic businessmen," he informed the President that the bill directly conflicted with his auto settlement, adding, "It seems important

[47] Tobin to Wagner, June 10, Rickert to Tobin, June 14, Tobin to Wagner, June 17, 1935, Levy papers; *Proposed Amendments to the National Labor Relations Act*, 76th Cong., 1st sess., H.R., Hearings before Comm. on Labor (Feb.–July 1939), p. 684; *National Labor Relations Act*, 76th Cong., 3d sess., Hearings before Sp. Comm. to Investigate NLRB (1940), p. 2389; Shishkin, Levy, Keyserling interviews.

[48] *Cong. Record*, LXXIX, pt. ix, 9370; *New York Times*, June 21, 1935; Levy interview.

[49] *Cong. Record*, LXXIX, pt. ix, 9731, 9778, 9864.

that the President avoid the inconsistency of signing a bill which does not conform with his definitely stated principles of employer-employee relations." Hence, he asked Roosevelt to instruct the conference that "a clear-cut provision should be inserted to guarantee the employee protection against coercion or intimidation from any source whatsoever."[50]

Roosevelt, however, did not intervene and the conference report of June 26th contained no such language. The House findings and policy and definitions were accepted with only verbal changes, while the amendment covering removal of board members was adopted without revision. On location the committee made the NLRB independent. Ramspeck achieved this by sacrificing his proviso to 9(b). As a compromise on the latter the conference replaced "other unit" with "or appropriate subdivision thereof," to read "employer unit, craft unit, plant unit, or appropriate subdivision thereof." Ramspeck felt that this achieved the same result since "employer unit" now became the largest segment in the series. The "free speech" amendment was stricken out on the counsel of Senator Borah who argued that it had no legal effect since the Constitution was supreme in any case. The Senate conferees, through Newspaper Guild instance, were concerned lest publishers use it to evade the Act. On June 27th the House accepted the conference report 132 to 42 and the Senate acted affirmatively the same day without a vote.[51]

On July 5, 1935, the President signed the National Labor Relations Act, giving the pens used to Wagner and Green. In a statement prepared by the Department of Labor and approved by Wagner, Roosevelt set forth the purposes of the Act: it would foster the employment contract, remove a chief cause of economic strife, and assure every worker "within its scope" freedom of choice and action. The NLRB would not mediate, that function remaining with the Conciliation Service. "It is important that the judicial function and the mediation function should not be confused." Emphasizing the narrow purpose of the Act, he predicted that it "may eventually eliminate one major cause of labor disputes, but it will not stop all labor disputes."[52]

Upon passage of the Act Green declared, "I am confident that it will

---

[50] Roper to Roosevelt, June 20, 1935, White House, O.F. No. 407, Labor. Roosevelt, however, wrote to Connery the same day: "I am delighted with the fine way you handled the big Bill in the House this week." June 20, 1935, White House, O.F. No. 407, Labor.

[51] *National Labor Relations Board*, 74th Cong., 1st sess., Conf. Rep. on S. 1958, Rep. No. 1371 (June 26, 1935); *New York Times*, June 25, 1935; *Justice*, June 1, 1935, 16; *Cong. Record*, LXXIX, pt. ix, 10258–59, 10299, 10300. The text of the National Labor Relations Act appears in the Appendix.

[52] *Public Papers and Addresses of Franklin D. Roosevelt*, ed. by Samuel I. Rosenman (New York: 1938), IV, 294–95; Arthur J. Altmeyer to McIntyre, July 1, 1935, White House, O.F. No. 716, NLRB; *New York Times*, July 6, 1935.

prove itself the Magna Charta of Labor of the United States." Industry, on the other hand, was convinced that the statute was unconstitutional. The steel and automotive industries announced that they would move to challenge its validity, while the lawyers committee of the American Liberty League pronounced the Act an affront to the Constitution. The *Baltimore Sun* felt it "safe to predict that the Wagner bill will be as ineffectual as was Section 7(a)."[53]

After two years of indecision the government had committed itself to a policy that embodied all four concepts set forth in Chapter II as well as an enforcement machinery. The result was primarily the work of the Senator whose name it bore. He mobilized the draftsmen, devised the political strategy, and carried the brunt of the fight with the public, Congress, and the White House. His principal technical assistants were Keyserling, Magruder, and Levy. Although the Act was not an "Administration" measure, the depression and the New Deal combined to create a climate of opinion that made passage possible. This mood along with the fortuitous timing of the Schechter decision weakened the opposition in Congress. It has been said that the Act could have been passed at no other time.[54] Roosevelt—little interested in details and subject to conflicting pressures—added his support at the penultimate moment. The growing cleavage between the New Deal and business in the spring of 1935 joined with the decline of NRA to remove old inhibitions. The court's action left the President little alternative since 7(a) and the code labor standards were wiped out and he felt the need for a substitute.

---

[53] AFL, *Weekly News Service*, June 22, 1935; *New York Times*, June 28, July 6, 1935; *La Follette Comm. Hearings*, pt. 18, 7870; National Lawyers Committee of the American Liberty League, *Report on the Constitutionality of the National Labor Relations Act* (New York: 1935); *Baltimore Sun*, June 21, 1935.

[54] Leon H. Keyserling, "Why the Wagner Act?" *The Wagner Act: After Ten Years*, ed. by Louis G. Silverberg (Washington: 1945), pp. 5–6.

X. A NATIONAL LABOR POLICY

THIS CONCLUDING CHAPTER deals with four topics: first, a summary of this monograph; second, an analysis of the legislation in relation to the New Deal as a whole; third, an evaluation of the arguments advanced in behalf of and in opposition to the National Labor Relations Act; and finally, the consequences of the statutes as expressed in the development of collective bargaining and federal regulation.

SUMMARY

In a brief span of years, 1933–1935, a national collective bargaining policy was shaped in the National Labor Relations Act, in the 1934 amendments to the Railway Labor Act, and, momentarily, in the Bituminous Coal Conservation Act. A framework of basic ideas appeared in each: that workers shall be free to associate and select representatives for collective bargaining; that their employers shall not interfere in the exercise of these rights; that employees may elect their own representatives with the choice of the majority governing all; and, finally, that employers shall recognize and deal with these spokesmen. The emergence of this policy came in response to the conditions of the times.

Governmental intervention, spurned earlier by unions and industry alike, arose from the inability of workers to organize themselves or of unions to organize them. The latter, in fact, relapsed into stagnation in the decade of the twenties. The symptoms were declining membership, hesitant organizing, parochial leadership, unimpressive results at the bargaining table, and the rise of dual unions. The causes were the indifference or hostility of workers to unions, rising real wages, economic concentration, craft and jurisdictional restrictions of the organizations themselves, and, perhaps most important, the antiunion practices of management. The last were of two types: the indirect effects of "welfare capitalism" and the direct attacks upon unions by such devices as discrimination, injunctions, espionage, strikebreaking, and company unions. The Great Depression accentuated this secular tendency to decline. At the same time, however, it diminished the influence of businessmen, caused union leaders to turn their backs on voluntarism, and created an experimental political climate.

The new policy was, in fact, old, since the underlying principles had been repeatedly though fragmentarily expressed in prior official actions: in a line of court decisions beginning with *Commonwealth v. Hunt,* in the reports of industrial commissions, in the policies of the first National War Labor Board, and in the Clayton, Railway Labor, and Norris-LaGuardia Acts. Within the union movement the railway organizations

and the Mine Workers led the way in asking for government intervention in collective bargaining. There were special reasons in both cases:
the public utility character of transportation with consequent limitations on the right to strike and the disastrous economic condition of
the bituminous coal industry. The former rounded out the statutory
system of the 1926 Railway Labor Act in the Bankruptcy and Emergency
Railroad Transportation Acts of 1933, and, finally, in the 1934 amendments. After 1928 the miners urged federal regulation to permit producers to fix prices and allocate tonnage outside the antitrust laws with
a correlative guarantee to workers of the right to organize in order to
stabilize wages and hours. The AFL came more slowly to request governmental assistance, reaching this position in the spring of 1933. President Roosevelt and his key advisers were little interested in collective
bargaining and omitted it from their program on taking office. Senator
Wagner, on the other hand, provided the link between the unions and
the New Deal.

The policy emerged gradually from the hopes and eventual wreckage
of that monument of the "first" New Deal, NRA. Sec. 7(a), though hastily
written and distressingly ambiguous, stimulated workers to organize
into trade unions, while employers countered with company unions.
The National Labor Board, under Wagner's guidance, despite its immediate ineffectiveness, shaped a "common law" of collective bargaining.
These policies grew from a pragmatic case-by-case search for workable
answers to concrete questions. This experience took statutory form in
the 1934 Wagner bill, a measure laid to rest by the President's stopgap
improvisation, Public Resolution No. 44. It, in turn, provided for the
first National Labor Relations Board, which, though beset by the difficulties that undermined NLB, pricked out further lines of interpretation. The National Labor Relations bill, brought in by Wagner in 1935,
was the end product of this experience. Despite industry and press opposition, Wagner won the approval of Congress. The Supreme Court,
by knocking out NRA, ensured the President's support.

The key statutes of the New Deal policy, the 1934 amendments to
the Railway Labor Act, and the Wagner Act, incorporated the same
fundamental principles dealing with the establishment of collective
bargaining. The only difference in substance was over the closed shop,
the former outlawing and the latter permitting it. This divergence arose
basically from differing historical conditions and attitudes within the
union movement. Organizations such as the building and printing trades
and the miners never shared the indifference of the railway unions to
the closed shop and would undoubtedly have opposed the Wagner Act
if Senator Wagner had held Joseph Eastman's views.

THE NEW DEAL AND THE LEGISLATION

The New Deal at its inception was not a radical reform movement. Although the policies of the "first" New Deal were characterized by a willingness to experiment, the Administration sought no basic changes in the structure of the American economy. In fact, it worked within the viewpoint and framework of the business community. There are grounds for holding that both Congress and the public were prepared to go further. The policies of "The Hundred Days" following March 4, 1933, however, sought to promote recovery rather than reform: rehabilitation of the banks, the departure from gold, the Agricultural Adjustment Act, the Emergency Railroad Transportation Act, scuttling the London Economic Conference, and, above all, the National Industrial Recovery Act. The last, the Administration's basic measure, wrote the aspirations of businessmen into national policy.[1]

Only in light of this analysis can the relationship of the New Deal to its collective bargaining legislation be understood. Industry, of course, opposed an affirmative national policy in this area. The Administration therefore could not espouse the legislation so long as it sought to work through business and the NRA system to promote recovery. The insertion of Sec. 7(a) in the Act was, in fact, of secondary importance to the government and was largely to create the impression of balanced treatment of business and labor. One may speculate upon what Roosevelt's attitude would have been had he foreseen the implications of the provision for union organization and his Administration. Wagner and the unions did perceive the possibilities and expanded 7(a) into the National Labor Relations Act. Much the same can be said for Eastman and the railway organizations in their sector of the economy. A basic problem for Wagner, however, was to convince the President that he should release himself from the viewpoint of business.

For this the Supreme Court bore a large responsibility. Many factors contributed to the conversion of the New Deal from a recovery to a reform movement—from the "first" to the "second" New Deal—but perhaps as important as any was the role of the judiciary. The Schechter case, of course, was its climax. By raising a constitutional bar against moderate change, the court influenced Roosevelt to seek more far-reaching solutions. It is no coincidence that the most significant reform measures of the New Deal followed in the wake of the decision in the poultry case. The Wagner Act, moreover, might not have been passed at all in the absence of the court's action.

---

[1] Broadus Mitchell, *Depression Decade, from New Era through New Deal, 1929–1941* (New York: 1947), pp. 132–33.

An Evaluation of the Arguments

The arguments advanced in favor of and in opposition to the National Labor Relations Act during its legislative history were of unusual importance. The debate did not cease with its passage, but, in fact, continues to the present time. Hence it is appropriate to weigh the validity of the arguments in some detail. They will be considered in this order: the supporting position, the industry opposition, and the Communist attack.[2]

The proponents' first contention was that the principles of Sec. 7(a) of the Recovery Act were not effectuated because of the breakdown of enforcement. The purpose of 7(a) was to guarantee to workers "the right to organize and bargain collectively through representatives of their own choosing" without "the interference, restraint, or coercion of employers." As this monograph has demonstrated, this objective was not realized because the penalties for noncompliance were inadequate.[3] Many employers were indifferent to removal of the Blue Eagle, while the Department of Justice failed to obtain court enforcement. The result was that workers were unable to organize when a determined employer stood in the way. In those industries in which organization made substantial advances—coal, men's and women's clothing—unions already had sufficient strength to gain recognition with little direct assistance from 7(a). Industry, moreover, did not contend that the statute was properly enforced.

The second affirmative contention was that economic concentration produced an imbalance of bargaining power between employer and unorganized worker. At the outset of the Industrial Revolution, when small business units prevailed, Adam Smith observed,

It is not . . . difficult to foresee which of the two parties must, upon all ordinary occasions, have the advantage in the dispute, and force the other into a compliance with their terms. The masters, being few in number, can combine much more easily . . . [and] can hold out much longer. . . . Many workmen could not subsist a week, few could subsist a month, and scarce any a year without employment. In the long-run the workman may be as necessary to his master as his master is to him, but the necessity is not so immediate.[4]

This imbalance was magnified when the employer grew in size, as he did in the United States after the Civil War. By 1935, 0.1 per cent of

[2] The debate over NLRA is reported in full in chap. viii. Only the Wagner Act arguments will be evaluated here. The contentions with regard to the amendments to the Railway Labor Act will not be treated for these reasons: (1) many arguments overlapped; (2) carrier opposition has not continued; and (3) the railways present special problems.

[3] Cf. pp. 59–60, 62, 68, 87, 100 of this monograph.

[4] *The Wealth of Nations* (Modern Library ed.), p. 66.

the corporations reporting to the Bureau of Internal Revenue owned 52 per cent of the assets of all corporations.[5] A related concentration occurred in employment. A selective survey in 1933 revealed that 0.8 per cent of the firms in manufacturing employed 27 per cent of manufacturing wage earners.[6] To gain a voice in establishing the terms of their employment, therefore, workers were required to act in concert through a bargaining agency with sufficient power to deal with the large employer. This, in fact, is the conventional rationale for the trade union.[7]

The third argument was that the Wagner bill invoked no novel principles but was based on official precedents. The historic sources of the statute's substantive provisions have been demonstrated in Chapter II and do not require repetition. On the procedural side, the draftsmen, haunted by concern with a constitutional test, followed the processes of existing administrative agencies that the courts had approved. The Supreme Court, as will be shown in succeeding pages, gave weight to this fact in sustaining the validity of the Act.

The fourth argument was that the attainment of both long- and short-run prosperity required a higher level of wages and a more even distribution of the national income, and that collective bargaining would promote both these objectives. This contention will be examined in two parts: (1) that bargaining produces higher wages which promote prosperity and (2) that it removes inequalities of income distribution, thereby also fostering prosperity. It should be noted first that economists have more effectively raised than answered questions in this area, wage theory being one of the most controverted and cloudy fields of economics.

Whether collective bargaining can raise the wage share of the national income is a question on which the available evidence is inconclusive. A persuasive case, however, has been made for the view that unions increase the real wages of their members as contrasted with unorganized employees.[8] Even if one assumed that unions went beyond this to raise the segment of the national income going to all of labor, it would be hazardous to predict the general economic effects. It would be necessary to contrast the uncharted influence of wage changes on consumer purchasing power with their little-known effects on investment. A wage movement, furthermore, is integrated with other economic factors and its impact upon employment and investment is heavily conditioned by

---

[5] Cited in *Investigation of Concentration of Economic Power,* 77th Cong., 1st sess., Sen., Final Rep. and Recommendations of the TNEC (March 31, 1941), p. 11.

[6] *Big Business, Its Growth and Its Place,* Twentieth Century Fund (New York: 1937), pp. 3–4.

[7] Harry A. Millis and Royal E. Montgomery, *Organized Labor* (New York: 1945), chap. i; A. H. Frey, "The Logic of Collective Bargaining and Arbitration," *Law and Contemporary Problems,* XII (1947), 265–66.

[8] Arthur M. Ross, *Trade Union Wage Policy* (Berkeley: 1948), pp. 113–33.

such considerations as the phase of the business cycle, the extent of union organization, and the state of competition. The effect of a change, therefore, cannot be considered apart from the economic context in which it takes place.

Although other economists disagree, a leading student has concluded, "The most desirable behavior of the wage level . . . would probably be stability during recession and a moderate rate of increase during recovery, so that over the long run the wage level would rise at about the same rate as man-hour output."[9] His finding is that collective bargaining tends to stabilize the wage level during depression and to raise wages during recovery at a rate in excess of that of productivity. To the limited extent, therefore, that the wage level influences the cycle, one might conclude that bargaining tends to smooth out fluctuations, particularly during depressions. The probability, however, is that "wage policy by itself is not a sufficiently potent weapon to control cyclical unemployment in a significant way."[10]

The effects of collective bargaining upon the second problem, inequalities of income distribution, are similarly clouded. It is probable that wage increases gained through bargaining result in a shifting of real income to wage earners from the fixed income group, thereby reducing inequalities. At the same time, inequalities are created between unionized workers and the lowest level of nonunion employees. Economists generally agree that removing income inequalities through the mechanism of wage changes is less effective than through governmental tax and expenditure policies.[11] Even if it were granted that bargaining significantly influenced income distribution in the direction of equality, there is little evidence that this would have a desirable effect upon the business cycle. Many economists believe that underemployment can result from an excess of savings over investment. Available data indicate that the increase in consumer expenditures (lessened savings) resulting from income redistribution are small. "The conclusion is drawn that . . . too much emphasis should not be placed on income redistribution for the solution of the savings-investment problem."[12] There is the added risk in the case of a sharp redistribution of income, as Millis pointed out during the debates, that investment will be discouraged.

The fifth contention in favor of the bill was that the history of government intervention in collective bargaining on the railroads provided a test for the soundness of the principles of the Wagner bill. After half

---

[9] Lloyd G. Reynolds, *Labor Economics and Labor Relations* (New York: 1949), p. 430.

[10] Joseph Shister, *Economics of the Labor Market* (Philadelphia: 1949), p. 487.

[11] Reynolds, *op. cit.*, p. 430.

[12] Harold Lubell, "Effects of Redistribution of Income on Consumers' Expenditures," *American Economic Review*, XXXVII (1947), 157.

a century of controversy the railway unions, carriers, and government evolved a solution to the right to organize and bargain in the Railway Labor Act as amended. Harry D. Wolf, a leading authority, has written,

> Collective bargaining on the railroads has reached a greater maturity and wider acceptance than in almost any other American industry. . . .
> Collective bargaining for them [the railroad unions and carriers] has passed through its period of "growing pains." The two sides have long lived together and each understands and respects the other pretty thoroughly.[13]

It was, accordingly, sensible of the draftsmen of NLRA to turn to a working statute and experienced administrators for assistance. The Supreme Court, as well, in sustaining the Wagner Act, turned to the railway legislation and cases for precedents.[14] Although there are special considerations that distinguish labor relations on the railroads, they do not explain the effectiveness of those provisions of the Railway Labor Act that deal with the right to organize and bargain, as the bitter historic struggle over recognition in this industry attests. This success resulted from gradual carrier acceptance of bargaining combined with the workability of the Act.

The sixth contention was that business unionism was a bulwark against Communism and therefore a means of supporting the existing system. Collective bargaining would redress grievances and thereby deflect workers from seeking to overthrow the social order. The history of the union movement in the United States supports this analysis. Selig Perlman has observed,

> Trade unionism despite an occasional revolutionary facet and despite a revolutionary clamor especially on its fringes, is a conservative social force. Trade unionism seems to have the same moderating effect upon society as a wide diffusion of private property. In fact, the gains of trade unionism are to the worker on a par with private property to its owner. . . .
> In practice . . . the trade union movements in nearly all nations have served as brakes upon the national socialist movements; and from the standpoint of society interested in its own preservation against catastrophic change, have played and are playing a role of society's policemen and watchdogs over the more revolutionary groups in the wage-earning class. . . .
> The hope of American Bolshevism will . . . continue to rest with the will of employers to rule as autocrats.[15]

David Dubinsky, who began his union career as a revolutionary Marxist, recently remarked that "trade unionism needs capitalism like a fish

---

[13] Twentieth Century Fund, *How Collective Bargaining Works* (New York: 1945), pp. 318, 374.

[14] *NLRB v. Jones & Laughlin Steel Corp.* (1937), 301 U.S. 1.

[15] *A History of Trade Unionism in the United States* (New York: 1922), pp. 303–06.

needs water."[16] Moreover, it is doubtful whether collective bargaining can exist under a Communist system. It is certainly implausible to describe the Soviet organizations as trade unions or to consider their behavior as collective bargaining in the Western sense.[17]

The seventh argument was that company-dominated unions were inadequate instruments of collective bargaining. These organizations had pronounced shortcomings, including the following: workers were denied the right to vote for a trade union in a free contest with a company union; management retained the power to fix wages, hours, and working conditions; relations between company unions and employers did not result in written agreements; company union officers, themselves employees, had no outside assistance in formulating and executing policy; the organizations did not enjoy the right to strike; and employers often wrote their constitutions and bylaws and paid the salaries of officers. Hence, it is clear that "most company unions have been organized and operated for the purpose of coöperating, not bargaining, with management."[18] Workers recognized these weaknesses by giving large majorities to trade unions over dominated organizations in free labor board elections, while many company unions collapsed following the passage of the Wagner Act.[19] The Supreme Court, as well, has recognized that company unions are unsatisfactory bargaining agencies. In unanimously sustaining the invalidation of such an organization, the court held,

> It has long been recognized that employees are entitled to organize for the purpose of securing the redress of grievances and to promote agreements with employers relating to rates of pay and conditions of work. . . . Such collective action would be a mockery if representation were made futile by interferences with freedom of choice.[20]

The eighth argument in support of the bill was to favor majority rule over proportional representation in selecting bargaining agents in board elections. Defense of the majority rule is at bottom pragmatic; sponsors of democratic institutions have learned by experience that it is a work-

---

[16] Benjamin Stolberg, *Tailor's Progress* (New York: 1944), p. 197. Cf. also G. W. Taylor, "The Function of Collective Bargaining," American Management Assn., *Personnel Series*, No. 81, 4–5.

[17] Morris L. Weisberg, "The Transformation of the Collective Agreement in Soviet Law," *Chicago Law Review*, XVI (1949), 444–81.

[18] Millis and Montgomery, *op. cit.*, p. 883.

[19] *Ibid.*, p. 853; Robert R. R. Brooks, *As Steel Goes, . . . Unionism in a Basic Industry* (New Haven: 1940), chap. iv.

[20] *Texas & New Orleans R. R. Co., v. Brotherhood of Railway and Steamship Clerks* (1930), 281 U.S. 548. The court has ruled that "we cannot ignore the judgment of Congress, deliberately expressed in legislation, that where the obstruction of the company union is removed, the meeting of employers and employees at the conference table is a powerful aid to industrial peace." *Virginian Ry. Co. v. System Federation No. 40* (1937), 300 U.S. 515. Cf. also *NLRB v. Pennsylvania Greyhound Lines* (1938), 303 U.S. 261.

able principle for decision-making. Hence its use is widespread in government, industry, unions, and social organizations. Its practical advantages over proportional representation in determining bargaining representatives are clear. The latter, by permitting splinter units, would foster jurisdictional controversies between unions and give the willing employer a lever in playing factions off one against the other. Either result would produce instability, which is not a purpose of collective bargaining.

This instability can be demonstrated by example. Assume a manufacturing plant with one hundred employees who divided in a representation election, fifty voting for the AFL union, thirty for an independent union, and twenty for no union. Each union then negotiates a contract with the employer for its own members. The AFL agreement provides for departmental seniority, the independent contract for plant-wide seniority, and the unaffiliated employees, of course, have no agreement. Business declines and the employer decides to lay off thirty workers. There is no uniform layoff rule he can adopt without discrimination, contract violation, and unstabilizing results. From his viewpoint, in fact, proportional representation makes sense only as a means of preventing unionization. Once bargaining begins, its presence invites disorder. The Taft-Hartley Act, it is worth noting, carries over the majority principle of NLRA.

Majority rule is a two-edged blade that cuts impartially. Unions find it advantageous when they enjoy majorities, but are denied bargaining rights when they win large minorities. Frances Perkins was surprised at AFL endorsement of the Wagner bill since many unions had earlier gained bargaining rights when fewer than a majority were enrolled.[21]

The Supreme Court has sustained the majority rule and its consequence, the exclusive right of the majority agent to represent all the employees in the unit, under both the Wagner and Railway Labor Acts. The court has held,

> The workman is free, if he values his own bargaining position more than that of the group, to vote against representation; but the majority rules, and if it collectivizes the employment bargain, individual advantages or favors will generally in practice go in as a contribution to the collective result.[22]

Majority rule, of course, entails a loss of some minority rights. Groups that favor a minority union or minorities that prefer no union are sad-

[21] *The Roosevelt I Knew* (New York: 1946), pp. 243–44.
[22] *J. I. Case Co. v. NLRB* (1944), 321 U.S. 332. Cf. also *Medo Photo Supply Corp. v. NLRB* (1944), 321 U.S. 678; *Order of Railroad Telegraphers v. Railway Express Agency, Inc.* (1944), 321 U.S. 342; *Virginian Ry. Co. v. System Federation No. 40* (1937), 300 U.S. 515.

dled with the majority bargaining agent. By the same token, citizens who vote for an unsuccessful Democratic candidate for Congress must accept representation by a victorious Republican. This is the expedient cost of a workable democratic system.

The ninth affirmative argument was that the right of employees to organize and bargain was sterile without a reciprocal obligation upon the employer to bargain with their representatives once selected. It will be recalled that the proponents of the bill unanimously supported this view as a general policy, but that some doubted the wisdom of its explicit incorporation in the statute. Each position will be discussed in turn.

The general proposition is clearly necessary for bargaining to exist at all. By definition collective bargaining, like any contractual relationship, entails a mutuality of obligation for agreement to be reached. To argue that the employer (or the union) may at will refrain from bargaining is to negate the process, to argue by analogy for a marital system in which only women and not men proceed to the altar. If the policy of the United States, as both the Wagner and Taft-Hartley Acts declare, is to encourage "the practice and procedure of collective bargaining," the conclusion is inescapable that employers and unions alike must bargain in good faith. The NLRA, in fact, would have been an empty shell in the absence of this assumption. Why prevent employers from interfering with the self-organization of their employees if they need not engage in bargaining? The duty to bargain gave the negative prohibitions of the Act (the unfair practices) an affirmative purpose. The Supreme Court has accepted this analysis, holding,

> Experience has abundantly demonstrated that the recognition of the right of employees to self-organization and to have representatives of their own choosing for the purpose of collective bargaining is often an essential condition of industrial peace. Refusal to confer and negotiate has been one of the most prolific causes of strife. This is such an outstanding fact in the history of labor disturbances that it is a proper subject of judicial notice and requires no citation of instances.[23]

Judging the wisdom of incorporating Sec. 8(5) in the statute presents difficulties, since there is a good deal to be said on each side. The language of 8(5) was so general as to leave many fundamental questions undetermined: Must a contract be reached? Must it be reduced to writing? Must it be for a definite term? This provision, moreover, on a limited scale injected NLRB into the conduct of bargaining as distinguished from its establishment. A union, for example, might regard an employer's rejection of a contract demand as refusal to bargain and file a

---

[23] *NLRB v. Jones & Laughlin Steel Corp.* (1937), 301 U.S. 1. Cf. also *Virginian Ry. Co. v. System Federation No. 40* (1937), 300 U.S. 515; *H. J. Heinz Co. v. NLRB* (1941), 311 U.S. 514

charge with the board, employing the agency as a negotiating lever. Further, 8(5), as pointed out below, gave substance to the "one-sidedness" attack on the Act since it imposed an affirmative obligation upon employers without a correlative duty for unions. On the other side, however, the basic argument was that a statutory requirement was needed to push the reluctant employer into actual negotiations. Although the law might deny him the use of espionage and strikebreakers and might protect his employees in forming a union, how could he be required to bargain in the absence of 8(5)? The Taft-Hartley Act, moreover, continued the duty to bargain, making it bilateral.[24] There is, unfortunately, no experience upon which to judge whether the board and the courts could have enforced the duty to bargain without 8(5). Hence there is no solid basis for deciding whether its explicit statement was wise.

The tenth argument was that the bill would not impose the closed shop. The statute did not require employers or employees to accept any form of union security. The purpose of the proviso to Sec. 8(3) was to forestall an interpretation that 8(3) itself outlawed the closed shop. The proviso was inserted because industry had so interpreted Sec. 7(a) of the Recovery Act. The Supreme Court, furthermore, has held, "The Act does not interfere with the normal exercise of the right of the employer to select its employees or to discharge them."[25] On the other hand, the statute, as will be developed below, encouraged unionism and collective bargaining. Since a cardinal aim of most American labor organizations is union security, the period following 1935 witnessed a marked increase in the number of contracts in which employers and unions voluntarily agreed to the closed shop or one of its variants. By 1946, of the 14.8 million workers covered by agreements, over 11 million worked under some form of union security.[26] An indirect result of the passage of the Act, therefore, was to encourage the spread of the closed shop.

The eleventh and final supporting argument was a defense of the National Labor Relations Act's constitutionality. Since the reverse was the leading objection, it is treated immediately following.

We turn, then, to industry's attack on the bill. The first argument,

---

[24] Prof. G. W. Taylor has declared, "I am very much disturbed about this notion that . . . we have got to make 8(5) bilateral. Granting that it is one-sided as it stands, its purpose in the Wagner Act ties back into organization, not ahead into real collective bargaining, and I for one feel that between making it bilateral and dropping it, I would drop it. . . . It is something like a protective tariff to help an infant industry that isn't an infant any more." Conference on the Training of Law Students in Labor Relations (mimeo., University of Michigan, June 16–26, 1947), I, 26.

[25] *NLRB v. Jones & Laughlin Steel Corp.* (1937), 301 U.S. 1.

[26] *Union-Security Provisions in Collective Bargaining,* Bureau of Labor Statistics, Bull. No. 908, p. 6.

and the one lent greatest weight by its sponsors, was that the measure was unconstitutional. It was advanced on two counts, first, that Congress was without broad authority to regulate labor relations under the commerce clause, and second, that the bill unconstitutionally deprived employers of several fundamental rights. These objections faced their acid test before the Supreme Court in the great cases handed down in April, 1937, and it is to those decisions that we must turn for authority.

A majority of the court in the Jones & Laughlin case rejected the industry argument on commerce.

> The grant of authority to the Board . . . purports to reach only what may be deemed to burden or obstruct . . . commerce and, thus qualified, it must be construed as contemplating the exercise of control within constitutional grounds. It is a familiar principle that acts which directly burden or obstruct interstate or foreign commerce, or its free flow, are within the reach of the congressional power. Acts having that effect are not rendered immune because they grow out of labor disputes. . . . It is the effect upon commerce, not the source of the injury which is criterior.

The court in the same case disposed of the argument that manufacturing was not commerce and hence not subject to federal regulation as follows:

> Giving full weight to respondent's contention with respect to a break in the complete continuity of the "stream of commerce" by reason of respondent's manufacturing operations, the fact remains that the stoppage of those operations by industrial strife would have a most serious effect upon interstate commerce. In view of respondent's far-flung activities, it is idle to say that the effect would be indirect or remote. It is obvious that it would be immediate and might be catastrophic. . . .
>
> The steel industry is one of the great basic industries of the United States, with ramifying activities affecting interstate commerce at every point. . . . We think that it presents in a most striking way the close and intimate relation which a manufacturing industry may have to interstate commerce and we have no doubt that Congress had constitutional authority to safeguard the right of respondent's employees to self-organization and freedom in the choice of representatives for collective bargaining.[27]

The court summarily disposed of the objections based on other constitutional rights. In the Associated Press case the tribunal, by reliance on the Railway Clerks decision, rejected the AP's argument that the Act deprived it of due process of law. With respect to the validity of NLRB procedures, the court in the Jones & Laughlin case ruled:

[27] *NLRB v. Jones & Laughlin Steel Corp.* (1937), 301 U.S. 1. At the same time the court found that a clothing manufacturer, an automobile trailer builder, and a press association were also in commerce. *NLRB v. Friedman-Harry Marks Co.* (1937), 301 U.S. 58; *NLRB v. Fruehauf Trailer Co.* (1937), 301 U.S. 49; *Associated Press v. NLRB* (1937), 301 U.S. 103. In the case of an avowed instrumentality of commerce, an interstate bus company, the court simply relied on the Railway Clerks and Virginian cases sustaining the Railway Labor Act. *Washington, Virginia & Maryland Coach Co. v. NLRB* (1937), 301 U.S. 142.

These provisions, as we construe them, do not offend against the constitutional requirements governing the creation and action of administrative bodies. . . . We construe the procedural provisions as affording adequate opportunity to secure judicial protection against arbitrary action in accordance with the well-settled rules applicable to administrative agencies set up by Congress to aid in the enforcement of valid legislation.

The steel company also argued that the NLRB directive to reinstate with back pay discriminatorily discharged employees deprived it of the right to trial by jury in the face of the Seventh Amendment. On this the court held,

Reinstatement of the employee and payment for time lost are requirements imposed for violation of the statute and are remedies appropriate to its enforcement. The contention under the Seventh Amendment is without merit.

Finally, the AP contended that Congressional regulation over the editorial employees of a news-gathering agency was an abridgement of freedom of the press in violation of the First Amendment. The court, however, ruled,

We hold the contention not only has no relevance to the circumstances of the instant case but is an unsound generalization. . . . The regulation here in question has no relation whatever to the impartial distribution of news.

In conclusion, the cases handed down by the Supreme Court in 1937 were a sweeping victory for the Act's draftsmen. Although the constitutional objections of industry failed to meet this decisive test, it would be unfair to dismiss them as totally lacking in merit. The argument on commerce was certainly one on which reasonable and disinterested men disagreed during the bill's legislative history. The court, in fact, divided five to four and several lower courts foreshadowed the minority view. The other group of arguments, however, had little or no validity.

The second industry contention was that NLRB procedures were arbitrary, depriving employers of rights not constitutional in origin. This criticism was to crop up repeatedly after 1935 in legislative proposals designed to restrict the agency. An exhaustive investigation of its merit concluded as follows: "One may conservatively insist . . . that the Board has made a largely successful effort to perform a difficult assignment by a procedure which, while minimizing the chance of mistake, fully preserves the basic values of traditional judicial processes."[28] Since the draftsmen carried over the procedures of existing agencies that had been sustained by the courts, NLRB processes were virtually identi-

[28] Walter Gellhorn and Seymour L. Linfield, "Politics and Labor Relations: an Appraisal of Criticisms of NLRB Procedure," *Columbia Law Review*, XXXIX (1939), 395.

cal with those of the other agencies. Hence the argument was at bottom an attack on the administrative process itself. A careful study by the Brookings Institution substantiated this view and concluded,

> To the contention that large fields of public policy are dominated and controlled by the regulatory boards and commissions, the answer is that they should be. Legislative matters as to transportation, communication, shipping, public waters, labor relations, and the like, are of such a nature as to require consistent, flexible, informed, intelligent, and developing administration over long periods of time.[29]

The third industry contention was that there was no need for the bill since Sec. 7(a) of NIRA and Public Resolution No. 44 adequately covered the law of collective bargaining. As this study as a whole has demonstrated, 7(a) and the Resolution were ambiguous, ineffective, and unenforceable against a determined employer. Further, they were due to expire with the Recovery Act in 1935, and actually were swept aside by the Schechter decision. The purpose of this argument was probably to delay Congressional action until the court had acted in the NRA case. Hence, there is no reason to lend it weight in retrospect.

The fourth argument was that the bill assumed an unalterable conflict between employer and employee, while, in fact, they had an identity of interest. The NLRA, of course, rested on the assumption that labor-management differences exist, but it certainly did not regard them as irreconcilable. The concrete conditions of industrialism create such disagreements without respect to the presence or absence of collective bargaining. In both circumstances symptoms of unrest occur: labor turnover, absenteeism, low productivity, industrial accidents, strikes, and lockouts. Although the worker and the employer share a basic aim, perpetuation of the enterprise, they have many areas of real difference. Under the pressure of competition, for example, the employer may prefer a lower wage, while the worker, faced with family needs, may desire a higher one. As Professor Benjamin M. Selekman has observed, "Industrial conflict is . . . a characteristic, rather than a catastrophic, aspect of human relations."[30] Recognition that such conflict exists does not inevitably lead to the conclusion that there must be class warfare in the Marxist sense. The Wagner Act, in fact, rested its faith in collective bargaining as an alternative to this extreme position. Its sponsors believed that through bargaining, free trade unions and free employers together could establish procedures for resolving their differences.[31]

---

[29] Frederick F. Blachly and Miriam E. Oatman, *Federal Regulatory Action and Control* (Washington: 1940), p. 171.

[30] *Labor Relations and Human Relations* (New York: 1947), p. 216.

[31] This position has been perceptively stated by Professor Harry Shulman in an arbitration under the Ford-UAW contract: "In any industrial plant, whatever may

The fifth industry argument was that the bill would cause strikes and thereby hamper recovery. The effect of the Act upon the volume of strikes will be discussed first, with the economic impact following. The Wagner Act, emphasizing the establishment rather than the conduct of bargaining, was intended to reduce the number of stoppages over union recognition and not to dispose of all causes of strikes.[32] The direct effect of the Act on the national strike-load is suggested by the BLS series on work stoppages caused by "union organization." The table (p. 144) compares such stoppages with all work stoppages for the years 1927–1947 by number and by number of workers involved.[33]

These statistics suggest two conclusions: first, that the half decade following passage of the Act witnessed a marked rise in the proportion of stoppages over "union recognition" as compared with both the late twenties and the early years of the Great Depression; and second, that the period between 1939 and the enactment of the Taft-Hartley Act revealed a sharp decline in the relative incidence of such stoppages to a level below that prevailing prior to passage of the Wagner Act.

---

be the form of the political or economic organization in which it exists, problems are bound to arise as to the method of making promotions, the assignment of tasks to individuals, the choice of shifts, the maintenance of discipline, the rates of production and remuneration, and the various other matters which are handled through the grievance procedure.

"These are not incidents peculiar to private enterprise. They are incidents of human organization in any form of society. On a lesser scale, similar problems exist in every family: who shall do the dishes, who shall mow the lawn, where to go on a Sunday, what movie to see, what is a reasonable spending allowance for husband or daughter, how much to pay for a new hat, and so on. The operation of the Union itself presents problems requiring adjustment quite similar to those involved in the operation of the Company. . . . Such 'disputes' are not necessarily evils. They are the normal characteristics of human society which both arise from, and create the occasion for the exercise of human intelligence. And the grievance procedure is the orderly, effective and democratic way of adjusting such disputes within the framework of the collective labor agreement. It is the substitute of civilized collective bargaining for jungle warfare." Harry Shulman and Neil W. Chamberlain, *Cases on Labor Relations* (Brooklyn: 1949), p. 45.

[32] Sec. 1 of the Act declared, "Experience has proved that protection by law of the right of employees to organize and bargain collectively safeguards commerce . . . by removing *certain recognized* sources of industrial strife. . . . It is hereby declared to be the policy of the United States to eliminate the causes of *certain substantial* obstructions to the free flow of commerce. . . ." [Italics mine.] Cf. also President Roosevelt's remarks on page 127.

[33] *Strikes in the United States, 1880–1936*, Bureau of Labor Statistics, Bull. No. 651, pp. 62–63, and *Handbook of Labor Statistics, 1947 Edition*, Bull. No. 916, p. 138. This series does not perfectly test the effectiveness of the Act. BLS defined "union organization" to include recognition; recognition and wages; recognition and hours; recognition, wages, and hours; closed shop; discrimination; and others. Hence some stoppages were included whose major cause was not recognition. In addition, NLRA applied only to industries in commerce, while the statistics include intrastate stoppages as well.

The historical bases for these tendencies are reasonably clear. The struggle for recognition was most intense in the period 1935–1939. The formation of the CIO, the invigoration of the AFL, the stimulus of the statute, and improved business conditions prior to 1938 combined to spur union organization. At the same time, employers were then more prone to resist than later and, in fact, for two years many flouted NLRA

Year	Work stoppages, per cent of total	Workers involved, per cent of total
1927	36.0	13.9
1928	36.5	29.5
1929	41.3	35.5
1930	31.8	41.7
1931	27.8	33.6
1932	19.0	22.4
1933	31.9	40.7
1934	45.9	51.5
1935	47.2	26.1
1936	50.2	51.4
1937	57.8	59.8
1938	50.0	32.6
1939	53.5	54.4
1940	49.9	33.1
1941	49.5	31.5
1942	31.2	22.4
1943	15.7	11.5
1944	16.3	18.6
1945	20.5	21.8
1946	32.4	11.5
1947	29.8	43.0

on the assumption that it would be invalidated. As a consequence workers were often compelled to resort to strikes rather than to the board to win recognition for their unions. The Act unquestionably was an influence in producing these stoppages, but it would hardly be fair to regard it as solely or even principally responsible. If employers had consented to work with its procedures, there would have been little need for these strikes. Such compliance, as a matter of fact, actually took effect after 1939. Many key organizational struggles were concluded, while employers increasingly accepted the NLRB. As a result the proportion of recognition strikes declined markedly. World War II undoubtedly speeded this development, but the trend does not seem to have been significantly reversed with its conclusion. The great wave of strikes following VJ-Day involved conditions of employment, primarily wages, rather than union organization.[34]

The indirect effects of the Act upon strikes as a whole are impossible to measure statistically. Roughly speaking, the national strike-load in the years after 1935 approximated that of the period during and immediately following World War I and substantially exceeded that of the twenties and early thirties. The historical causes are so diverse as to defy precise attribution to NLRA. This much can be said: The Act stimulated the expansion of unions and more strikes occur in their presence than in their absence. To the extent that there were more strikes after 1935 than in the preceding decade the statute may be held partly responsible, though it is not possible to estimate the degree of its responsibility.[35]

We may conclude that evaluating the effect of the Act upon strikes presents formidable statistical difficulties. In the direct and more measurable area the industry argument probably had merit in the short run and was unsupported in the more significant long run. With respect to indirect effects it is inadvisable to hazard a conclusion beyond the generality that the statute was one among several influences contributing to a larger volume of strikes than in the immediately preceding period.

We turn, then, to the argument that strikes have damaging economic effects. The problems of measurement encountered above are here compounded since there are no statistics upon which to base an evaluation. While a prolonged strike in a vital industry can affect the economy in the immediate sense, it would be sheer speculation to point out the long-run effects of strikes upon such factors as production and employment. Most labor economists, for example, would agree that even the costs of strikes cannot be measured.[36] There is, therefore, no basis upon which either to accept or reject this contention.

The sixth industry argument was that the bill would create a "monopoly" for the AFL. In 1946, according to BLS, 48 per cent of workers eligible for union coverage actually worked under collective bargaining agreements. In other words, a majority remained unorganized a decade after passage of the Act. Further, of the 15,414,000 union members in 1947, only 7,578,000 were affiliated with AFL, while 6,000,000 were mem-

[34] *Eleventh Annual Report of the National Labor Relations Board, 1946* (Washington: 1947), p. 1.

[35] D. O. Bowman, *Public Control of Labor Relations* (New York: 1942), pp. 433–44.

[36] In this connection Professor Edwin E. Witte has noted, "The years of great coal strikes have generally been years in which the coal miners worked an unusually large number of days. With an average of below two hundred days of work in the bituminous fields per year, the miners can strike for nearly a hundred days and yet work and earn as much during the year as when they do not strike." *The Government in Labor Disputes* (New York: 1932), p. 2.

bers of CIO unions and 1,836,000 of independent organizations.[37] Hence the contention was without merit.

The seventh argument, that the bill would impose and foster the closed shop, has already been considered.

The eighth argument was that the bill was "one-sided," imposing responsibilities upon employers without corresponding duties for unions. On its face this criticism appears reasonable since the unfair practices applied only to employers. The argument, however, must be examined within its economic context. Employers were free to form partnerships, corporations, and associations which had among their purposes the conduct of relationships with employees. The case in which workers or unions denied employers the right so to associate was virtually non-existent. As was shown in Chapter I, on the other hand, employers frequently intervened to deny correlative rights to their employees. Hence the source of the difficulty lay in the employer rather than in the worker or union. The only unfair practice that in part sustained the charge was the fifth, the duty to bargain, since it could be interpreted to go beyond the narrow question of association. Here again, as a practical matter, the case of the union that refuses to bargain is rare since the fundamental purpose of the union is to engage in bargaining. Apparent "one-sidedness," by analogy, is characteristic of many statutes in which the source of the difficulty is itself unilateral. Traffic laws regulating the speed of automobiles, for example, do not prescribe the speed at which pedestrians shall walk. Realistically considered, therefore, the one-sidedness argument had little validity with respect to the problems with which the Act dealt when it took effect. The criticism, however, acquired some merit with the passage of time. The Act restricted only employer activities and did not regulate union behavior. As labor organizations gained in power under its protection, their acts affected an ever-widening area, sometimes with undesirable effects upon workers, employers, and the public. This analysis suggests that the Wagner Act required amendment, if not alteration, to meet new conditions.

The ninth industry argument was a defense of the company union as an effective and fair instrument for conducting relations between employers and employees. The character of the company union has been described and there is no need for repetition. It may be significant that the Taft-Hartley Act, though imposing many restrictions upon trade unions, did not legalize company-dominated organizations.

The tenth contention was an attack on the majority rule for depriving minorities of rights. Here again the issue has been discussed above.

We now turn to the Communist attack on the bill, in essence an

---

[37] Bureau of Labor Statistics, Bull. No. 916, *op. cit.,* pp. 130, 133.

expression of the fear that the NLRB would become an instrument for capitalist suppression of the working class. In light of the growth of unionism since 1935 and the vigorous opposition of business to the Act and its administration this argument cannot be considered seriously. The contentions that the bill would outlaw strikes, establish compulsory arbitration, and foster company unions have no foundation whatever. The insincerity of these views was revealed after passage of the statute when the party line was reversed and firmly supported both the law and the board.[38] There is, accordingly, no reason to lend weight to the Communist Party's argument against the bill.

From the foregoing analysis it is clear that the supporters of the National Labor Relations bill had a stronger total argument than its industry opponents. The disparity between the two positions, however, tended to narrow somewhat with the passage of time as the Act succeeded increasingly in accomplishing its purposes. One may conclude that the statute had an historical function to fulfill. The Communist position, on the other hand, may be dismissed as having no merit.

The National Labor Relations bill, enacted in face of opposition from business and the press (thirty of thirty-six commenting newspapers), won support in large part because it drew upon deeply rooted democratic sources. Behind it lay a groundwork of political theory stemming from the eighteenth century Enlightenment, democratic standards against which to measure new conditions. In essence these ideas stated that citizens were entitled to representatives of their own choosing, that democratic secret ballot elections under universal suffrage with majority rule were the best means of selection, and that concentration of power was potentially dangerous. In the last the concept of checks and balances migrated from the political to the economic area. In modern times the concentration of wealth, and so of power, became the locus of concern and the legislation sought to polarize society in order to create an equilibrium. This concept, of course, was the antithesis of a monolithic system, whether Marxian or fascist.

The other side of the coin was that industry's position was weakened, since its spokesmen could not openly place themselves in opposition to these democratic ideas. As a consequence much of the industry appeal was not to reason but to fear symbols such as "monopoly," "closed shop," "arbitrary procedures." As Thurman Arnold has observed, "In the conflict to recognize collective bargaining, it was difficult indeed for any responsible conservative to treat the situation realistically," since the

---

[38] Cf., for example, the testimony of the left-wing United Electrical Workers on the Taft-Hartley bill. *Amendments to the National Labor Relations Act*, 80th Cong., 1st sess., H.R., Hearings before Comm. on Edu. and Labor (March, 1947), V, 3517 ff.

issue to him was one of faith. "Until this religious problem was solved, the real problem had to be ignored."[39]

The bitterness of the argument, unfortunately, left deep scars that were seriously to impair the administration of the Act. If collective bargaining is anything it is pragmatic. One cannot argue a difference of three cents an hour in wages in metaphysical absolutes. Yet the hardening of position on both sides during the legislative history served to promote this result.

THE CONSEQUENCES OF THE LEGISLATION

The period following the passage of the New Deal collective bargaining legislation witnessed fundamental changes in the labor affairs of the nation. Union membership spurted from approximately three million in 1933 to almost fifteen and one-half million in 1947. Collective bargaining became the accepted procedure for determining the wages, hours, and working conditions of roughly half of that part of the labor force which unions sought to organize. Many unaffiliated employees, as well, felt the impact of events in the bargained area. There are about one hundred thousand collectively bargained agreements, while grievance procedures and arbitration have generally been accepted for their administration. At the same time, union influence has grown correspondingly in political and social life.

The National Labor Relations Act and the Railway Labor Act laid the legal foundations for this expansion. The legislation served both as a stimulus to organization and as a shield against interference with its achievement. This is not to say that the statutes alone were responsible for the development, for their effect was indirect rather than compulsory. The slow recovery of business after 1933 played a role, while the economic expansion accompanying World War II lent generous assistance. The creation of the CIO, leading to unionization of the mass production industries, was another factor, while rival unionism roused the AFL to greater vigor.

Federal intervention, however, exacted a price for this accretion in the size and power of unions: regulation. Even the Wagner Act, written with care to side-step interference in the structure and conduct of labor organizations, impinged on their affairs. The NLRB was to exert such control in determining the appropriate unit, deciding the conditions under which elections would be held, stipulating the form of the ballot, and implementing majority rule. The soul-searching of the AFL Executive Council in 1935 was evidence that the union leaders themselves recognized the risks.

[39] *The Folklore of Capitalism* (New Haven: 1937), p. 88.

The words of Harry Millis carried this ring when he wrote President Roosevelt that the Wagner Act is "not a complete labor code. In the long run it will need to be amended in the light of experience."[40] Experience revealed that government assistance in time converted itself into control in the public interest. The railways received grants of land to encourage their development and their activities were eventually subjected to broad regulation; power companies, street railways, water works, and gas companies won monopoly charters and subsequently suffered the same fate. Once the first step was taken the issue was transformed: "It is no longer a question as to whether the state will intervene, but rather what form of intervention the state shall take."[41]

In the collective bargaining area the cycle of federal intervention—from assistance to regulation—has been telescoped into a short period, a scant twelve years separating the birth dates of the Wagner and Taft-Hartley Acts. The fundamental issue of policy in 1935, whether the government should step in, has been resolved, liberals and conservatives alike being in agreement here.[42] The permanent shape of that regulation, however, is a major challenge to the wisdom and imagination of the nation for it raises one of the most important and bitterly controverted issues of the times.

---

[40] July 21, 1935, White House, O.F. No. 716, NLRB. Chief Justice Hughes observed in this connection that "the Constitution does not forbid 'cautious advance step by step,' in dealing with the evils which are exhibited in activities within the range of legislative power." *NLRB v. Jones & Laughlin Steel Corp.* (1937), 301 U.S. 1.

[41] Bowman, *op. cit.*, p. 470.

[42] In the Senate debate over the Taft-Hartley bill only Senator George W. Malone (R., Nev.) took a consistently conservative position. He supported President Truman's veto on the ground that "the solution does not lie in superimposing another layer of complicated Federal law and machinery on top of an act which itself should be repealed." His words fell on deaf ears. *Cong. Record*, XCIII, No. 119 (daily ed.), June 23, 1947, pp. 7680–81.

APPENDIX:

NATIONAL LABOR RELATIONS ACT

APPENDIX

NATIONAL LABOR RELATIONS ACT

FINDINGS AND POLICY

Section 1. The denial by employers of the right of employees to organize and the refusal by employers to accept the procedure of collective bargaining lead to strikes and other forms of industrial strife or unrest, which have the intent or the necessary effect of burdening or obstructing commerce by (a) impairing the efficiency, safety, or operation of the instrumentalities of commerce; (b) occurring in the current of commerce; (c) materially affecting, restraining, or controlling the flow of raw materials or manufactured or processed goods from or into the channels of commerce, or the prices of such materials or goods in commerce; or (d) causing diminution of employment and wages in such volume as substantially to impair or disrupt the market for goods flowing from or into the channels of commerce.

The inequality of bargaining power between employees who do not possess full freedom of association or actual liberty of contract, and employers who are organized in the corporate or other forms of ownership association substantially burdens and affects the flow of commerce, and tends to aggravate recurrent business depressions, by depressing wage rates and the purchasing power of wage earners in industry and by preventing the stabilization of competitive wage rates and working conditions within and between industries.

Experience has proved that protection by law of the right of employees to organize and bargain collectively safeguards commerce from injury, impairment, or interruption, and promotes the flow of commerce by removing certain recognized sources of industrial strife and unrest, by encouraging practices fundamental to the friendly adjustment of industrial disputes arising out of differences as to wages, hours, or other working conditions, and by restoring equality of bargaining power between employers and employees.

It is hereby declared to be the policy of the United States to eliminate the causes of certain substantial obstructions to the free flow of commerce and to mitigate and eliminate these obstructions when they have occurred by encouraging the practice and procedure of collective bargaining and by protecting the exercise by workers of full freedom of association, self-organization, and designation of representatives of their own choosing, for the purpose of negotiating the terms and conditions of their employment or other mutual aid or protection.

DEFINITIONS

Sec. 2. When used in this Act—

(1) The term "person" includes one or more individuals, partnerships, associations, corporations, legal representatives, trustees, trustees in bankruptcy, or receivers.

(2) The term "employer" includes any person acting in the interest of an employer, directly or indirectly, but shall not include the United States, or any State or political subdivision thereof, or any person subject to the Railway Labor Act, as amended from time to time, or any labor organization (other than when acting as an employer), or anyone acting in the capacity of officer or agent of such labor organization.

(3) The term "employee" shall include any employee, and shall not be limited to the employees of a particular employer, unless the Act explicitly states otherwise, and shall include any individual whose work has ceased as a consequence of, or in connection with, any current labor dispute or because of any unfair labor practice, and

who has not obtained any other regular and substantially equivalent employment, but shall not include any individual employed as an agricultural laborer, or in the domestic service of any family or person at his home, or any individual employed by his parent or spouse.

(4) The term "representatives" includes any individual or labor organization.

(5) The term "labor organization" means any organization of any kind, or any agency or employee representation committee or plan, in which employees participate and which exists for the purpose, in whole or in part, of dealing with employers concerning grievances, labor disputes, wages, rates of pay, hours of employment, or conditions of work.

(6) The term "commerce" means trade, traffic, commerce, transportation, or communication among the several States, or between the District of Columbia or any Territory of the United States and any State or other Territory, or between any foreign country and any State, Territory, or the District of Columbia, or within the District of Columbia or any Territory, or between points in the same State but through any other State or any Territory or the District of Columbia or any foreign country.

(7) The term "affecting commerce" means in commerce, or burdening or obstructing commerce or the free flow of commerce, or having led or tending to lead to a labor dispute burdening or obstructing commerce or the free flow of commerce.

(8) The term "unfair labor practice" means any unfair labor practice listed in section 8.

(9) The term "labor dispute" includes any controversy concerning terms, tenure or conditions of employment, or concerning the association or representation of persons in negotiating, fixing, maintaining, changing, or seeking to arrange terms or conditions of employment, regardless of whether the disputants stand in the proximate relation of employer and employee.

(10) The term "National Labor Relations Board" means the National Labor Relations Board created by section 3 of this Act.

(11) The term "old Board" means the National Labor Relations Board established by Executive Order Numbered 6763 of the President on June 29, 1934, pursuant to Public Resolution Numbered 44, approved June 19, 1934 (48 Stat. 1183), and reëstablished and continued by Executive Order Numbered 7074 of the President of June 15, 1935, pursuant to Title I of the National Industrial Recovery Act (48 Stat. 195) as amended and continued by Senate Joint Resolution 133 approved June 14, 1935.

NATIONAL LABOR RELATIONS BOARD

Sec. 3. (a) There is hereby created a board, to be known as the "National Labor Relations Board" (hereinafter referred to as the "Board"), which shall be composed of three members, who shall be appointed by the President, by and with the advice and consent of the Senate. One of the original members shall be appointed for a term of one year, one for a term of three years, and one for a term of five years, but their successors shall be appointed for terms of five years each, except that any individual chosen to fill a vacancy shall be appointed only for the unexpired term of the member whom he shall succeed. The President shall designate one member to serve as chairman of the Board. Any member of the Board may be removed by the President, upon notice and hearing, for neglect of duty or malfeasance in office, but for no other cause.

(b) A vacancy in the Board shall not impair the right of the remaining members to exercise all the powers of the Board, and two members of the Board shall, at all times, constitute a quorum. The Board shall have an official seal which shall be judicially noticed.

(c) The Board shall at the close of each fiscal year make a report in writing to

Congress and to the President stating in detail the cases it has heard, the decisions it has rendered, the names, salaries, and duties of all employees and officers in the employ or under the supervision of the Board, and an account of all moneys it has disbursed.

Sec. 4. (a) Each member of the Board shall receive a salary of $10,000 a year, shall be eligible for reappointment, and shall not engage in any other business, vocation, or employment. The Board shall appoint, without regard for the provisions of the civil-service laws but subject to the Classification Act of 1923, as amended, an executive secretary, and such attorneys, examiners, and regional directors, and shall appoint such other employees with regard to existing laws applicable to the employment and compensation of officers and employees of the United States, as it may from time to time find necessary for the proper performance of its duties and as may be from time to time appropriated for by Congress. The Board may establish or utilize such regional, local, or other agencies, and utilize such voluntary and uncompensated services, as may from time to time be needed. Attorneys appointed under this section may, at the direction of the Board, appear for and represent the Board in any case in court. Nothing in this Act shall be construed to authorize the Board to appoint individuals for the purpose of conciliation or mediation (or for statistical work), where such service may be obtained from the Department of Labor.

(b) Upon the appointment of the three original members of the Board and the designation of its chairman, the old Board shall cease to exist. All employees of the old Board shall be transferred to and become employees of the Board with salaries under the Classification Act of 1923, as amended, without acquiring by such transfer a permanent or civil service status. All records, papers, and property of the old Board shall become records, papers, and property of the Board, and all unexpended funds and appropriations for the use and maintenance of the old Board shall become funds and appropriations available to be expended by the Board in the exercise of the powers, authority, and duties conferred on it by this Act.

(c) All of the expenses of the Board, including all necessary traveling and subsistence expenses outside the District of Columbia incurred by the members or employees of the Board under its orders, shall be allowed and paid on the presentation of itemized vouchers therefor approved by the Board or by any individual it designates for that purpose.

Sec. 5. The principal office of the Board shall be in the District of Columbia, but it may meet and exercise any or all of its powers at any other place. The Board may, by one or more of its members or by such agents or agencies as it may designate, prosecute any inquiry necessary to its functions in any part of the United States. A member who participates in such an inquiry shall not be disqualified from subsequently participating in a decision of the Board in the same case.

Sec. 6. (a) The Board shall have authority from time to time to make, amend, and rescind such rules and regulations as may be necessary to carry out the provisions of this Act. Such rules and regulations shall be effective upon publication in the manner which the Board shall prescribe.

RIGHTS OF EMPLOYEES

Sec. 7. Employees shall have the right to self-organization, to form, join, or assist labor organizations, to bargain collectively through representatives of their own choosing, and to engage in concerted activities, for the purpose of collective bargaining or other mutual aid or protection.

Sec. 8. It shall be an unfair labor practice for an employer—

(1) To interfere with, restrain, or coerce employees in the exercise of the rights guaranteed in section 7.

(2) To dominate or interfere with the formation or administration of any laboɪ organization or contribute financial or other support to it: *Provided,* That subject to rules and regulations made and published by the Board pursuant to section 6 (a), an employer shall not be prohibited from permitting employees to confer with him during working hours without loss of time or pay.

(3) By discrimination in regard to hire or tenure of employment or any term or condition of employment to encourage or discourage membership in any labor organization: *Provided,* That nothing in this Act, or in the National Industrial Recovery Act (U.S.C., Supp. VII, title 15, secs. 701–712), as amended from time to time, or in any code or agreement approved or prescribed thereunder, or in any other statute of the United States, shall preclude an employer from making an agreement with a labor organization (not established, maintained, or assisted by any action defined in this Act as an unfair labor practice) to require as a condition of employment membership therein, if such labor organization is the representative of the employees as provided in section 9 (a), in the appropriate collective bargaining unit covered by such agreement when made.

(4) To discharge or otherwise discriminate against an employee because he has filed charges or given testimony under this Act.

(5) To refuse to bargain collectively with the representatives of his employees, subject to the provisions of Section 9 (a).

REPRESENTATIVES AND ELECTIONS

Sec. 9. (a) Representatives designated or selected for the purposes of collective bargaining by the majority of the employees in a unit appropriate for such purposes, shall be the exclusive representatives of all the employees in such unit for the purposes of collective bargaining in respect to rates of pay, wages, hours of employment, or other conditions of employment: *Provided,* That any individual employee or a group of employees shall have the right at any time to present grievances to their employer.

(b) The Board shall decide in each case whether, in order to insure to employees the full benefit of their right to self-organization and to collective bargaining, and otherwise to effectuate the policies of this Act, the unit appropriate for the purposes of collective bargaining shall be the employer unit, craft unit, plant unit, or subdivision thereof.

(c) Whenever a question affecting commerce arises concerning the representation of employees, the Board may investigate such controversy and certify to the parties, in writing, the name or names of the representatives that have been designated or selected. In any such investigation, the Board shall provide for an appropriate hearing upon due notice, either in conjunction with a proceeding under section 10 or otherwise, and may take a secret ballot of employees, or utilize any other suitable method to ascertain such representatives.

(d) Whenever an order of the Board made pursuant to section 10 (c) is based in whole or in part upon facts certified following an investigation pursuant to subsection (c) of this section, and there is a petition for the enforcement or review of such order, such certification and the record of such investigation shall be included in the transcript of the entire record required to be filed under subsections 10 (e) or 10 (f), and thereupon the decree of the court enforcing, modifying, or setting aside in whole or in part the order of the Board shall be made and entered upon the pleadings, testimony, and proceedings set forth in such transcript.

PREVENTION OF UNFAIR LABOR PRACTICES

Sec. 10. (a) The Board is empowered, as hereinafter provided, to prevent any person from engaging in any unfair labor practice (listed in section 8) affecting commerce.

This power shall be exclusive, and shall not be affected by any other means of adjustment or prevention that has been or may be established by agreement, code, law, or otherwise.

(b) Whenever it is charged that any person has engaged in or is engaging in any such unfair labor practice, the Board, or any agent or agency designated by the Board for such purposes, shall have power to issue and cause to be served upon such person a complaint stating the charges in that respect, and containing a notice of hearing before the Board or a member thereof, or before a designated agent or agency, at a place therein fixed, not less than five days after the serving of said complaint. Any such complaint may be amended by the member, agent, or agency conducting the hearing or the Board in its discretion at any time prior to the issuance of an order based thereon. The person so complained of shall have the right to file an answer to the original or amended complaint and to appear in person or otherwise and give testimony at the place and time fixed in the complaint. In the discretion of the member, agent or agency conducting the hearing or the Board, any other person may be allowed to intervene in the said proceeding and to present testimony. In any such proceeding the rules of evidence prevailing in courts of law or equity shall not be controlling.

(c) The testimony taken by such member, agent or agency or the Board shall be reduced to writing and filed with the Board. Thereafter, in its discretion, the Board upon notice may take further testimony or hear argument. If upon all the testimony taken the Board shall be of the opinion that any person named in the complaint has engaged in or is engaging in any such unfair labor practice, then the Board shall state its findings of fact and shall issue and cause to be served on such person an order requiring such person to cease and desist from such unfair labor practice, and to take such affirmative action, including reinstatement of employees, with or without back pay, as will effectuate the policies of this Act. Such order may further require such person to make reports from time to time showing the extent to which it has complied with the order. If upon all the testimony taken the Board shall be of the opinion that no person named in the complaint has engaged in or is engaging in any such unfair labor practice, then the Board shall state its findings of fact and shall issue an order dismissing the said complaint.

(d) Until a transcript of the record in a case shall have been filed in a court, as hereinafter provided, the Board may at any time, upon reasonable notice and in such manner as it shall deem proper, modify or set aside, in whole or in part, any finding or order made or issued by it.

(e) The Board shall have power to petition any circuit court of appeals of the United States (including the Court of Appeals of the District of Columbia), or if all the circuit courts of appeals to which application may be made are in vacation, any district court of the United States (including the Supreme Court of the District of Columbia), within any circuit or district, respectively, wherein the unfair labor practice in question occurred or wherein such person resides or transacts business, for the enforcement of such order and for appropriate temporary relief or restraining order, and shall certify and file in the court a transcript of the entire record in the proceeding, including the pleadings and testimony upon which such order was entered and the findings and order of the Board. Upon such filing, the court shall cause notice thereof to be served upon such person, and thereupon shall have jurisdiction of the proceeding and of the question determined therein, and shall have power to grant such temporary relief or restraining order as it deems just and proper, and to make and enter upon the pleadings, testimony, and proceedings set forth in such transcript a decree enforcing, modifying, and enforcing as so modified, or setting aside in whole or in part the order of the Board. No objection that has not been urged before the Board, its member, agent or agency, shall be considered by the court, unless the failure or neglect to urge such objection shall be excused because of extraordinary circumstances. The findings of the Board as to the facts, if supported by evidence, shall be conclusive. If either party shall apply to the court for leave to adduce additional evidence and shall show to the satisfaction of the court that such additional evidence is material and that there were reasonable grounds for the failure to adduce such evidence in the hearing before the Board, its member, agent, or agency, the court may order such additional evidence to be taken before the Board, its member, agent, or agency, and to be made a part of the transcript. The Board may modify its findings as to the facts, or make new findings, by reason of additional evidence so taken and filed, and it shall file such modified or new findings, which, if supported by evidence, shall be conclusive, and shall file its recommendations, if any, for the modification or setting aside of its original order. The jurisdiction of the court shall be exclusive and its judgment and decree shall be final, except that the same shall be subject to review by the appropriate circuit court of appeals if application was made to the district court as hereinafter provided, and by the Supreme Court of the United States upon writ of certiorari or certification as provided in sections 239 and 240 of the Judicial Code, as amended (U.S.C., title 28, secs. 346 and 347).

(f) Any person aggrieved by a final order of the Board granting or denying in whole or in part the relief sought may obtain a review of such order in any circuit court of appeals of the United States in the circuit wherein the unfair labor practice in question was alleged to have been engaged in or wherein such person resides or transacts business, or in the Court of Appeals of the District of Columbia, by filing in such court a written petition praying that the order of the Board be modified or set aside. A copy of such petition shall be forthwith served upon the Board, and thereupon the aggrieved party shall file in the court a transcript of the entire record in the proceeding, certified by the Board, including the pleading and testimony upon which the order complained of was entered and the findings and order of the Board. Upon such filing, the court shall proceed in the same manner as in the case of an application by the Board under subsection (e), and shall have the same exclusive jurisdiction to grant to the Board such temporary relief or restraining order as it deems just and proper, and in like manner to make and enter a decree enforcing, modifying, and enforcing as so modified, or setting aside in whole or in part the order of the Board; and the findings of the Board as to the facts, if supported by evidence, shall in like manner be conclusive.

(g) The commencement of proceedings under subsection (e) or (f) of this section shall not, unless specifically ordered by the court, operate as a stay of the Board's order.

(h) When granting appropriate temporary relief or a restraining order, or making and entering a decree enforcing, modifying, and enforcing as so modified or setting aside in whole or in part an order of the Board, as provided in this section, the jurisdiction of courts sitting in equity shall not be limited by the Act entitled "An Act to amend the Judicial Code and to define and limit the jurisdiction of courts sitting in equity, and for other purposes," approved March 23, 1932 (U.S.C., Supp. VII, title 29, secs. 101–115).

(i) Petitions filed under this Act shall be heard expeditiously, and if possible within ten days after they have been docketed.

INVESTIGATORY POWERS

Sec. 11. For the purpose of all hearings and investigations, which, in the opinion of the Board, are necessary and proper for the exercise of the powers vested in it by section 9 and section 10—

(1) The Board, or its duly authorized agents or agencies, shall at all reasonable times have access to, for the purpose of examination, and the right to copy any evidence of any person being investigated or proceeded against that relates to any matter under investigation or in question. Any member of the Board shall have power to issue subpenas requiring the attendence and testimony of witnesses and the production of any evidence that relates to any matter under investigation or in question, before the Board, its member, agent, or agency conducting the hearing or investigation. Any member of the Board, or any agent or agency designated by the Board for such purposes, may administer oaths and affirmations, examine witnesses, and receive evidence. Such attendance of witnesses and the production of such evidence may be required from any place in the United States or any Territory or possession thereof, at any designated place of hearing.

(2) In case of contumacy or refusal to obey a subpena issued to any person, any District Court of the United States or the United States courts of any Territory or possession, or the Supreme Court of the District of Columbia, within the jurisdiction of which the inquiry is carried on or within the jurisdiction of which said person guilty of contumacy or refusal to obey is found or resides or transacts business, upon application by the Board shall have jurisdiction to issue to such person an order requiring such person to appear before the Board, its member, agent, or agency, there to produce evidence if so ordered, or there to give testimony touching the matter under investigation or in question; and any failure to obey such order of the court may be punished by said court as a contempt thereof.

(3) No person shall be excused from attending and testifying or from producing books, records, correspondence, documents, or other evidence in obedience to the subpena of the Board, on the ground that the testimony or evidence required of him may tend to incriminate him or subject him to a penalty or forfeiture; but no individual shall be prosecuted or subjected to any penalty or forfeiture for or on account of any transaction, matter, or thing concerning which he is compelled, after having claimed his privilege against self-incrimination, to testify or produce evidence, except that such individual so testifying shall not be exempt from prosecution and punishment for perjury committed in so testifying.

(4) Complaints, orders, and other process and papers of the Board, its member, agent, or agency, may be served either personally or by registered mail or by telegraph or by leaving a copy thereof at the principal office or place of business of the person required to be served. The verified return by the individual so serving the same setting forth the manner of such service shall be proof of the same, and the return post office receipt or telegraph receipt therefor when registered and mailed or telegraphed as aforesaid shall be proof of service of the same. Witnesses summoned before the Board, its member, agent, or agency, shall be paid the same fees and mileage that are paid witnesses in the courts of the United States, and witnesses whose depositions are taken and the persons taking the same shall severally be entitled to the same fees as are paid for like services in the courts of the United States.

(5) All process of any court to which application may be made under this Act may be served in the judicial district wherein the defendant or other person required to be served resides or may be found.

(6) The several departments and agencies of the Government, when directed by the President, shall furnish the Board, upon its request, all records, papers, and information in their possession relating to any matter before the Board.

Sec. 12. Any person who shall willfully resist, prevent, impede, or interfere with any member of the Board or any of its agents or agencies in the performance of duties pursuant to this Act shall be punished by a fine of not more than $5,000 or by imprisonment for not more than one year, or both.

LIMITATIONS

Sec. 13. Nothing in this Act shall be construed so as to interfere with or impede or diminish in any way the right to strike.

Sec. 14. Wherever the application of the provisions of section 7 (a) of the National Industrial Recovery Act (U.S.C., Supp. VII, title 15, sec. 707 (a), as amended from time to time, or of section 77 B, paragraphs (1) and (m) of the Act approved June 7, 1934, entitled "An Act to amend an Act entitled 'An Act to establish a uniform system of bankruptcy throughout the United States' approved July 1, 1898, and Acts amendatory thereof and supplementary thereto" (48 Stat. 922, pars. (1) and (m), as amended from time to time, or of Public Resolution Numbered 44, approved June 19, 1934 (48 Stat. 1183), conflicts with the application of the provisions of this Act, this Act shall prevail: *Provided,* That in any situation where the provisions of this Act cannot be validly enforced, the provisions of such other Acts shall remain in full force and effect.

Sec. 15. If any provision of this Act, or the application of such provision to any person or circumstance, shall be held invalid, the remainder of this Act, or the application of such provision to persons or circumstances other than those as to which it is held invalid, shall not be affected thereby.

Sec. 16. This Act may be cited as the "National Labor Relations Act."

APPROVED, July 5, 1935.

BIBLIOGRAPHY

BIBLIOGRAPHY

PRIMARY SOURCES

1. MANUSCRIPTS

Federal Coördinator of Transportation papers. National Archives.
Leon H. Keyserling papers. Washington, D.C.
Labor Department papers. National Archives.
Philip Levy papers. Washington, D.C.
National Labor Board papers. National Archives.
National Labor Relations Board papers. National Archives.
National Recovery Administration papers. National Archives.
Boris Shishkin papers. Washington, D.C.
White House Office File. Franklin D. Roosevelt Library, Hyde Park, N.Y.
Charles E. Wyzanski, Jr., papers. Boston, Mass.

2. PUBLIC DOCUMENTS

Amendments to the National Labor Relations Act, Hearings before the Committee on Education and Labor, House of Representatives, 80th Congress, 1st session.
Board to Settle Disputes between Carriers and Their Employees, Report of the Committee on Interstate Commerce, Senate, Report No. 1065, May 21, 1934, 73d Congress, 2d session.
Congressional Record, 1932–1947.
Decisions of the National Labor Board. 2v. Washington, 1934.
Decisions of the National Labor Relations Board. 2v. Washington, 1935.
Defining and Limiting the Jurisdiction of Courts Sitting in Equity, Hearings before the Committee on the Judiciary on H.R. 5315, House of Representatives, 72d Congress, 1st session.
Department of Labor Appropriation Bill for 1937, Hearing before the Subcommittee of the House Committee on Appropriations, House of Representatives, 74th Congress, 2d session.
Eleventh Annual Report of the National Labor Relations Board. Washington, 1947.
Emergency Railroad Transportation Act, 1933, Hearings before the Committee on Interstate and Foreign Commerce, House of Representatives, 73d Congress, 1st session.
Emergency Railroad Transportation Act, 1933, Report of the Committee on Interstate and Foreign Commerce, House of Representatives, Report No. 193, June 2, 1933, 73d Congress, 1st session.
Emergency Railroad Transportation Act, 1933, Report of the Committee on Interstate and Foreign Commerce, House of Representatives, Report No. 213, June 9, 1933, 73d Congress, 1st session.
Emergency Railroad Transportation Act, 1933, Hearings before the Committee on Interstate Commerce on S. 1580, Senate, 73d Congress, 1st session.
Emergency Railroad Transportation Act, 1933, Report of the Committee on Interstate Commerce, Senate, Report No. 87, May 22, 1933, 73d Congress, 1st session.
Federal Register, 1933–1935.
Final Report of the Commission on Industrial Relations. Washington, 1915.
Final Report of the Industrial Commission. Washington, 1902.
First Annual Report of the National Mediation Board. Washington, 1935.

Investigation of Concentration of Economic Power, Final Report and Recommendations of the Temporary National Economic Committee, Senate, March 31, 1941, 77th Congress, 1st session.

Investigation of Economic Problems, Hearings before the Committee on Finance pursuant to S. Res. 315, Senate, 72d Congress, 2d session.

Labor Disputes Act, Hearings before the Committee on Labor on H. R. 6288, House of Representatives, 74th Congress, 1st session.

National Industrial Recovery, Hearings on H. R. 5664 before the Committee on Ways and Means, House of Representatives, 73d Congress, 1st session.

National Industrial Recovery, Report of the Committee on Ways and Means on H. R. 5755, House of Representatives, Report No. 159, May 23, 1933, 73d Congress, 1st session.

National Industrial Recovery, Hearings before the Committee on Finance on S. 1712 and H. R. 5755, Senate, 73d Congress, 1st session.

National Industrial Recovery Bill, Report of the Committee on Finance to accompany H. R. 5755, Senate, Report No. 114, June 5, 1933, 73d Congress, 1st session.

National Industrial Recovery, Conference Report on H. R. 5755, House of Representatives, Report No. 243, 73d Congress, 1st session.

National Labor Relations Act, Hearings before the Special Committee to Investigate the National Labor Relations Board, House of Representatives, 76th Congress, 3d session.

National Labor Relations Board, Comparison of S. 2926 and S. 1958 and Proposed Amendments, Committee on Education and Labor, Senate, 74th Congress, 1st session.

National Labor Relations Board, Conference Report on S. 1958, Report No. 1371, June 26, 1935, 74th Congress, 1st session.

National Labor Relations Board, Hearings before the Committee on Education and Labor on S. 1958, Senate, 74th Congress, 1st session.

National Labor Relations Board, Report of the Committee on Education and Labor on S. 1958, Report No. 573, Senate, 74th Congress, 1st session.

National Labor Relations Board, Report of the House Labor Committee to accompany H. R. 7978, House of Representatives, Report No. 969, May 20, 1935, 74th Congress, 1st session.

National Labor Relations Board, Report of the Labor Committee on H. R. 7978, House of Representatives, Report No. 1147, June 10, 1935, 74th Congress, 1st session.

Proposed Amendments to the National Labor Relations Act, Hearings before the Committee on Labor, House of Representatives, 76th Congress, 1st session.

Railway Labor Act Amendments, Hearings before the Committee on Interstate and Foreign Commerce on H. R. 7650, House of Representatives, 73d Congress, 2d session.

Regulations of Railroads, Senate, Document No. 119, January 22, 1934, 73d Congress, 2d session.

Report from the Committee on Judiciary to accompany S. 158, Senate, Report No. 114, March 30, 1933, 73d Congress, 1st session.

Report of the Committee on Interstate Commerce, Senate, Report No. 470, April 1, 1935, 74th Congress, 1st session.

Thirty-Hour Bill, Hearings before the Committee on Labor on S. 158, H. R. 4557 and Proposals Offered by the Secretary of Labor, House of Representatives, 73d Congress, 1st session.

Thirty-Hour Week Bill, Report of the Committee on Labor on S. 158, House of Representatives, Report No. 124, May 10, 1933, 73d Congress, 1st session.

Thirty-Hour Work Week, Hearings before the Subcommittee of the Committee on the Judiciary on S. 5267, Senate, 72d Congress, 2d session.

To Amend the Railway Labor Act, Hearings before the Committee on Interstate Commerce on S. 3266, Senate, 73d Congress, 2d session.

To Amend the Railway Labor Act, Report of the Committee on Interstate and Foreign Commerce, House of Representatives, Report No. 1944, June 11, 1934, 73d Congress, 2d session.

To Create a National Industrial Adjustment Board, Report of the Committee on Education and Labor on S. 2926, Senate, Report No. 1184, May 26, 1934, 73d Congress, 2d session.

To Create a National Labor Board, Hearings before the Committee on Education and Labor on S. 2926, Senate, 73d Congress, 2d session.

United States Statutes at Large, 1888–1937.

United States Strike Commission, *Report on the Chicago Strike of June–July 1894.* Washington, 1894.

United States Supreme Court Reports, 1908–1936.

Violations of Free Speech and Rights of Labor, Hearings before a Subcommittee of the Committee on Education and Labor pursuant to S. Res. 266, Senate, 76th Congress, 1st session.

Violations of Free Speech and Rights of Labor, Report of the Subcommittee of the Committee on Education and Labor, Senate, Report No. 46, 1937–1938, 75th Congress, 1st session.

3. CONVENTION PROCEEDINGS

Conference on the Training of Law Students in Labor Relations. Mimeo., 2v., University of Michigan, June 16–26, 1947.

Proceedings of the Constitutional Conventions of the United Mine Workers of America, 1934–1938.

Reports of Officers to the Sessions of the International Typographical Union, 1931–1933.

Reports of Proceedings of the Annual Conventions of the American Federation of Labor, 1919–1936.

Tenth Biennial Convention of the Amalgamated Clothing Workers of America, 1930–1934.

SECONDARY WORKS

1. BOOKS

Alsop, Joseph, and Robert Kintner. *Men around the President.* New York: 1939.

Arnold, Thurman. *The Folklore of Capitalism.* New Haven: 1937.

Baker, Ralph Hillis. *The National Bituminous Coal Commission, Administration of the Bituminous Coal Act, 1937–1941.* Baltimore: 1941.

Berle, A. A., Jr., and Gardiner C. Means. *The Modern Corporation and Private Property.* New York: 1932.

Blachly, Frederick F., and Miriam E. Oatman. *Federal Regulatory Action and Control.* Washington: 1940.

Bowman, D. O. *Public Control of Labor Relations.* New York: 1942.

Brooks, Robert R. R. *As Steel Goes, . . . Unionism in a Basic Industry.* New Haven: 1940.

———. *When Unions Organize.* New Haven: 1938.

Calkins, Clinch. *Spy Overhead, the Story of Industrial Espionage.* New York: 1937.

Carsel, Wilfred. *A History of the Chicago Ladies Garment Workers Union.* Chicago: 1940.

Coleman, McAlister. *Men and Coal.* New York: 1943.

Commons, John R., and John B. Andrews. *Principles of Labor Legislation.* 4th rev. ed. New York: 1936.

Commons, John R., and associates. *History of Labour in the United States.* New York: 1918, 1935. 4 vols.

Daugherty, C. R., M. G. deChazeau, and S. S. Stratton. *The Economics of the Iron and Steel Industry.* New York: 1937. 2 vols.

Douglas, Paul H. *Real Wages in the United States, 1890–1926.* Cambridge, Mass.: 1930.

Frankfurter, Felix, and Nathan Greene. *The Labor Injunction.* New York: 1930.

Gilbert, Hilda Kessler. The United States Department of Labor in the New Deal Period. Unpublished Ph.D thesis, University of Wisconsin, 1942.

Griffin, John I. *Strikes, a Study in Quantitative Economics.* New York: 1939.

GT-99. *Labor Spy.* Indianapolis: 1937.

Higgins, George Gilmary. *Voluntarism in Organized Labor in the United States, 1930–1940.* Washington: 1944.

Howard, Sidney. *The Labor Spy.* New York: 1924.

Huberman, Leo. *The Labor Spy Racket.* New York: 1937.

Johnson, Hugh S. *The Blue Eagle from Egg to Earth.* New York: 1935.

Laidler, Harry W. *Concentration of Control in American Industry.* New York: 1931.

Leiserson, William M. *Right and Wrong in Labor Relations.* Berkeley, Calif.: 1938.

Levinson, Edward. *I Break Strikes.* New York: 1935.

Lindley, Ernest K. *The Roosevelt Revolution: First Phase.* New York: 1933.

Lippmann, Walter. *Interpretations, 1931–1932.* Edited by Allan Nevins. New York: 1932.

Lorwin, Lewis L. *The American Federation of Labor, History, Policies, and Prospects.* Washington: 1933.

Lorwin, Lewis L., and Arthur Wubnig. *Labor Relation Boards.* Washington: 1935.

Lynd, Robert S., and Helen Merrell Lynd. *Middletown, a Study in Contemporary American Culture.* New York: 1929.

McDonald, David J., and Edward A. Lynch. *Coal and Unionism, a History of the American Coal Miners' Union.* Silver Spring, Md.: 1939.

Millis, Harry A., and Royal E. Montgomery. *Organized Labor.* New York: 1945.

Mitchell, Broadus. *Depression Decade, from New Era through New Deal, 1929–1941.* New York: 1947.

Moley, Raymond. *After Seven Years.* New York: 1939.

Perkins, Frances. *The Roosevelt I Knew.* New York: 1946.

Perlman, Selig. *A History of Trade Unionism in the United States.* New York: 1922.

Public Papers and Addresses of Franklin D. Roosevelt. Edited by Samuel I. Rosenman. New York: 1938. 9 vols.

Rauch, Basil. *The History of the New Deal.* New York: 1944.

Reynolds, Lloyd G. *Labor Economics and Labor Relations.* New York: 1949.

Richberg, Donald R. *The Rainbow.* Garden City, N.Y.: 1936.

Roos, C. F. *NRA Economic Planning.* Bloomington, Ill.: 1937.

Rosenfarb, Joseph. *The National Labor Policy and How It Works.* New York: 1940.

Ross, Arthur M. *Trade Union Wage Policy.* Berkeley: University of California Press, 1948.

Ross, Malcolm. *Death of a Yale Man.* New York: 1939.

Seidman, Joel. *The Needle Trades.* New York: 1942.

Selekman, Benjamin M. *Labor Relations and Human Relations.* New York: 1947.

Shister, Joseph. *Economics of the Labor Market.* Philadelphia: 1949.

Shulman, Harry, and Neil W. Chamberlain. *Cases on Labor Relations.* Brooklyn: 1949.

Smith, Adam. *The Wealth of Nations.* Modern Library ed.

Spencer, William H. *Collective Bargaining under Section 7(a) of the National Industrial Recovery Act.* Chicago: 1935.

Stolberg, Benjamin. *Tailor's Progress.* New York: 1944.

Toner, Jerome L. *The Closed Shop.* Washington: 1942.

Tugwell, Rexford G. *The Industrial Discipline and the Governmental Arts.* New York: 1933.

Twentieth Century Fund. *Big Business, Its Growth and Its Place.* New York: 1937.

————. *How Collective Bargaining Works.* New York: 1945.

————. *Labor and the Government.* New York: 1935.

Unofficial Observer. *The New Dealers.* New York: 1934.

Wecter, Dixon. *The Age of the Great Depression, 1929–1941.* New York: 1948.

Witte, Edwin E. *The Government in Labor Disputes.* New York: 1932.

Wolf, Harry D. *The Railroad Labor Board.* Chicago: 1927.

Wolman, Leo. *Ebb and Flow in Trade Unionism.* New York: 1936.

2. ARTICLES

Adamic, Louis. "The Collapse of Organized Labor," *Harper's Magazine,* CLXIV (1932), 167–178.

Anderson, Paul Y. "Food, Drink, and Politics," *Nation,* CXXXV (1932), 54–55.

Bernstein, Irving. "Labor and the Recovery Program, 1933," *Quarterly Journal of Economics,* LX (1946), 270–288.

Beyer, Otto S., and Edwin M. Fitch. "Annual Earnings of Railroad Employees, 1924 to 1933," *Monthly Labor Review,* XLI (1935), 1–12.

Brissenden, Paul F. "Genesis and Import of the Collective-Bargaining Provisions of the Recovery Act," *Economic Essays in Honor of Wesley Clair Mitchell.* New York: 1935.

Carey, Homer F. and Herman Oliphant. "The Present Status of the Hitchman Case," *Columbia Law Review,* XXIX (1929), 441–460.

Cooper, Lyle W. "The American Labor Movement in Prosperity and Depression," *American Economic Review,* XXII (1932), 641–659.

Douty, H. M. "The Trend of Industrial Disputes, 1922–1930," *Journal of the American Statistical Association,* XXVII (1932), 168–172.

"Employer Interference with Lawful Union Activity," *Columbia Law Review,* XXXVII (1937), 816–841.

Flynn, John T. "Whose Child is the NRA?" *Harper's Magazine,* CLXIX (1934), 385–394.

Fraenkel, Osmond K. "Recent Statutes Affecting Labor Injunctions and Yellow-Dog Contracts," *Illinois Law Review,* XXX (1936), 854–883.

Frey, Alexander H. "The Logic of Collective Bargaining and Arbitration," *Law and Contemporary Problems,* XII (1947), 264–280.

Garrison, Lloyd K. "7-A and the Future," *Survey Graphic,* XXIV (1935), 53–57.

————. "The National Labor Boards," *Annals of The American Academy of Political and Social Science,* CLXXIV (1936), 138–146.

————. "The National Railroad Adjustment Board," *Yale Law Journal,* XLVI (1937), 567–598.

Gellhorn, Walter, and Seymour L. Linfield. "Politics and Labor Relations: an Appraisal of Criticisms of NLRB Procedure," *Columbia Law Review,* XXXIX (1939), 339–395.

Gompers, Samuel. "The President's Industrial Conference," *American Federationist*, XXVI (1919), 1121–1125.

Green, William. "Labor's Opportunity and Responsibility," *American Federationist*, XL (1933), 692–694.

Hamilton, Walton H. "Collective Bargaining," *Encyclopedia of the Social Sciences*, III, 628–629.

Harrison, George M. "Railway Labor Act," *American Federationist*, XLI (1934), 1053–1057.

Keyserling, Leon H. "Why the Wagner Act?" *The Wagner Act: After Ten Years*. Edited by Louis G. Silverberg. Washington: 1945. Pp. 5–34.

Lauck, W. Jett. "Coal Labor Legislation: A Case," *Annals of the American Academy of Political and Social Science*, CLXXXIV (1936), 130–137.

Lewis, John L. "Labor and the National Recovery Administration," *Annals of the American Academy of Political and Social Science*, CLXXII (1934), 58–63.

Lubell, Harold. "Effects of Redistribution of Income on Consumers' Expenditures," *American Economic Review*, XXXVII (1947), 157–170.

Magruder, Calvert. "A Half Century of Legal Influence upon the Development of Collective Bargaining," *Harvard Law Review*, L (1937), 1071–1117.

Mangold, William R. "On the Labor Front," *New Republic*, LXXXI (1935).

McKillips, B. L. "Company Unions on the Railroads," *Nation*, CXLII (1936), 48–50.

Millis, Walter. "Presidential Candidates," *Yale Review*, XXII (1932), 1–18.

Montgomery, Royal E. "Labor," *American Journal of Sociology*, XLVII (1942), 929–940.

Perkins, Frances. "Eight Years as Madame Secretary," *Fortune*, XXIV (1941), 76–79.

Seidman, Joel I. "The Yellow-Dog Contract," *Quarterly Journal of Economics*, XLVI (1932), 348–361.

Slichter, Sumner H. "The Current Labor Policies of American Industries," *Quarterly Journal of Economics*, XLIII (1929), 393–435.

———. "Labor and the Government," *Yale Review*, XXV (1936), 258–274.

Stanley, Louis. "The Collapse of the A. F. of L.," *Nation*, CXXXI (1930), 367–369.

Stone, I. F. "Robert F. Wagner," *Nation*, CLIX (1944), 507–508.

"Strikebreaking," *Fortune*, XL (1935), 56–61.

"U. S. Steel III: Labor," *Fortune*, XIII (1936), 92–97.

Villard, Oswald Garrison. "The Democratic Trough at Chicago," *Nation*, CXXXV (1932), 26–27.

———. "Pillars of Government, Robert F. Wagner," *Forum & Century*, XCVI (1936), 124–128.

Watkins, Myron W. "Trustification and Economic Theory," *American Economic Review*, XXI, supp. (1931), 54–76.

Weisberg, Morris L. "The Transformation of the Collective Agreement in Soviet Law," *Chicago Law Review*, XVI (1949), 444–481.

White, Owen P. "When the Public Needs a Friend," *Collier's*, XCIII (1934), 18.

3. PAMPHLETS

American Management Association. *The Function of Collective Bargaining*, by George W. Taylor. Personnel Series, No. 81.

Bureau of Labor Statistics. *National War Labor Board*. Bulletin No. 287. Washington: 1922.

Bureau of Labor Statistics. *Handbook of American Trade-Unions*. Bulletin No. 618. Washington: 1936.

Bureau of Labor Statistics. *Characteristics of Company Unions, 1935*. Bulletin No. 634. Washington: 1937.

Bureau of Labor Statistics. *Strikes in the United States, 1880–1936.* Bulletin No. 651. Washington: 1937.

Bureau of Labor Statistics. *Union Wages, Hours, and Working Conditions in the Printing Trades, June 1, 1939.* Bulletin No. 675. Washington: 1940.

Bureau of Labor Statistics. *Union-Security Provisions in Collective Bargaining.* Bulletin No. 908. Washington: 1947.

Bureau of Labor Statistics. *Extent of Collective Bargaining and Union Recognition, 1946.* Bulletin No. 909. Washington: 1947.

Bureau of Labor Statistics. *Handbook of Labor Statistics, 1947 Edition.* Bulletin No. 916. Washington: 1948.

National Bureau of Economic Research. *Employment during the Depression,* by Meredith B. Givens. Bulletin No. 47. New York: 1933.

National Bureau of Economic Research. *National Income, 1929–32,* by Simon Kuznets. Bulletin No. 49. New York: 1934.

National Bureau of Economic Research. *Wages during the Depression,* by Leo Wolman. Bulletin No. 46. New York: 1933.

National Industrial Conference Board. *Collective Bargaining through Employee Representation.* New York: 1933.

National Industrial Conference Board. *Individual and Collective Bargaining under the N.I.R.A.* New York: 1933.

National Labor Relations Board, Division of Economic Research. *Governmental Protection of Labor's Right to Organize.* Bulletin No. 1. Washington: 1936.

National Lawyers Committee of the American Liberty League. *Report on the Constitutionality of the National Labor Relations Act.* New York: 1935.

Office of National Industrial Recovery Administration, Division of Review. *Section 7(a): Its History, Interpretation and Administration,* by Raymond S. Rubinow. Work Materials No. 45, pt. E. Washington: 1936.

Social Science Research Council, Division of Industry and Trade. *Railway Labor Survey,* by J. Douglas Brown and associates. Washington: 1933.

4. NEWSPAPERS

Akron Beacon-Journal, 1934–1935.

Atlanta Constitution, 1933.

Baltimore Sun, 1933–1934.

Boston Herald, 1933–1935.

Boston Transcript, 1935.

Charlotte (N.C.) *Observer,* 1935.

Chicago Daily News, 1934.

Chicago Journal of Commerce, 1934–1935.

Chicago Tribune, 1933–1935.

Cincinnati Enquirer, 1934.

Cleveland Plain Dealer, 1933–1935.

Dallas Morning News, 1935.

Detroit Free Press, 1934.

Detroit News, 1935.

Des Moines Register, 1935.

Division of Press Intelligence, Press Intelligence Bulletin, 1935 (National Archives)

Indianapolis News, 1935.

Kansas City Times, 1935.

Los Angeles Times, 1933–1934.

Minneapolis Journal, 1934.

Minneapolis Tribune, 1934.

New York Evening Journal, 1933.

New York Evening Post, 1934–1935.

New York Evening Sun, 1934–1935.

New York Herald Tribune, 1933–1935.

New York Journal of Commerce, 1934.

New York Post, 1933.

New York Times, 1930–1936.

New York World-Telegram, 1932–1935.

Philadelphia Evening Bulletin, 1933–193.

Philadelphia Inquirer, 1934–1935.

Philadelphia Public Ledger, 1934.

Philadelphia Record, 1934–1935.

Pittsburgh Post-Gazette, 1934.

Portland Oregonian, 1935.

Providence Journal, 1934.

Richmond News-Leader, 1935.

San Francisco Argonaut, 1934.

St. Louis Post-Dispatch, 1933–1935.
Springfield (Mass.) *Daily News*, 1934.
Wall St. Journal, 1934–1935.
Washington Daily News, 1934–1935.

Washington Herald, 1935.
Washington Post, 1933–1935.
Washington Star, 1934–1935.

5. PERIODICALS

Advance, 1934.
Amalgamated Journal, 1934–1935.
American Federationist, 1930–1936.
American Federation of Labor, *Weekly News Service*, 1931–1935.
Business Week, 1933–1935.
Coal Age, 1934–1935.
The Guaranty Survey, 1934.
International Juridical Association, *Monthly Bulletin*, 1934–1935.
International Typographical Journal, 1931–1933.
Iron Age, 1934.

Justice, 1935.
Kiplinger Washington Letter, 1934–1935.
Labor, 1933–1934.
Literary Digest, 1935.
Nation, 1932–1935.
Nation's Business, 1933–1935.
New Republic, 1932–1935.
Railroad Telegrapher, 1933–1934.
Railroad Trainman, 1934.
Railway Age, 1933–1934.
Railway Clerk, 1933–1934.
United Mine Workers Journal, 1931–1935.
United States News, 1933–1934.

INDEX

INDEX

FACULTY ADVISORY COMMITTEE